Beyond The AI Demo

Enough of POCs. Let's Talk Production

ROHIT AGARWAL

notionpress.com

INDIA • SINGAPORE • MALAYSIA

ISBN

Hardcase 979-8-90510-605-7
Paperback 979-8-90342-851-9

Contents

Foreword.....5

Preface.....11

Acknowledgements.....15

Chapter 01: Cutting Through the AI Hype: The Real Story Behind Agentic Intelligence.....17

Chapter 02: The Data Backbone for Our Agentic AI Examples.....43

Chapter 03: Architectural Fundamentals of Agentic System.....60

Chapter 04: The SQL-Focused Agent: From Queries to Conversations.....87

Chapter 05: A Balanced Agentic Approach: Deterministic Queries with Generative Enrichment.....108

Chapter 06: From Language to Action: The Journey to the Model Context Protocol.....127

Chapter 07: From Summarizers to Cognitive Agents: Designing Multi-Layered AI Systems.....143

Chapter 08: Evolving Beyond PADM: Towards Smarter Agentic Patterns.....183

Chapter 09: Towards True Agency: Reasoning, Reflection, and Refinement.....225

Chapter 10: The GAP Advantage: Deterministic Agentic Systems at Scale 265

Final Thoughts 307

Appendix A: Extending the SQL Agent with Langflow *313*

Appendix B: Amazon Bedrock: Scaling Generative AI for Real-World Enterprise Systems *325*

Appendix C: Cost Estimates for Amazon Bedrock in Production *341*

Appendix D: Parseboard Tool: Technical Guide *348*

Foreword

The AI landscape has rapidly evolved from specialized research labs to the center of the global boardroom. While the excitement around "transformational" AI is undeniable, many organizations still grapple with a fundamental question: *how do we operationalize AI at scale?*

History reminds us that innovation alone is not enough—mainstream adoption requires structure, repeatable patterns, and robust frameworks. This is where Rohit's book **Beyond The AI Demo** makes a significant contribution. It begins by demystifying the evolution of AI, from traditional machine learning to Agentic AI, while offering a grounded perspective on why this shift is driven not only by technology but also by organizational and social pressures.

A defining strength of the book is its candid examination of why most AI initiatives fail to move beyond proof of concept. Rohit clearly articulates common challenges such as weak business alignment, domain mismatch, cost mismanagement, and lack of observability—issues that resonate with practitioners across industries.

The book strikes a strong balance between theory and practice, reflecting deep hands-on experience. It emphasizes that scaling intelligent systems is not merely a model problem, but fundamentally an architectural one—requiring thoughtful integration of data, infrastructure, orchestration, and cost discipline.

With practical evaluation frameworks such as the "4R" metrics and a comparative view of agentic architectures and their trade-offs, this work provides a clear path from experimentation to production.

– Sridhar Turaga

SVP - Data, Analytics & AI at CitiusTech

We are living through a rare moment, the kind that only comes a few times in a generation, where a technology is genuinely reshaping what organizations can accomplish. Not incrementally, but fundamentally. Agentic AI is not a better search engine or a smarter autocomplete. It is a new category of capability: systems that can reason through complexity, act on incomplete information, and operate at a scale no human team could match alone.

The opportunity is real. But so is the gap between seeing it and seizing it.

Most organizations today are somewhere in the middle, convinced enough to invest, but struggling to move from experimentation to something that actually runs in production. The demos are working. The business case is clear. And yet full deployment keeps getting pushed to the next quarter.

Rohit Agarwal wrote this book for exactly that moment.

What the world needs is someone willing to say the quieter, less comfortable things. That most AI projects stall not because the technology fails, but because the people building them underestimated what "production" actually means. That governance and cost discipline are not afterthoughts; they are the whole game. That the distance between an impressive demo and a reliable system is often wider than the distance between no AI and the demo itself.

Rohit says those things. Clearly, and without flinching.

Rohit's instincts about enterprise technology are evident from the very first chapter. His writing carries the weight of someone who has navigated these challenges firsthand, not theorized about them from a distance. You can tell he has seen well-funded AI initiatives stall at their first compliance review, watched cost curves bend in directions nobody anticipated, and understood what it truly takes to move a system from a controlled test environment into the unpredictability of live production.

This book is shaped by that hard-won perspective. And it shows.

What I found most useful, and I think practitioners will agree, is that Rohit does not treat Agentic AI as a single thing to be adopted or avoided. He treats it as a design space with real tradeoffs, where the right choice depends on your problem, your data, your risk tolerance, and your budget. That framing alone is more valuable than most of what gets written about AI at the enterprise level.

The chapters on cost management and observability are particularly worth your time. These are the areas where even well-resourced teams routinely make avoidable mistakes, and Rohit covers them with the kind of specificity that only comes from having lived through the consequences.

The CPG examples scattered throughout might seem niche at first glance, but they are well chosen. Few industries combine the data volume, operational complexity, and zero tolerance for error that Consumer Packaged Goods demands. If the frameworks here hold up under those conditions, and the evidence suggests they do, they will hold up in yours.

I do not think Agentic AI is magic. Neither does Rohit. But I do think it represents a meaningful shift in what software can do inside an organization, and the teams that figure out how to build it properly, not just quickly, are going to have a real and durable advantage.

This book is a solid place to start figuring that out.

– Bhuwan Lodha

CEO- AI Division at Mahindra Group

Developing agentic AI solutions is the easy part. The hard part is operating these systems. Security, safety, reliability, responsibility, scalability and efficiency are all requirements that often contradict each other. As an AI engineer, it is your job to find the right balance. In his book **Beyond the AI Demo**, Rohit Agarwal provides the right framework for designing multi-agent systems that excel in operations. Starting with a simple chat-with-your-data application, he demonstrates the trade-offs within his 4 R framework for agentic design: Reliability, Respect, Reach and Restraint. To strengthen one or more of these four dimensions, he introduces design patterns, gradually increasing the complexity of the solution chapter by chapter. This enables you to learn about different architectures through a real-world example, as well as how to assess their respective pros and cons. It is a real pleasure to follow Rohit's journey from start to finish, and his in-depth exploration of technical details that make a difference. Having known Rohit for many years as an excellent and frequent speaker at Machine Learning Week Europe, I can say that this book reflects the pragmatic and progressive mindset of an AI expert and explorer. If you want to exploit the potential of Agentic AI, this book is your travel guide to this new territory.

– Martin Szugat

Managing Partner at Datentreiber

Program Director, Machine Learning Week Europe

Artificial intelligence has moved quickly from curiosity to boardroom priority. Yet for most organizations, the real challenge is no longer understanding the promise of AI. It is making it work in the real world.

That is what makes **Beyond The AI Demo** such an important book. Rohit Agarwal focuses on the questions that matter most to business leaders: how to move beyond impressive proofs of concept and build Agentic AI systems that are reliable, scalable, secure, and commercially viable.

What I particularly value in this book is its practical clarity. It does not get lost in hype. It addresses the hard realities of production: architecture, governance, cost, trust, and execution. Rohit brings discipline to a space that too often rewards excitement over substance.

This is a thoughtful and timely contribution for leaders, architects, and innovators who want to turn AI ambition into real operational value. The organizations that will lead in the years ahead will not be those that talk most about AI, but those that deploy it responsibly and effectively.

Beyond The AI Demo helps show the way.

– Vivek Mehrotra

Director, Cybersecurity & Enterprise Architecture at Smiths Detection
Author, *The Orchestration Age*

Preface

When I first started working with large language models, I was convinced we were witnessing something historic. The machines had finally begun to *reason*. I watched teams build prototypes that could summarize reports, answer complex questions, and even suggest business decisions. For a while, it felt like anything was possible.

But then came the hard part, which is production.

Suddenly, those same impressive demos began to crack under the weight of reality. Costs ballooned. APIs throttled. Data security teams raised alarms. And that sleek, "intelligent" system that wowed everyone in the demo room? It froze the first time it encountered a live customer query.

That's when it hit me that **the real challenge in AI isn't building intelligence; it's operationalizing it.**

Taking an Agentic AI system from proof of concept (POC) to production is not a technical sprint, it's a design marathon. It requires balancing creativity with control, autonomy with accountability, and innovation with cost discipline.

This book was born from that realization and from countless conversations with engineers, data scientists, and product leaders who were all struggling with the same question:

> "How do we make Agentic AI actually work reliably, securely, and at scale?"

Because somewhere between the conference keynotes and corporate roadmaps, the fundamentals got lost. AI became a buzzword, not a blueprint. Every company claimed to be "doing AI," but very few could explain *how* or *why*.

I wrote this book to change that.

It's not about chasing hype or building another flashy demo. It's about something far more practical and far more difficult: "**Choosing the right Agentic AI approach for your problem, and building it in a way that you can afford, trust, and scale.**"

Why this Book Exists

AI is no more optional. It has become the backbone of digital transformation. But as organizations rush to adopt it, they often fall into the same traps:

- Using the wrong AI paradigm for the wrong problem
- Underestimating the true cost of LLM usage at scale
- Overlooking the governance and security layers that make enterprise AI sustainable

This book is meant to help you avoid those mistakes. It's for **practitioners**, the architects, data engineers, decision-makers, and innovators, who want to move beyond proof-of-concept AI into **production-grade, agentic systems** that truly deliver business value.

What You'll Learn

Across the chapters, we'll unpack the journey from experimentation to execution.

You'll learn how to:

- Choose the right **Agentic AI design pattern** for your use case which can be anything from simple retrieval-augmented systems to fully autonomous reasoning agents
- Manage **costs** strategically, by understanding where and how LLMs consume compute and how to optimize API utilization

- Protect **data** through architectural safeguards that balance intelligence with compliance
- Build for **scalability and observability**, so that your system performs reliably in production and not just in the demo room

Our examples come from the **Consumer Packaged Goods (CPG)** industry not because it's trendy, but because it represents the perfect proving ground: complex data, high volume, and low tolerance for error. Through these scenarios, we'll see how Agentic AI can automate reasoning-based workflows, scale customer intelligence, and deliver decisions.

A Note on Approach

This isn't a book about coding an agent from scratch. It's a design conversation and a guided exploration of the architectural and strategic decisions that separate sustainable systems from short-lived prototypes. We'll discuss tools, APIs, data pipelines, and observability not as isolated components, but as parts of a living ecosystem.

The focus is not *how to make AI talk*, but *how to make it think responsibly, act reliably, and scale affordably.*

Because AI isn't magic. It's engineering at enterprise scale.

The Promise

By the end of this book, you won't just understand what *Agentic AI* means. You'll know how to build it with confidence. You'll see how to move from *prototype to platform*, from *ideas to implementation*, and from *talking about AI* to actually *delivering with it.*

My hope is that this book becomes your field guide and a companion for navigating complexity, cutting through the noise, and choosing the right path forward in this next phase of intelligence.

The age of Agentic AI has only just begun. Let's make it work, for real.

– Rohit Agarwal

Acknowledgements

This book would not have been possible without the support and encouragement of several people who stood by me throughout this journey.

First and foremost, I would like to thank my wife, Richa, and my son, Sanyam, for their patience, understanding, and constant support. Writing this book demanded time and focus, and their unwavering encouragement made all the difference.

I am also grateful to my colleagues—Samarth, Prithviraj, and Khushi—for the many insightful technical discussions that helped shape my thinking and refine the ideas presented in this book. Their perspectives and questions pushed me to go deeper and be more precise.

Special thanks to Nidhi Agrawal for her prompt proofreading and valuable edits to the manuscript at short notice.

Above all, I would like to thank Lalit Bhise, whose motivation and belief in me played a pivotal role in getting this book started and, more importantly, completed. His encouragement gave me the confidence to take this step.

This is my first venture into serious writing, and I hope it is just the beginning of many more to come.

CHAPTER 01

Cutting Through the AI Hype: The Real Story Behind Agentic Intelligence

"When uncertainty became the norm, AI had to learn not just to predict but to decide."

The COVID-19 pandemic was not just a global health crisis; it was a technological reset button. In the span of months, the world experienced what would have otherwise taken a decade of digital transformation. Businesses that once operated in boardrooms and factories suddenly found themselves running on Zoom, cloud servers, and algorithms.

Before COVID, the artificial intelligence landscape was largely dominated by **conventional AI** that was built on rule-based systems, statistical models, and machine learning pipelines that excelled at specific, well-defined tasks. They could forecast demand, detect fraud, or optimize logistics but they thrived only in **stable, predictable** environments.

When the world changed overnight, these systems faltered. They couldn't adapt, reason, or respond to new realities because they weren't built to.

Then came the **post-pandemic explosion of AI hype**. In just a few years, the term "AI" went from a niche technical topic to dinner-table conversation. ChatGPT became the face of modern intelligence; every startup became an "AI company," and every corporate boardroom began asking the same question:

"How can we use AI to transform our business?"

But amidst this frenzy, **clarity** was lost.

The headlines glorified Generative AI models for writing poems, composing emails, and generating images, but few people paused to ask:

Can this really solve business problems at scale?

Why do so many AI pilots never move past experimentation?

Why do billions of dollars poured into AI yield so little measurable return?

The truth is, we are standing at an **inflection point** in the AI journey. The world is now waking up to the limitations of "static intelligence" and discovering the next evolution:

> "Agentic AI, a new paradigm that moves beyond prediction and generation toward autonomy, reasoning, and action."

Agentic AI is not just another model. It's a system capable of understanding goals, reasoning through uncertainty, deciding what to do next, and calling on tools or other agents to execute those actions, much like a human professional would.

If conventional AI was like a calculator, and Generative AI like an artist, then Agentic AI is like a *strategist*, the one who can plan, adapt, and act.

Yet despite the enormous promise, we are also seeing familiar signs of **disillusionment**. A quick Google Search for *'references of cases where AI projects failed to deliver ROI'* returns multiple studies from diverse organizations with differing failure statistics, but they all point to one undeniable conclusion: ***not everything is on track***.

Hype cycles continue to outpace practical understanding. Most organizations adopt these technologies out of **FOMO** not strategy. They see demos of AI writing code or creating content and imagine overnight transformation, only to realize that moving from *prototype to production* is a different kind of challenge altogether.

That's exactly why this book exists.

This book isn't about the hype. It's about the **how**. It's about cutting through the noise to uncover what truly works when you try to build and scale **Agentic AI** in the real world.

We'll go beyond definitions to explore **how to design, deploy, and manage these systems responsibly**. Along the way, we'll dissect the **mistakes that derail most AI projects**, the **frameworks that make them succeed**, and the **mindset shift** organizations must adopt to turn experiments into real business value.

This is not a "**how to code an agent**" manual. It's a **design conversation**; a high-level exploration of the **components, subsystems, and architectural choices** that shape intelligent agents. Our focus is on understanding how the pieces fit together, not on writing the code that glues them. This book will provide a comprehensive understanding of the design choices that influence the performance of agentic systems.

The goal is simple and urgent: to help you understand the **technology, its potential, and its limits**, so you can build systems that **deliver results, not just demonstrations**.

Because AI isn't magic. It's **engineering, reasoning, and design.** And the age of **Agentic Intelligence** has only just begun.

The Evolution of Intelligence: From Equations to Conversations

The story of Artificial Intelligence is a journey of relentless curiosity. A tale of humans trying to build machines that could *think*. What began as an abstract dream has now seeped into every corner of modern life: from the phones we carry to the cars we drive and the conversations we have with systems like *ChatGPT*.

But how did we get here? How did AI evolve from obscure research papers to becoming a household companion?

To make sense of this journey, we'll trace it across **six pivotal eras** where each one is pushing machines a little closer to understanding the world like we do.

1. The Age of Equations (1990s - Early 2000s)

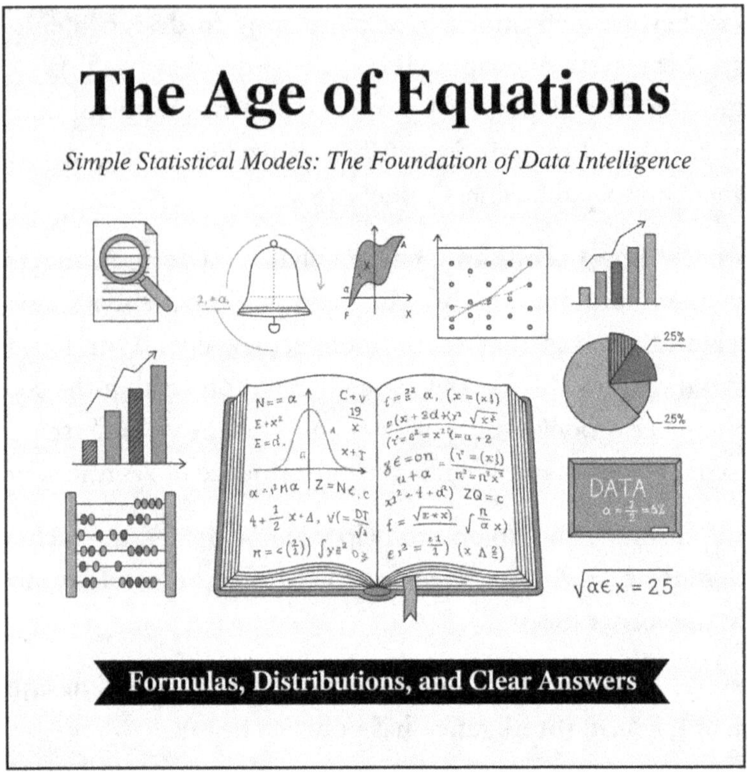

- **Data was scarce.** Storing a few gigabytes was a luxury; compute power was painfully limited.
- **Models were humble:** regression, time-series analysis, and a few statistical tricks.
- **AI meant math, not magic.** It was built by statisticians, the people of logic, not hype.
- **Intelligence lived in formulas**, not neural networks.

This was AI's quiet childhood which was precise, predictable, but far from "intelligent."

2. The Machine Learning Boom (2006 - 2012)

- The **Netflix Prize (2006)** changed everything. The $1M challenge to improve recommendations ignited a global data revolution.

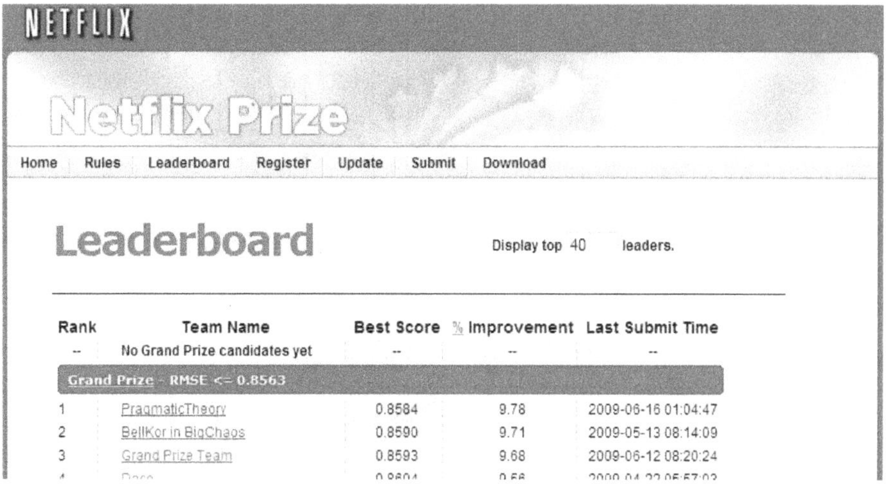

- **Data became abundant.** Storage was cheap, compute was accessible, and algorithms like random forests, gradient boosting, ensemble models, and collaborative filtering flourished.
- The term **"Machine Learning"** emerged, and with it, a new profession: the *Data Scientist.*
- Businesses realized **data could predict behavior.**
    - "If you liked this, you'll love that" became e-commerce gold.
    - Amazon, Netflix, Spotify—all rode this personalization wave.
- But intelligence was still trapped in **structured data,** that is, rows, columns, and tables. Machines could crunch numbers but couldn't yet *see* or *understand.*

3. The Deep Learning Era (2012 - 2017)

- The breakthrough came from **ImageNet (2012)** and a model named **AlexNet** that used *Convolutional Neural Networks (CNNs)* to recognize images.

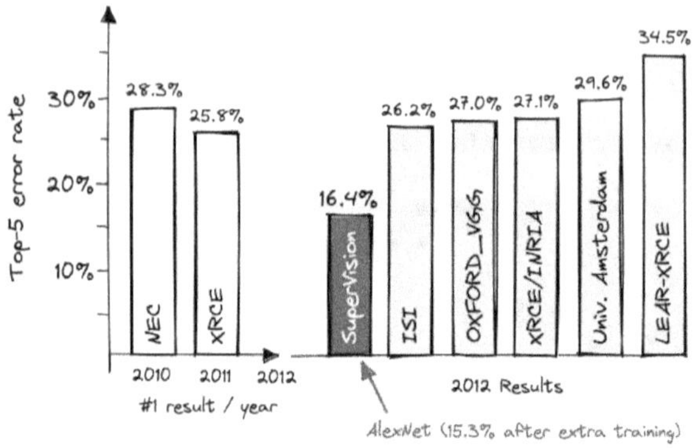

- **Deep Learning** was born. Machines could now *see,* identify objects, and even detect faces.
- **GPUs** (originally for gaming) powered this revolution, accelerating neural network training 100× faster than CPUs.
- AI was reborn as a **visual thinker**. It could recognize cats, cars, and handwriting with near-human accuracy.
- But while vision was solved, **language remained elusive.** Machines could label an image, but not interpret a sentence.

4. The Language Revolution (2017 - 2021)

- Google's paper *"Attention Is All You Need"* introduced the **Transformer**, teaching models to grasp **context** (how words relate to one another).
- **BERT (2018)** took it further by pre-training on massive text datasets, enabling models to understand meaning without manual labeling.
- Transformers turned raw text into **understanding**. Machines could now summarize, answer questions, and even reason in basic forms.

*Figure: Before BERT, Google would just show results about **how to get a prescription filled**. After BERT, Google understands that **"for someone"** means you're trying to **pick up a prescription for another person**, and it now shows results that actually help with that. (Image: https://huggingface.co/blog/bert-101)*

- This was the birth of **Generative AI**. Models that didn't just analyze text but could *create it.*

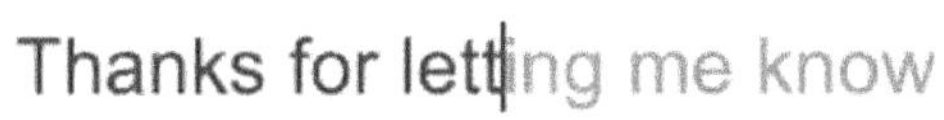

Figure: The ubiquitous auto suggestions that we see while writing mails or typing text in editor

- However, this revolution was still confined to researchers and developers and not accessible publicly.

5. The ChatGPT Moment (2022 - Present)

- **OpenAI's ChatGPT** made AI universally accessible without any code, set up, and just a chat box.
- For the first time, anyone could have a *conversation* with intelligence.
- Students wrote essays, marketers drafted campaigns, engineers debugged code in natural dialogue.
- This democratization triggered the **AI gold rush**. Every company suddenly wanted a "copilot."
- But cracks soon appeared: hallucinations, inconsistencies, and lack of grounding in real data.
    - LLMs could *talk convincingly* but didn't *know for sure.*

6. The Rise of Agentic AI (2024 - Future)

- The next frontier is **Agentic AI** systems that can *reason, plan, and act.*
- Unlike traditional chatbots, these agents:
    - Use **tools and APIs** to fetch live information.
    - Validate outputs instead of hallucinating.
    - Execute tasks and make decisions autonomously.
- Agentic AI marks a shift from *conversation* to *cognition.* It's where AI stops being reactive and starts being *responsible.*

In Summary

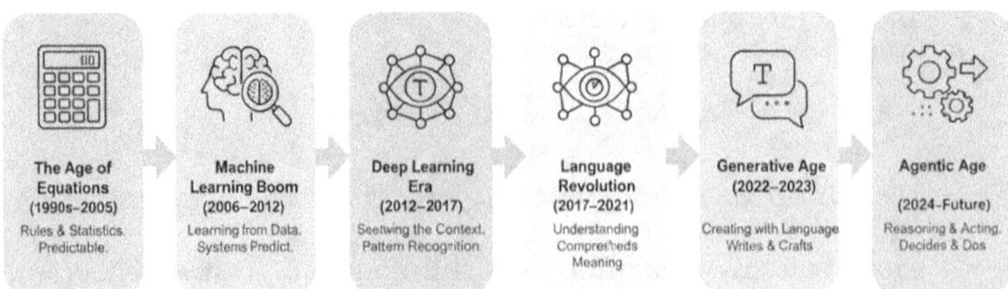

Era	Defining Capability	Breakthrough Moment	What It Meant for AI
Age of Equations (1990s–2005)	Rule-based & Statistical Models	Regression, Forecasting, Time-Series	Intelligence was math (predictable but rigid).
Machine Learning Boom (2006–2012)	Learning from Data	Netflix Prize, Random Forests, Gradient Boosting	Data became the new oil. Systems learned to predict.
Deep Learning Era (2012–2017)	Seeing the World	ImageNet, CNNs, GPUs	Machines learned to recognize faces, objects, patterns.
Language Revolution (2017–2021)	Understanding Context	Transformers, BERT	Machines began to comprehend meaning and nuance.
Generative Age (2022–2023)	Creating with Language	ChatGPT, OpenAI, LLMs	AI could now talk, write, and create but not think.
Agentic Age (2024–Future)	Reasoning & Acting	Tool-Using Agents, Autonomous Orchestration	AI stops predicting. It starts deciding and doing.

Understanding Agentic AI

Let's begin with a straightforward example.

In traditional systems, when you ask a question, you get an answer. But with **Agentic AI**, the interaction goes a step further—from responding to *doing*.

Instead of asking , *"What's a 5 day itinerary for Italy?,"* you might say, *"Book me a 5-day trip to Italy with a focus on food and history, under $3000."*

In this case, the system doesn't just generate a description. It retrieves real-time data, checks flight and hotel availability, reviews options, and presents a complete plan ready for action.

That's the key distinction: **Agentic AI doesn't just inform, it executes.**

What Really is Agentic AI?

In architectural terms, **Agentic AI** is not a single model. It's a **pattern.** A pattern that brings together three essential components:

1. **An LLM (Large Language Model)**: the brain that understands and generates natural language.
2. **A Reasoning or Decision Layer**: the logic that decides *what needs to be done next.*
3. **A Set of Tools or Functions**: external systems the LLM can call to actually *do* things.

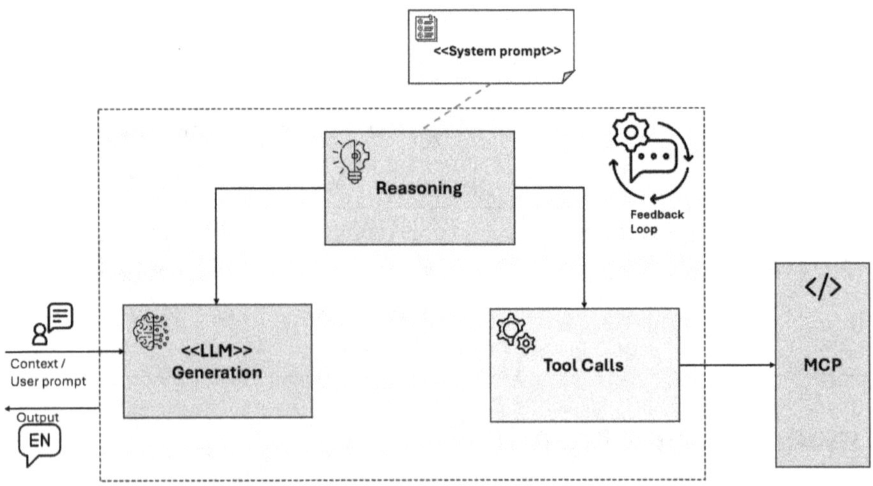

With all three components operating together in a continuous loop, the agent is able to solve tasks autonomously. This feedback loop is essential. It allows the agent to evaluate the outcome of each step and adjust its approach when the initial result is incomplete or incorrect. As we will see in later chapters, this feedback mechanism is at the heart of agentic capability itself, and much of the ongoing research in agent architectures is focused on refining, strengthening, and accelerating this loop with each new design.

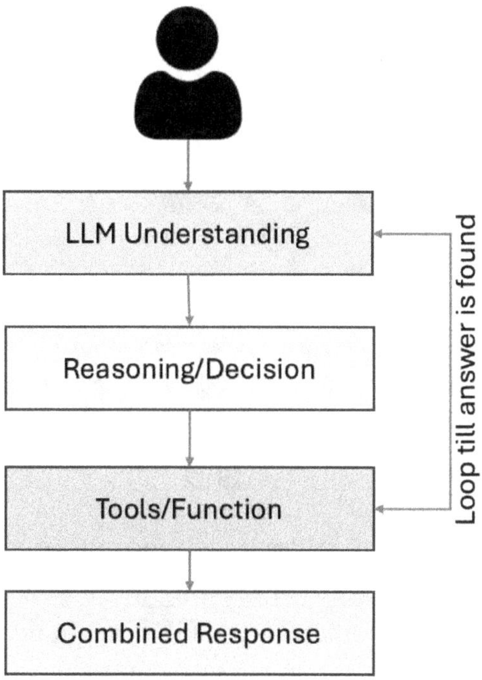

How LLMs Fit Into the Picture

Today, most of what we call "AI" begins and ends with the **LLM**. These massive models with names like GPT-4, Claude, Gemini are built on billions of parameters. Think of parameters as compressed knowledge with each one storing tiny fragments of how the world works.

As **Andrej Karpathy** once said,

> *"An LLM is basically a zip file of the internet with a good search function."*

That's your **parametric memory**—the information the model carries within its parameters.

When you ask, *"What's the capital of France?"* it doesn't look up external data, it *just retrieves from its learned parameters.*

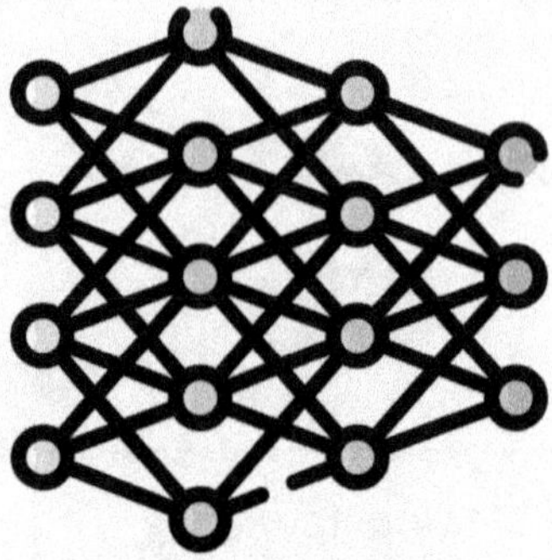

Figure: The parameters are the variables /nodes which are trained during the LLM training. 7B, 32B is the number of these parameters. The world knowledge is gained and stored in these parameters as part of the training

But here's the catch!!

Unlike Google, which constantly re-crawls and updates the web, an LLM's memory is **frozen at the time of training**. So if you create a webpage today, Google will find it tomorrow but GPT might never know it exists.

That's where the cracks start to show.

The Itinerary Problem: Where Static Intelligence Fails

Let's take the previous example.

You ask:

> "Plan a 7-day trip to Italy from Bangalore."

An LLM will do a great job because it's been trained on thousands of travel blogs, itineraries, and articles.

It will create something that looks like this:

```
Day 1: Arrive in Rome -- explore the Colosseum.
Day 2: Vatican City tour.
Day 3-4: Florence -- art and cuisine.
Day 5-7: Venice -- canals, gondolas, and gelato.
```

Pretty impressive.

But now, add some **real-world constraints**:

> *"Plan and book my 7-day Italy trip, under $3000, with stays in 4-star hotels near historical landmarks."*

Now the LLM hits a wall.

- It doesn't know current flight prices.
- It can't compare hotels or check today's availability.
- It can't access your travel budget or book anything.

That's because this information doesn't live in its parameters. It lives **outside**.

And this is exactly where **Agentic AI steps in**.

The Augmentation: Reasoning + Tools

To bridge the gap between *knowledge* and *action*, the LLM must be **augmented** with **two key capabilities**:

- **Reasoning (or Decision-Making):**
- The ability to recognize *what it doesn't know* and decide *what to do next.*
- For example:
    - "This query needs real-time data—fetch it."
    - "This requires code execution—run a function."
    - "This information is internal—check the company database."

This layer is what gives the system self-awareness and control flow, or, simply put, the ability to "think" before "doing" it.

Tools or Function Calls:

- Once the reasoning layer decides the next action, the model calls an external **tool** to execute it.

- These could be:
    - APIs (for flights, hotels, stock data, etc.)
    - Code interpreters (for math or logic problems)
    - Knowledge bases (for enterprise data)

The connection between LLMs and tools is made through standardized protocols like **MCP (Model Context Protocol)** which allows models to discover, list, and invoke external services safely. We will cover in detail on MCP in the later chapters.

Putting It All Together

Let's revisit our Italy example:

> "*Plan and book my 7-day Italy trip within a $3000 budget, focusing on history and food.*"

Here's how an **Agentic AI** handles it:

1. **LLM (Understanding or Perception):** Recognizes the intent, that is, "plan and book trip."
2. **Reasoning (Decision):** Determines it needs flight, hotel, and restaurant data which must be fetched externally.
3. **Tools (Action):** Calls APIs for flight prices, checks hotel availability, reads restaurant reviews.
4. **LLM (Integration):** Merges the real-time results with its parametric memory to generate a coherent plan; a complete itinerary aligned with the user's budget and preferences.

That's not just answering, that's *executing*. And that's what makes a system **agentic**.

The Invisible Magic of Function Calls

In programming, every action is executed with a function call that is called within the business logic for e.g.

Function	Action
calculate_discount (price, discount_perc)	Calculates the discount given the original price and the discount%
get_weather(city)	Finds the weather of the given city
book_hotel(location, budget)	Given the location and the budget the function will book the hotel

Agentic AI does the same thing but now, the **function call is generated automatically by the LLM**. The user just says, *"Book me a hotel in Florence,"* and under the hood, the system translates it into:

```
book_hotel(city="Florence", rating="4-star", budget=1000)
```

It's invisible, seamless, and feels almost magical — but it's pure architecture.

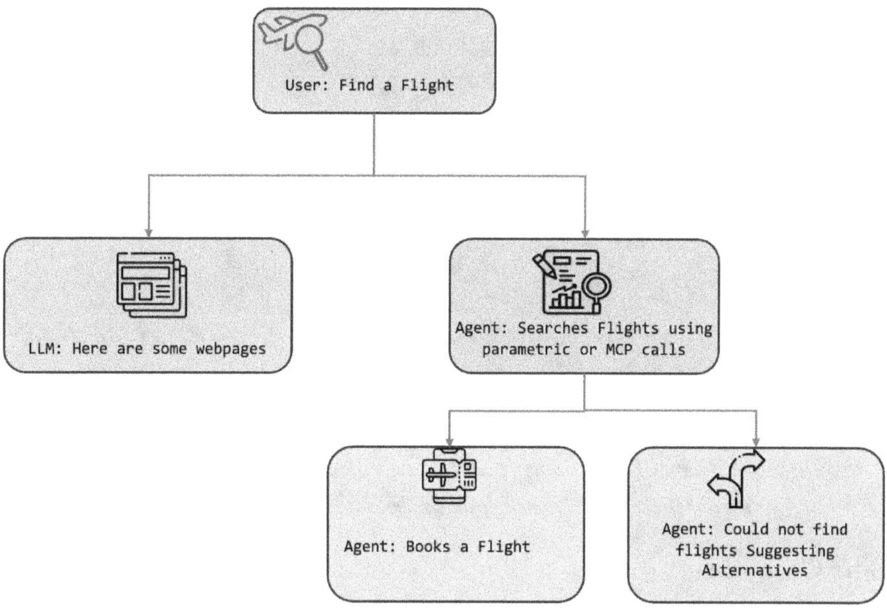

Figure: Suggests the difference between the LLM approach and the Agentic Approach for searching the flights which is one of the key steps for designing an Itinerary. The LLM approach acts as a powerful search engine to find out the relevant content while the Agentic Approach is trying to book the most relevant flights

Why This Matters

This architectural shift changes everything. It's the difference between an LLM that *talks* and an AI that *acts*. Between *answers* and *outcomes*.

When reasoning and tools come together, the LLM stops being a storyteller and becomes a **problem solver** who is capable of chaining logic, calling functions, and collaborating with other systems autonomously.

ChatGPT's Code Interpreter, for example, was an early glimpse of this, allowing the model to run math, analyze data, and generate charts. Each time you ask it to "calculate," "draw," or "compare," you're witnessing **Agentic behavior**—the AI deciding what to do, calling the right tool, and merging the results—all without you seeing the process.

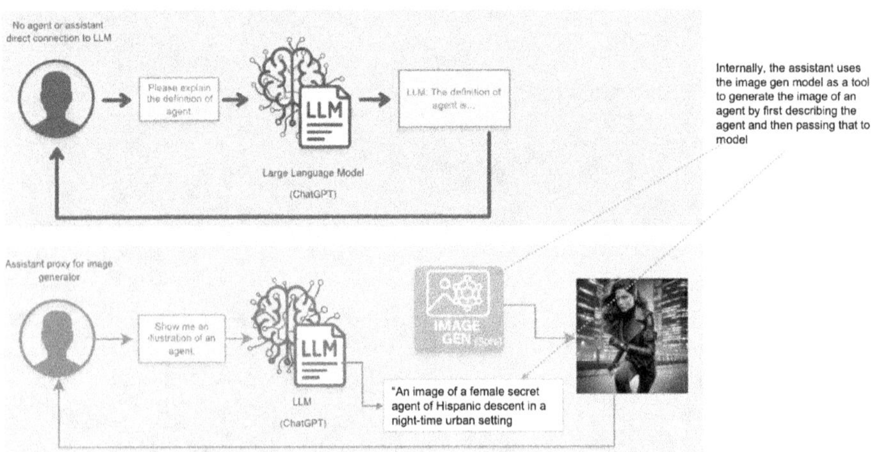

Figure: Shows the difference between the pure LLM and the agentic workflow . It also highlights how some of the commonly used LLM systems like ChatGPT automatically performs the agentic workflows without actually telling the user.

The Core Idea

Agentic AI = LLM + Reasoning + Tools

It's not a product. It's not a buzzword. It's architecture.

A system design where the LLM:

- Understands the goal
- Thinks through how to achieve it
- Acts by invoking tools
- And integrates the results into a complete, human-like response.

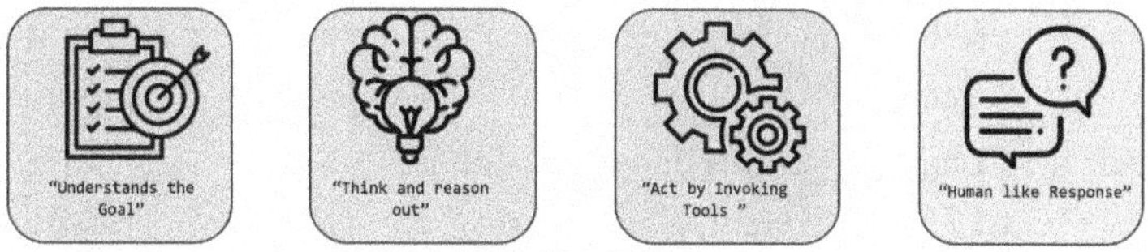

Agentic AI Capabilities

It's the difference between asking a question and getting something *done.*

Agentic AI transforms an LLM from a *passive responder* into an *active problem solver.* It no longer just talks. It thinks, plans, and acts.

In essence, **Agentic AI is an LLM-based system that completes a task either using its own knowledge or by calling other tools, functions, or agents to finish the job.**

Agentic AI doesn't just answer questions; it *understands goals, plans intelligently, uses the right resources, and achieves outcomes.*

This table clearly explains the difference between the Conventional AI, Generative AI , and Agentic AI

Era / Type	Core Idea	What It Does	Example Use Cases	Key Limitation	Analogy
Conventional AI (Rule-Based & Classical ML)	Follows pre-defined rules or learns from structured data	Predicts or classifies based on past patterns	Fraud detection, spam filters, demand forecasting	Can't adapt beyond its training or rules	An obedient accountant that follows instructions perfectly, but never questions them.

Era / Type	Core Idea	What It Does	Example Use Cases	Key Limitation	Analogy
Generative AI (GenAI)	Learns patterns from huge datasets to create new content	Generates text, images, audio, and code	ChatGPT, DALL·E, Gmail's smart compose	Creative but not goal-driven because it responds, but doesn't act	A creative artist who paints or writes beautifully, but waits for your prompt.
Agentic AI	Combines LLMs + reasoning + tools for real-world action	Understands intent, plans actions, uses tools/APIs to complete tasks	Booking a trip, managing schedules, automating workflows	Still evolving: reasoning and control boundaries are active research	A proactive assistant that plans, reasons, and gets the job done for you.

If It's So Powerful, Why Isn't Everyone Using It in Production?

Now, if Agentic AI is *so transformative*, you might wonder *why isn't every company using it successfully?*

The reality is far less glamorous. A **recent MIT study** revealed that **95% of all AI projects fail to deliver any ROI**. (Source: Forbes, Aug 2025) A similar trend has been observed in India too. Despite the hype, boardroom presentations, and glossy demos, most AI pilots quietly fade into oblivion within months.

So, what's really happening?

Why is something so powerful, so full of promise, *struggling to create tangible business value*? Let's unpack a few hard truths.

1. The FOMO Problem (Chasing AI Without a Purpose)

Figure: Generated using Gemini

The biggest reason for failure is surprisingly human—**FOMO (Fear of Missing Out).**

Everyone wants to say they're "doing something with AI." Executives announce AI initiatives in press releases, teams scramble to integrate LLMs into workflows often without any clear business case.

The result? **Expectation mismatch.**

Agentic AI is a marvel. It can reason, automate, and even write complex code.

But that doesn't mean *every* workflow needs it. Before adopting it, every organization must ask a simple question:

> *"Is this solving a real business problem, or are we just doing it because everyone else is?"*

For instance, using an LLM to automate internal FAQs may sound futuristic. But a well-designed search system might do the job faster, cheaper, and more reliably.

2. Generic Intelligence Meets Domain Complexity

Figure: Generated using Gemini

Most LLMs are **trained for general-purpose intelligence** like summarizing text, writing emails, creating content, or answering open-ended questions. They perform brilliantly in these creative and linguistic tasks.

But drop them into a **specialized domain**, say, manufacturing, supply chain optimization, or financial compliance, and they stumble.

These areas demand **domain-specific reasoning** and **high factual accuracy**. A generic LLM doesn't "understand" the nuances of industrial machinery or financial regulations the way experts do.

Until companies train or fine-tune these models with proprietary data and strict validation, they'll continue to face accuracy, reliability, and compliance challenges.

3. The Perfection Illusion (Expecting AI to Be Infallible)

Figure: Generated using Gemini

Here's another common trap: unrealistic expectations.

Many business leaders assume that once they deploy AI, it will **always be right** like a superhuman oracle. But AI, even Agentic AI, is fundamentally **probabilistic**, not deterministic. It's designed to predict the *most likely* answer, not the *perfect* one. A 90% accuracy rate might sound impressive to a data scientist, but to a CEO spending millions, it feels like failure.

The truth?

Every AI system will have an inherent margin of error just as humans do. Expecting perfection from a probabilistic model is like expecting weather forecasts to always be 100% accurate.

4. Wrong Tool for the Right Problem

Figure: Generated using Gemini

Not every problem needs an LLM. This is perhaps the most ignored principle in today's AI gold rush. Many organizations deploy massive models for problems that could be solved with **simple statistical or rule-based methods**.

A logistic regression, a decision tree, or even a few SQL queries could sometimes outperform a fancy LLM but because these don't *sound* like AI, they're dismissed as "too simple."

This mindset that "*complex equals intelligent*" has led to countless expensive failures. Simplicity, ironically, is often the smartest strategy.

From Proof of Concept to Production Reality

This book isn't about building another flashy AI demo or recycling what's already been done. It's about something far more difficult and far more important:

"How to take an Agentic AI system from proof of concept (POC) to production"

That might sound straightforward, but in reality, it's the hardest part of the AI journey. Look around, and you'll find endless blogs, whitepapers, and conference talks showcasing use cases **but very few that explain how to actually make those systems work *at scale*.** As we discussed earlier, most projects never make it beyond the POC stage. They stay trapped in the lab—impressive in PowerPoint, but unusable in production.

This book aims to change that. It's written for the **practitioners—the builders, architects, and decision-makers**—who are done with hype and want to know how to make Agentic AI work in the real world and to solve the business problems. To do that, we take a grounded, industry-first approach.

We focus on the **Consumer Packaged Goods (CPG)** industry, a domain that perfectly illustrates the complexity, data diversity, and operational scale where Agentic AI can truly shine. Through these examples, you'll see how intelligent systems can enable smarter decision-making, automate reasoning-based workflows, and deliver scalable question-answering systems capable of serving millions.

The book follows a practical flow that mirrors how real-world systems are built:

1. Understanding the Domain and the Opportunity

We start with the *why*. Before choosing tools or architectures, we ground ourselves in real business problems that Agentic AI can meaningfully solve.

2. Exploring the Data

Every intelligent system is only as strong as its data. Here, we'll examine the data behind our examples: its structure, its limitations, and its potential for reasoning-driven AI.

3. Architectural Foundations for Agentic AI

Before scaling, you need strong foundations. This section explores the core principles of production-grade architecture: **scalability, data protection, cost efficiency, reproducibility, and governance**. These aren't optional extras. They're what determine whether your AI remains a toy or becomes a trusted enterprise system.

4. Six Paths to Building Agentic AI Systems

At the heart of this book are six distinct approaches to designing and deploying Agentic AI for the CPG industry. Each chapter examines their architectures, trade-offs, and true "agentic" nature (versus mere marketing). It takes you through a full exploration: the technical architecture, how the components interact, and where each method excels or falls short.

Furthermore, we'll dive into ***cost-effectiveness (especially around LLM API usage), scalability, data protection, and error handling*** identifying where hallucinations and failures could undermine reliability. The goal isn't just to describe architectures but to *stress-test* them for real-world viability.

Moving from POC to production is not a simple matter of moving code from one server to another.It requires deliberate choices across several key pillars:

- **Tools:** From IDEs and version control to CI/CD pipelines and observability stacks, your toolchain must support the full lifecycle: build, deploy, monitor, and evolve.
- **APIs:** Integration is everything. We'll discuss selecting and managing APIs (internal and third-party) with a focus on reliability, security, and clear documentation.
- **LLMs:** The model you choose defines both your capabilities and your costs. We'll evaluate performance, ethical considerations, and pricing strategies to help balance ambition with sustainability.

- **Scalability:** True production systems must adapt to changing loads. We'll explore design patterns for horizontal and vertical scalability that prevent bottlenecks as usage grows.
- **Accuracy:** Domain grounding is critical. We'll look at why many LLM-based solutions fail here and how to prevent issues like "hallucinating" products your company doesn't even sell.
- **Observability:** When outputs can't be fully predicted, you need robust monitoring. We'll discuss human-in-the-loop review, automated evaluation, and how LLMs can audit other LLMs at scale.

Here is a infographics to remember

In short, the journey from POC to production demands a holistic, system-level perspective that balances technology, cost, and trust. We have gone through it and the book is a reflection of that journey. You'll see the incremental steps, lessons, and trade-offs we faced while developing production-ready Agentic AI systems not as a marketing story, but as a realistic playbook for anyone building at scale.

By the end, you won't just understand what *Agentic AI* means. You'll know how to design, deploy, and scale it responsibly. You'll have a clear view of the full lifecycle: from prototype to platform, from proof of concept to production. And most importantly, you'll be equipped to build systems that don't just talk smart but also **think, act, and deliver** at enterprise scale.

CHAPTER 02

The Data Backbone for Our Agentic AI Examples

"Without data, you're just another person with an opinion."
—W. Edwards Deming

To make this book both practical and relevant and to truly reflect the journey from *proof of concept* (POC) to *production at scale*. Every example and case study in the coming chapters is grounded in one of the most dynamic and data-rich industries in the world: the **Consumer Packaged Goods (CPG)** industry.

The CPG industry is, in many ways, the pulse of everyday life. It includes the products that find their way into every household—from your morning cup of coffee to the detergent you use for laundry, the shampoo on your bathroom shelf, and the snacks in your pantry. These are the brands and items we interact with daily, often without even realizing it.

Figure: The various products that we need to consume in daily life. They can be classified mostly as Beverages, Home care, Personal Care, Commodities, Dairy, Medicines

What makes this industry fascinating from an AI standpoint is not just the sheer volume of products, but the **diversity of its retail landscape**. In an offline setting (retail shops) CPG products are sold across two very distinct worlds:

- **Modern Trade (Organized Retail):** These are the supermarkets, hypermarkets, and retail chains, basically well-lit stores where products are neatly stacked, barcoded, and tracked. Customers walk through aisles, pick up what they need, and often make decisions influenced by promotions, product placement, and recommendations.

- **General Trade (Unorganized Retail):** On the other end of the spectrum lies the traditional shop or the small neighborhood store or the "***Kirana***" as it's known in India. Here, products are not always visible. The shelves are crowded, the inventory is often managed manually, and the customer usually asks the shopkeeper for what they want rather than picking it off a shelf.

Modern Trade Shop

General Trade (Kirana Stores in India)

The Hidden Complexity of the Shelf

Before any product reaches your shopping basket or your kitchen shelf, it must first **exist** on the store shelf. That simple fact hides an entire universe of operational complexity. Behind every well-stocked store is a coordinated supply chain: a daily choreography of manufacturing, distribution, and sales execution.

At the front lines of this system stand the sales representatives , the "*feet on the street*". They visit stores, check which products are missing, record orders, and make sure the right items are available at the right time. Their work ensures that both the organized supermarket and the unassuming corner store can serve their communities without interruption.

This **flow of goods, data, and decisions** forms the heartbeat of the CPG ecosystem. It's dynamic, distributed, and endlessly rich in data, making it a perfect stage for exploring how agentic AI can make real impact.

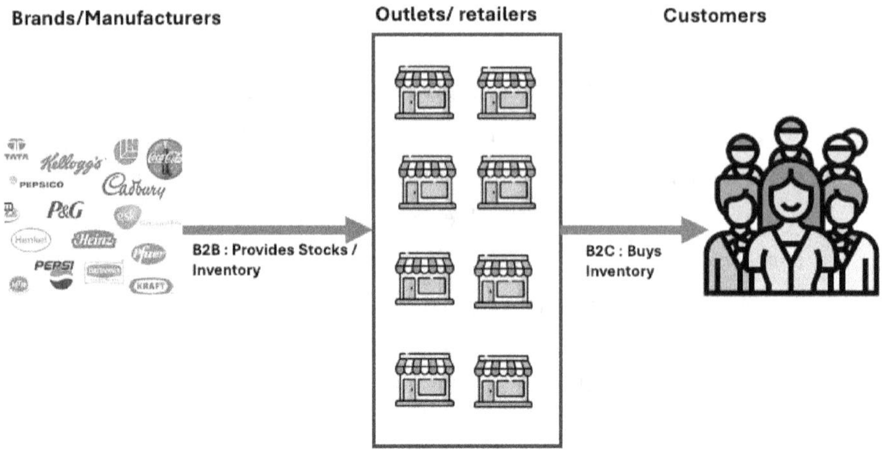

Figure: The diagram illustrates the flow of products from manufacturers or brands to the end consumer, mediated by retailers. The interaction between brands and retailers is categorized as a ***B2B*** *(business-to-business) transaction, whereas the interaction between retailers and consumers is a* ***B2C*** *(business-to-consumer) transaction.*

The scenarios we'll explore are set in this dynamic B2B ecosystem, where sales representatives act as the vital link between manufacturers and retailers. Their job is to make sure stores are always ready to meet the needs of shoppers, managing inventories so each outlet, from the sprawling supermarket to the bustling corner kirana, can serve its unique community of customers. It's this flow of goods, data, and decisions that defines the CPG world.

CPG Core Entities

At the center of our dataset, and indeed of every CPG operation, are two foundational entities:

1. **Products (SKUs):** the individual items that consumers buy. These can vary from everyday staples like Rice, Wheat, Milk to Household needs like Detergent, Soap to Personal Care like Shampoos, Body wash and so on.
2. **Outlets:** the diverse stores and shops that bring those products to people. These range from high-volume supermarkets carrying

thousands of items to small, family-run stores where every inch of shelf space is carefully negotiated.

Together, products and outlets form the backbone of CPG analytics. Understanding their interactions: what's selling where, what's missing, what's moving too slowly, is what drives smarter supply chains, targeted promotions, and better business decisions. Any software that stores the data for the CPG analytics will have to deal with these entities.

Some of the key attributes or these entities are:

SKU/ Product

Attribute	Type	Explanation
skuId	int	SKU key
name	string	Name of the SKU
size	string	What is the size of the sku e.g. 100ml, 1L, 100gm, etc.
price	float	5$, 2.5$
Expiry date	date	Till which date the product can be sold

Outlets/ Retail Shop

Attribute	Type	Explanation
outletId	int	Outlet identifier
name	string	Name of the outlet like **abc supermarket**
address	string	1001, charleston street , KA
phone	string	+91977967332
latitude	float	12.8799
longitude	float	77.87682

At the intersection of **products** and **outlets** lies the heartbeat of the CPG industry, **sales**. Every product placement, every restock, every negotiation between a brand representative and a retailer eventually translates into one simple, measurable event: a sale.

In practice, this process unfolds through the daily work of sales representatives. These field executives visit multiple outlets, check which products are available, take new orders, and record transactions. Each of these interactions becomes a **sales record**, forming the most vital data link between a manufacturer and the marketplace.

To capture this activity, the system maintains a dedicated **Sales Table,** which is a structured log of every transaction that occurs between a product and an outlet. This table provides a single source of truth for understanding what is selling, where, when, and in what quantity.

Attribute	**Type**	**Explanation**
skuId	int	SKU that has been sold
outletId	int	Outlet to which the SKU is sold
qty	int	Quantity of the SKU sold
amount	float	Amount=Quantity * price of the SKU
salesDate	date	Date of sales

Here is a ER Diagram for the same

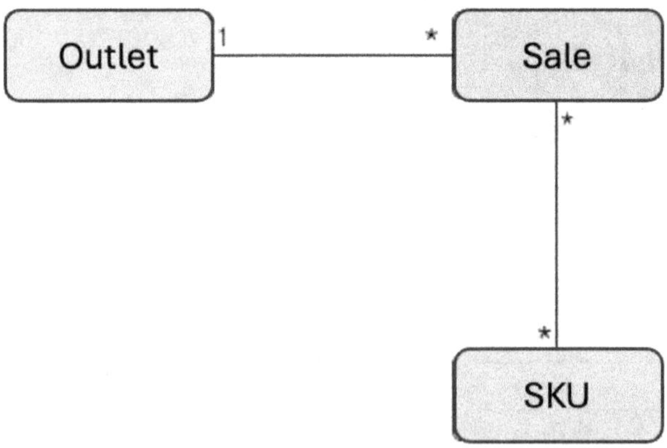

These simple attributes together unlock a wealth of analytical power. They allow us to track trends across time and geography, identify top-performing SKUs or outlets, detect stockouts, forecast demand, and even measure the effectiveness of promotions or field strategies.

In the chapters that follow, this Sales Table, alongside the Products and Outlets tables, will serve as our foundation. It's through these interconnected datasets that we'll explore how agentic systems think, plan, and act: writing queries, interpreting results, and helping organizations make smarter, faster, and more scalable decisions.

Why Does this Dataset Matters?

By grounding our discussion in this consistent, relatable dataset and following the journeys of these products and outlets, we'll build a shared mental model that connects data to real-world behavior.

You'll see how concepts grow organically: from small experiments on a few stores and SKUs to full-scale, production-ready agentic systems that can operate across thousands of locations. The examples in this book are drawn from this living ecosystem, giving every chapter a clear anchor in both business reality and data reality.

Turning Data into Direction

For leading consumer brands and manufacturers, names like **Procter & Gamble**, **Unilever**, and their many global peers, data isn't just a record of what has happened. It's a **strategic compass**, guiding everything from production schedules to marketing decisions.

Each day, these organizations sift through millions of sales and inventory records, not simply to count what's been sold, but to **discover patterns**. These signals are hidden in the noise that can shape their next move. The real value lies not in the data itself, but in the *questions* it helps answer.

It's not just about measuring performance; it's about asking:

> *What's working? What's faltering? And where's the next opportunity waiting to be found?*

The questions range from the practical to the visionary:

- **Which SKUs are top sellers at a particular outlet?**
    - Identifying the products that perform best in each store helps tailor inventory recommendations and promotional strategies.

- **Which SKUs have poor stock rotation?**
  - Poor stock rotation indicates products that are not selling through to end consumers and are rarely reordered by outlets, signaling a need for intervention.
- **Which SKUs have experienced a surge in demand?**
  - Tracking products with recent spikes in sales over the past three months highlights trending items that may require greater supply or promotional effort.
- **Which SKUs are losing demand?**
  - Monitoring declining sales trends over a similar three-month period reveals which products are falling out of favor and may require strategic adjustments.
- **Which SKUs are nearing expiration?**
  - Identifying near-expiry items allows brands to prioritize pushing these products out to outlets, ensuring they reach consumers before becoming unsellable.
- **Which outlets have purchased the largest quantities of inventory?**
  - Recognizing high-volume buyers helps brands focus on nurturing key business relationships.
- **Which outlets have shown improvement over time?**
  - Analyzing positive sales trends at certain outlets over the past three months can reveal growth opportunities and best practices.
- **Which outlets are struggling?**
  - Outlets exhibiting declining purchase trends over time can be targeted for support, training, or special offers to help reverse downward trajectories.

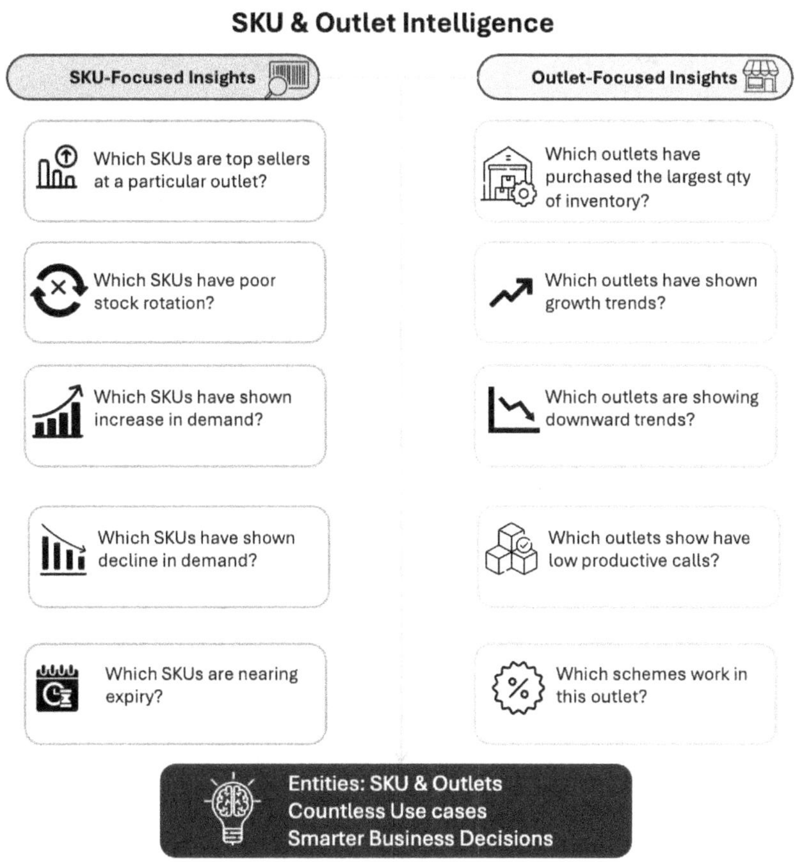

This list is by no means exhaustive; there are numerous other questions analysts might pose. In practice, many analyses combine several of these queries, generating even more sophisticated insights to inform brand strategy. In the coming chapters we will see how these queries are used to create prompts for Agentic Outputs.

Bizom: Retail Intelligence Platform for consumer packaged goods (CPG) brands

Bizom (http://bizom.in) is a B2B retail execution platform used by consumer goods brands to manage sales operations across large and fragmented retail networks, particularly in emerging markets such as India. It supports workflows including sales force automation (SFA), distributor operations, and retail-level data capture, generating detailed records of day-to-day commercial activity.

The platform operates at scale, with hundreds of brands and a large field workforce using it to record orders, inventory movement, outlet visits, and fulfillment outcomes across millions of retail outlets. As a result, Bizom accumulates a continuous stream of structured transactional and operational data that reflects how products move from distributors to stores and how sales decisions are made on the ground.

For the purposes of this book, Bizom serves as a concrete and realistic data environment. The datasets derived from it such as products, outlets, sales transactions, and field activity , provide a consistent backbone for exploring agentic AI patterns. Rather than focusing on the platform itself, the examples use this data to illustrate how intelligent agents can reason over large-scale, real-world B2B sales systems and translate data into actionable decisions

Let's zoom into how B2B sales actually work in India and in much of Southeast Asia and Africa as well. Retail here runs on relationships and visits. Sales representatives physically go from shop to shop, talk to the store owner, take orders, and send them to distributors who fulfill them within a couple of days.

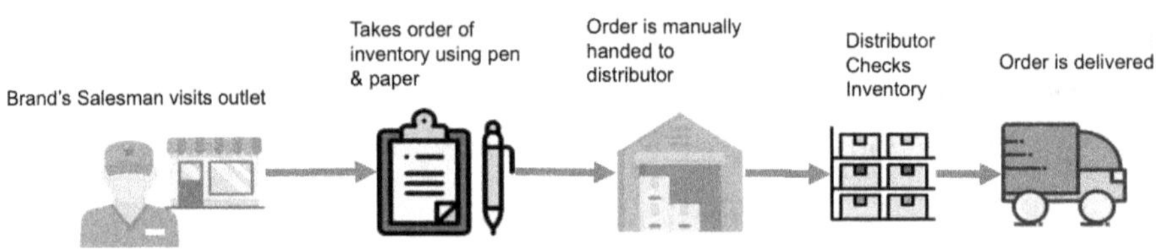

For a long time, this process was completely manual. A salesman would note down ***orders on a piece*** of paper, hand it over to the distributor, wait a day or two, and then the distributor would take another few days to deliver, assuming the stock was even available. Often it wasn't, which meant more delays, partial deliveries, or lost sales. A full cycle from visit to fulfillment could easily stretch to **a week.**

Bizom changed that entire flow.

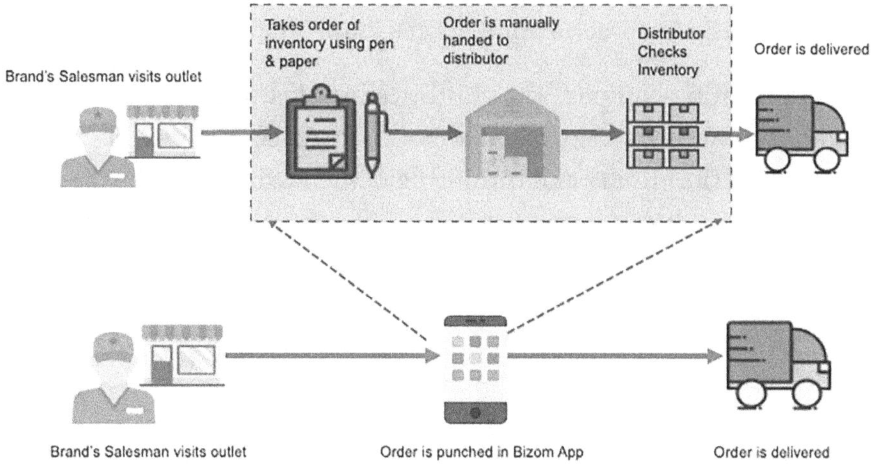

Now, when a salesperson walks into a shop, they walk in with intelligence, literally. The Bizom app shows **exactly which SKUs** this store is likely to sell, along with **recommended quantities**, calculated from real sales data. Only the products that are actually in stock at the distributor are shown, eliminating wasted order attempts. Once the shopkeeper confirms, the order is sent instantly to the distributor system with no waiting, no walking paper slips across town. The entire order fulfillment process gets completed in 2-3 days compared to earlier 7-8 days.

In a system as complex as this, data-driven insights are the secret sauce that turn routine visits into informed, impactful conversations. There are countless moments in the sales process where the right information can tip the scales, moments where a well-timed suggestion or a clear view of the trends can turn a simple store check-in into a true value-add for the retailer. For the purposes of this book, we're focusing on one such scenario: **the sales representative's visit to an outlet.**

Agentic Workflows in Bizom

Picture this: before even stepping inside, the salesperson is armed with a visual snapshot of an engaging image summarizing exactly what matters.

- What are the sales trends in this outlet?
- Which SKUs are flying off the shelves?
- How did last week's numbers stack up?

By transforming complex sales histories into instantly readable visuals, Bizom empowers its users to make every second count, sparking smarter decisions on the ground and turning data into action, store by store. This information is shown in the form of an image to make it interesting

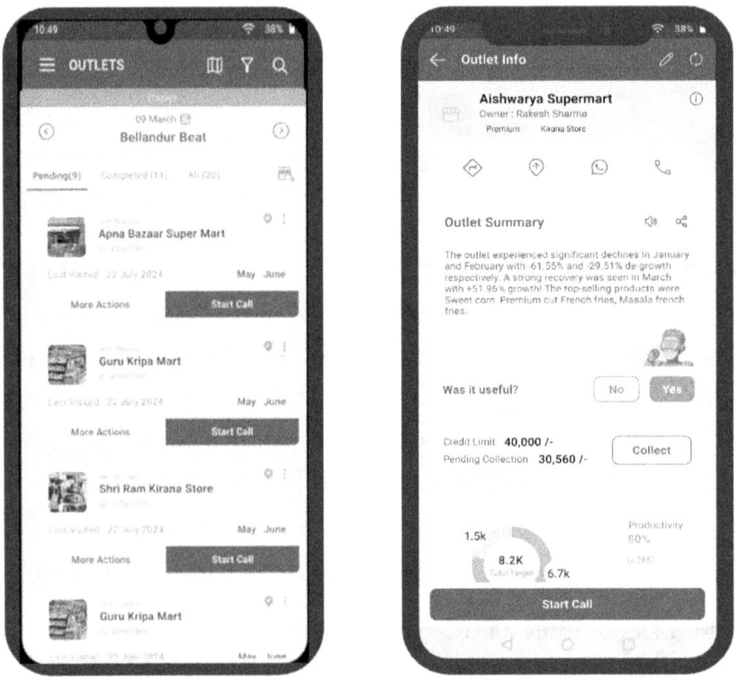

***Figure:** Bizom's Outlet Order Screen. When a salesperson selects a store to visit, Bizom presents a concise outlet summary, showing recent sales trends, high-velocity SKUs that are likely to sell, and indicators of potential growth opportunities. This snapshot helps the salesperson walk into the conversation informed, confident, and ready to make meaningful recommendations.*

Of course, the real power lies in the flexibility to ask the right questions at the right time.

Brands don't want to be boxed into a handful of standard reports or rigid dashboards. They want the freedom to dig deeper, to frame their own questions and follow their own hunches as the market shifts around them. That's why the system needs to be **adaptable**, ready to accommodate a wide variety of brand-specific queries.

Whether it's diving into seasonal trends, pinpointing the fastest-growing outlets, or uncovering the slow burners on the shelf, the platform must empower users to seek out insights that matter most to their unique business goals. In this new landscape, the ability to explore, customize, and evolve these questions isn't just a nice-to-have, it's a game-changer.

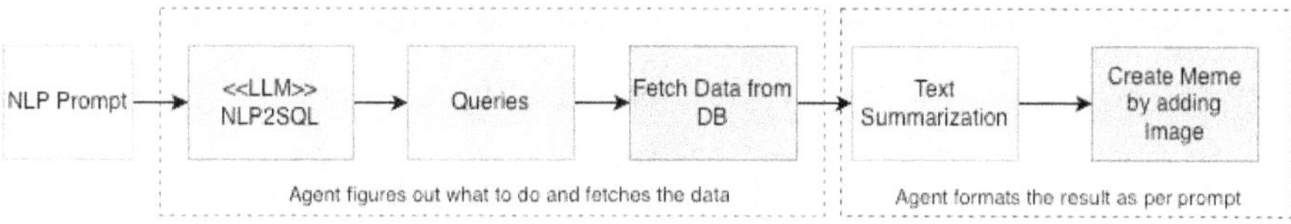

Figure: High Level Architecture of Agentic Flow

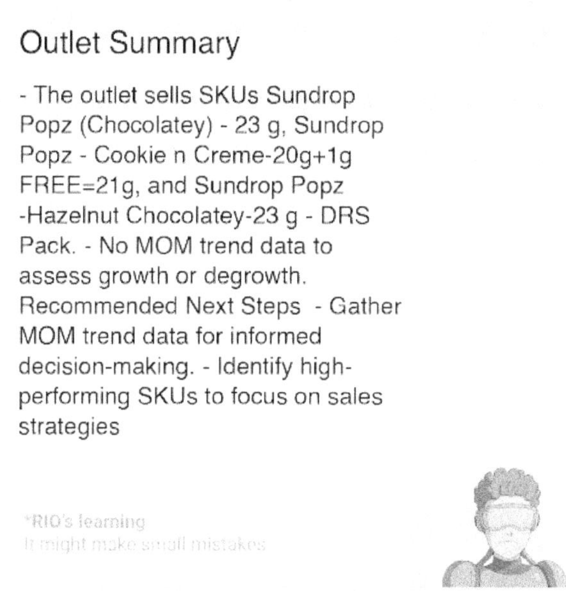

Figure: Agentic Output as Shown in Bizom

At the heart of this solution is the ability to **translate free-text questions which are posed in natural, everyday language, directly**

into precise SQL queries. This is a fundamental leap from the conventional approach, where every insight is hardwired: for each new question, a developer must carefully craft (and later, recraft) underlying queries.

Yes, you could build a similar reporting system with traditional tools, but in that world, every new business question is a ticket in the development queue—a cycle of requests, code changes, and waiting.

What sets this new approach apart is its remarkable adaptability. With **prompt-based** configuration, the conversation is wide open. Want to ask a different question or reframe an analysis? Just adjust the prompt without any need to overhaul the codebase. The system instantly interprets the revised question and generates the right output on the fly. The result is a more agile, dynamic platform that keeps pace with the curiosity and evolving priorities of the brand, all without the bottleneck of manual intervention. It's not just smart, it's genuinely future-ready.

Here is an example prompt for generating the **Outlet Level Summary**

```
You are agent which is capable of performing data analytics.
Now consider the skus: {topSKUs} and the Month on Month (MOM) trends {growthTrends} for an
outlet.
Your task is to analyse this information and summarize it in 40 words. Use bullet points and
headings
At the end also suggest what can be done to improve the current situation. e.g "Sell more
lines," "Increase quantity," or "Prevent degrowth". You may be able to generate your own
recommended next steps at this outlet.
Also all the numbers are in indian rupees.
Given this info now consider my question. Do not add anything on your own . Stick to what
has been provided in the data.
Do not show any foot notes like Note: after the summary
Please format the output under the following headings:
1. Top Selling SKUS
2. Growth Trends
3. Outlet Summary

***Generate summary for the outlet in max 40 words***
```

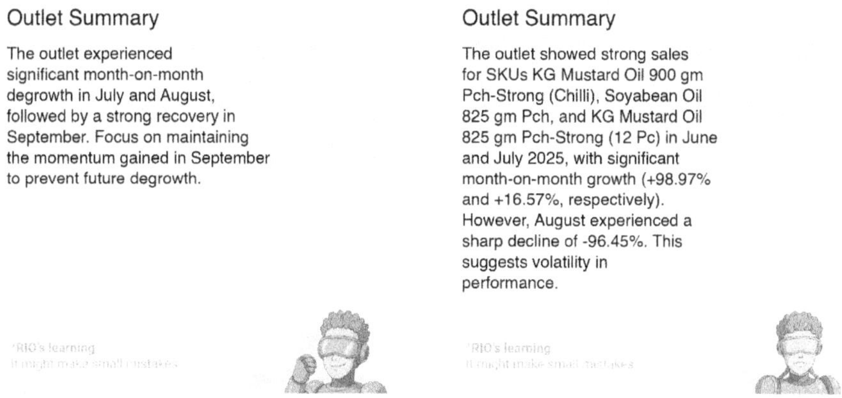

Figure: The sample shows how the outlet summary would look like. Based on the content of the summary the mood of the mascot "RIO" will also change

If the prompt is changed little bit it becomes a End Of Day report which is a summary shown at the end of the day to the salesman

```
You are an expert assistant generating a crisp End-of-Day (EOD) summary for a sales agent.
Here are today's metrics:
Visited {row['NumberofOutletVisited']}/{row['totalOutlets']} outlets
Orders placed: {row['pc']} / Orders cancelled: {row['nc']} / Total orders: {row['tc']}
Total sales: {totalSales}, Average daily sales: {averageSales}
Improved outlet: {row['improvedOutletName']}
Struggling outlet: {row['strugglingOutletName']}
Best outlet today: {row['mostValuableOutletName']}
Top growth product is {str(int(row['growth_sku_id']))} with growth
{row['growth_net_change']}
Dip product is {str(int(row['dip_sku_id']))} with dip {row['dip_net_change']}

Generate a **motivational and emotion-rich** EOD detailed summary:
A human touch
Outlet and product names
All currency is in rupees
Mention of rejections if any
No footnotes
Ready? Now make a detailed report with all above mentioned numbers and metrics(without
missing any metric)
***Please Do NOT use emojis or currency symbols and make all the text value within 30
words***
```

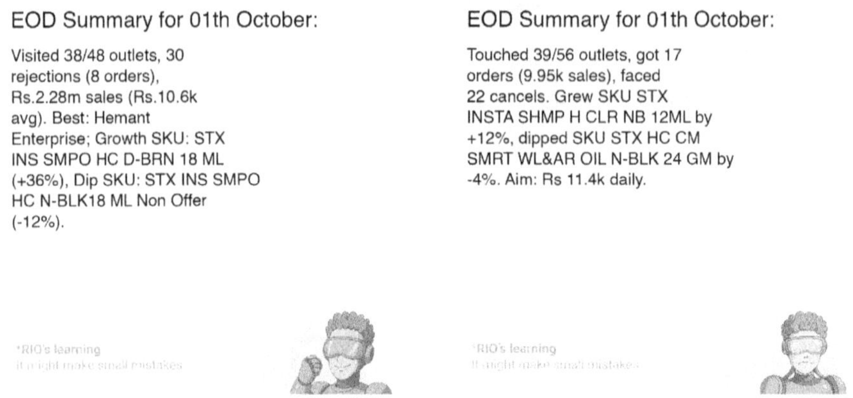

Figure: The mascot, RIO, visually represents the day's summary. On the left, an excited RIO indicates a positive day, while on the right, a less excited RIO signifies a mixed day.

Note: These images are the way to show the agentic output on Bizom platform and all our queries that we present in this book are aimed to get the right content on these images

What Happens When Every Outlet Gets Smarter

Today, most workflows in Bizom are powered by embedded agents that enhance the overall user experience and automate decision-making. While implementing such systems for a few hundred outlets may seem straightforward, scaling the same architecture to Bizom's network of over ten million outlets introduces an entirely different level of engineering complexity. Each outlet represents a distinct data node with its own sales patterns, assortment, and operational context. Embedding intelligence at this granularity means orchestrating millions of localized computations including retrieving data, analyzing trends, and making context-aware recommendations in near real time.

At such a scale, traditional approaches to analytics or automation begin to break down. Factors like computation cost, latency, and data synchronization become architectural constraints, not afterthoughts. Designing agents that can operate reliably in this distributed environment requires a structured understanding of how agentic systems evolve from simple retrieval and reasoning agents to complex, multi-step planning and orchestration layers.

In the coming chapters, we'll explore this evolution in depth. We'll see how different types of agents, each with their own design goals, reasoning depth, and interaction models can be assembled to handle real-world complexities such as large-scale search, contextual grounding, and tool coordination. The objective is not just to build agents that can "respond," but to engineer systems that can reason efficiently, operate predictably, and scale sustainably across millions of interactions.

By understanding these patterns, we move from theoretical promise to practical design, transforming the concept of agentic AI from a lab prototype into a production-grade capability that can power intelligence at enterprise scale.

CHAPTER 03

Architectural Fundamentals of Agentic System

"First we shape our architecture, then our architecture shapes us."
– Adapted from Winston Churchill

Before we move into use cases, workflows, and more advanced agentic patterns, it's worth pausing for a moment and looking underneath the surface. Because in Agentic AI, what ultimately determines success isn't just *what* a system can do, it's *how* it's put together.

This chapter is about those foundational choices.

Every system built around large language models carries a set of architectural decisions, whether they're made deliberately or by accident. Where the model runs. How it accesses data. How much freedom it's given to reason, act, and adapt. These choices quietly shape everything that follows like how reliably the system behaves, how far it can scale, how much it costs to operate, and whether it can be trusted with real business decisions.

We'll start by examining the infrastructure beneath agentic systems, exploring how different hosting strategies influence scalability, consistency, and economics. From there, we'll look at how queries are created and executed: how prompts, context, and orchestration determine whether an LLM merely *sounds* right or actually *is* right. And finally, we'll step into the agentic dimension itself, asking a deceptively simple but critical question: at what point does a system stop being a sophisticated query–response engine and start behaving like an autonomous agent?

By grounding ourselves in these fundamentals, this chapter lays out a framework for thinking in trade-offs rather than absolutes. It helps separate architectures that generate impressive outputs from those that sustain intelligent behavior under real-world constraints. In other words, it sets the foundation for understanding not just how to build with LLMs but how to build systems that deserve to be trusted.

Design Principles: 4 R's of Agentic Design

To be an acceptable Agentic solution by the industry , it is essential to have the mix of 4 R's in the system which is

1. **Reliability (Consistency)**: how deterministic is the output.
2. **Respect (Privacy & Ethics)**: how it handles data with integrity and user trust.
3. **Reach (Scalability)**: how far the system can extend across users, geographies, or workloads.
4. **Restraint (Cost Efficiency)**: how intelligently it allocates resources, balancing ambition with sustainability.

Reliability

One of the most fascinating—and sometimes unsettling—traits of large language models is their ability to **sound perfectly confident while being completely wrong**.

This phenomenon, known as ***hallucination***, occurs when an LLM generates information that is factually incorrect, nonsensical, or entirely fabricated yet presented in a tone of absolute certainty.

A hallucinating model can invent details, statistics, names, or even processes that don't exist, and sometimes weave truth and fiction together so seamlessly that it becomes difficult for users to tell the difference.

Take a simple example: you might ask a model, *"How do you create a user in Bizom?"*, referring to the well-known Sales Force Automation (SFA) platform used by millions of outlets across India. Unless the model has been trained specifically on Bizom's proprietary data, it won't actually know the answer. But rather than admit uncertainty, it will often fabricate a plausible-sounding set of instructions presented with total confidence. This is hallucination in action: the system doesn't lie deliberately; it simply **fills the void with its best statistical guess,** mistaking probability for truth.

> *Recently, A leading consulting firm allegedly used AI to produce a $400K client report, skipping senior consultants. The catch? The report cited a nonexistent court ruling, exposing blatant AI hallucination. The client caught the error during validation. It is a costly reminder that unchecked AI output can carry real financial and reputational risks* ***[1]***

While **hallucination** exposes the **accuracy** problem, another challenge lies deeper: **consistency**. Even when an LLM *does* know the right answer, it may not give the same response twice. Unlike traditional software systems, which behave **deterministically**, LLMs are **probabilistic** by design. They predict the next word in a sequence by weighing multiple possible continuations and selecting one based on likelihood.

Ask, "*The cat sits on a* __", and it might say *mat*, *chair*, or *sofa*, each perfectly reasonable. This creativity makes LLMs engaging and flexible, but it also makes them unpredictable.

Now, imagine this behavior in a business context like the CPG world we discussed earlier. A simple query such as "*What were the sales of SKU 123 in outlet 345?*" will likely yield a consistent answer, because it maps cleanly to a single, structured data request. But the moment we introduce complexity, say, "*What are the sales of the top three SKUs across the top five outlets in my area?*", the model must reason through multiple logical steps: identify top outlets, fetch their leading SKUs, aggregate sales, and rank results. If it changes the order of these operations or skips a step, the final output will vary, even if the input remains the same.

This isn't hallucination but it's **inconsistency**, a byproduct of the model's probabilistic reasoning. The LLM knows *how* to answer, but doesn't always execute the reasoning path identically. And while occasional variability may be acceptable in creative tasks, it's deeply problematic in environments where accuracy, auditability, and trust matter.

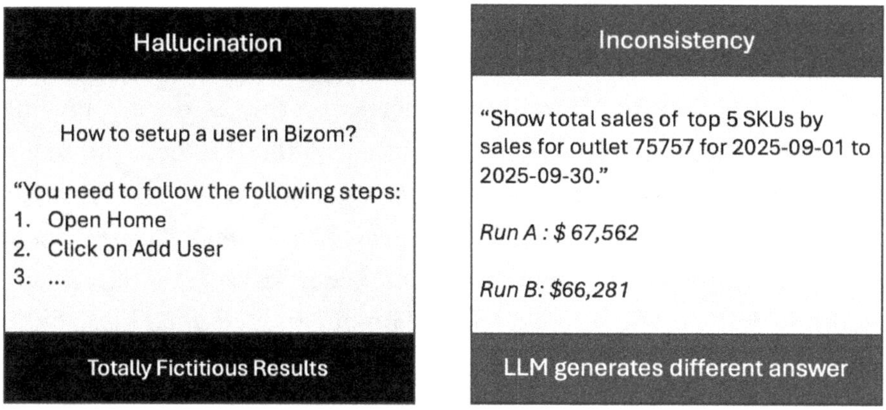

For decision-making systems, especially those replacing manual processes, addressing both hallucination and inconsistency is non-negotiable. We must design architectures that minimize randomness, verify facts, and enforce logical repeatability without suppressing the intelligence of the model itself.

In the chapters ahead, we'll explore how reliability can be *engineered* through layers of orchestration, validation, and memory that bring discipline to the model's creativity. Because for agentic systems to earn trust, they must not only *think*, they must think *reliably*.

Note: https://amatria.in/blog/hallucinations is a great resource to understand the Hallucination problem in greater detail.

Reach

The transition from proof of concept (POC) to a fully operational production system hinges largely on our ability to scale the solution to meet real-world demands.

In theory, a model that performs beautifully in the lab should also work in production. In practice, scale has a way of revealing everything we didn't account for viz. the silent bottlenecks, the cost curves, the latency spikes, the unexpected interdependencies that only emerge under real load.

When we talk about production scale, we're no longer dealing with hypothetical traffic or controlled demos but we're talking about the messy, relentless volume of real business usage. In consumer goods, that scale can easily mean ten million outlets operating across a sprawling commercial ecosystem. Now imagine each of those outlets running a modest agentic task every day: *Find the top-selling SKUs for this outlet. Identify which items haven't sold in the past three months. Summarize it all in fifty words*. On its own, the request seems trivial. At scale, it isn't. Multiply that workflow across ten million outlets, and what looks like a simple analysis turns into roughly thirty million LLM calls per day.

Figure: The production scale complexity and size is most of the time 1000x the POC

Handling 30 million daily requests is a substantial challenge, even for the heavy weight of the cloud-hosted solution providers. Behind the scenes, providers must provision enough hardware, primarily GPUs, to ensure that processing remains timely and reliable, regardless of whether the hardware is managed in-house or by a third party. The need for such robust scalability becomes even more pronounced in industries larger than CPG, where the volume of data and required analyses can be many times higher.

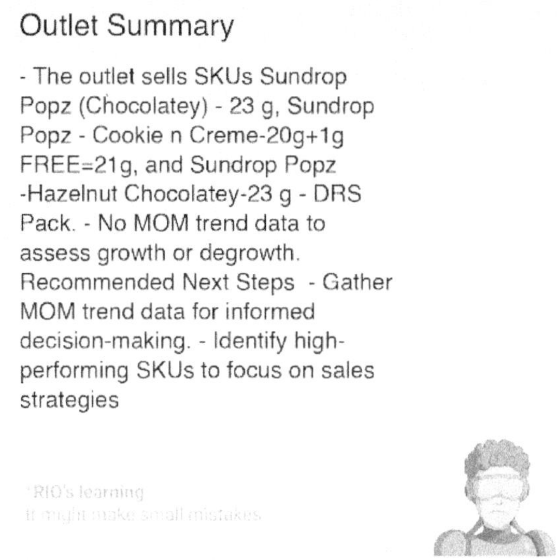

Figure: Similar summary has to be generated for millions of outlets every day which is a massive undertaking from LLM usage point of view

But scaling isn't just about **handling more**; it's also about **handling complex problems**. As queries evolve from simple lookups to multi-layered reasoning involving joins, comparisons, and contextual enrichment, the cognitive load on the system compounds. Each layer of complexity multiplies the number of intermediate steps, model invocations, and validation checks, stretching both computational and architectural limits. This is the **Complexity Scalability.**

> **Note:** POCs usually run on a happy-path scenario—a simple workflow that shows the tech in the best light and helps get stakeholders on board. But real life is rarely that smooth, and that gap between the POC and reality is where many projects end up falling short on the promised ROI.

True reach, therefore, is not merely about throughput. It's about maintaining clarity, efficiency, and correctness as the **intelligence itself scales in depth and sophistication**.

We will discuss some of the strategies to address both **volume** and **complexity scalability** challenges in the chapters that follow.

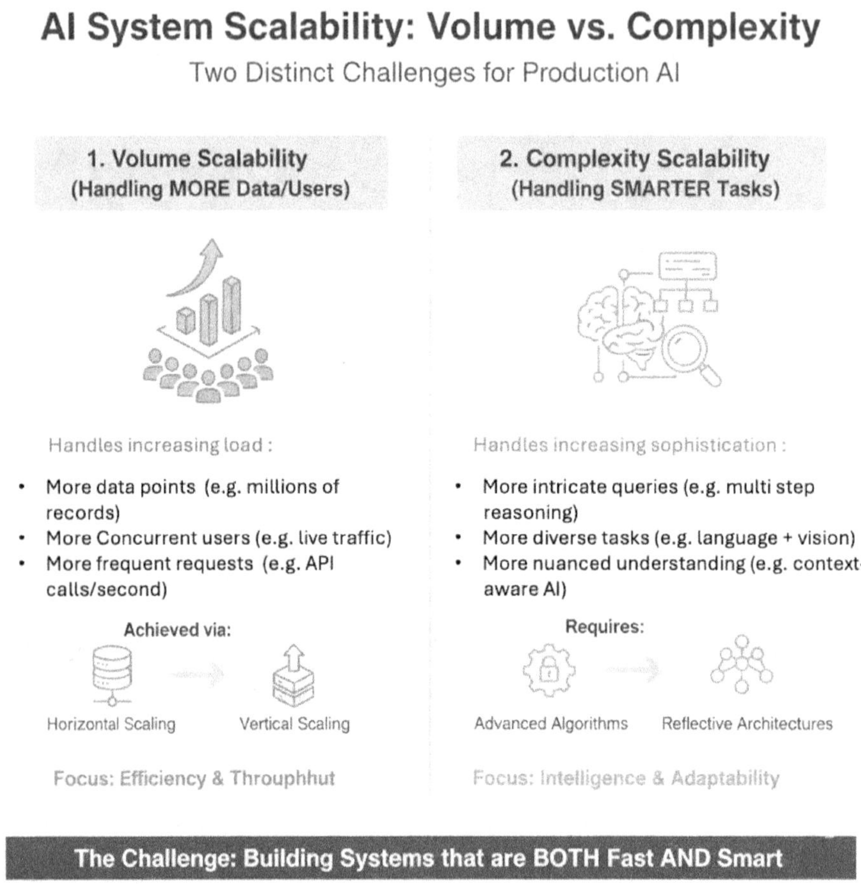

Respect

Every technological shift brings with it a familiar hesitation, the quiet pause before adoption, rooted in one word: ***trust***. Whether it was the dawn of the internet, the rise of mobile devices, or the migration to the cloud, organizations have always hesitated to move sensitive data beyond their walls. The arrival of large language models (LLMs) is no different. In fact, it amplifies these concerns.

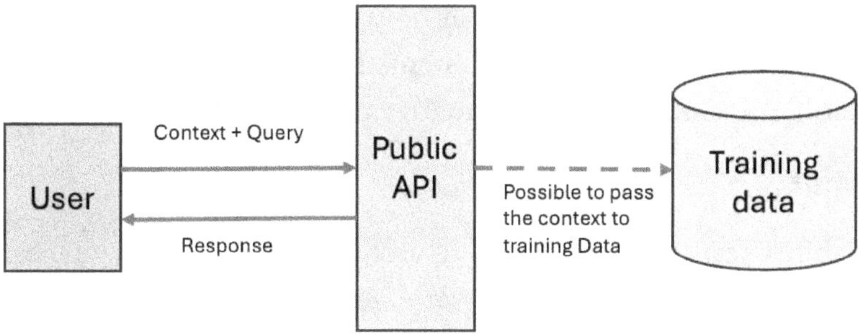

***Figure:** When users share sensitive context, such as database schemas, financial reports, or proprietary data, these inputs may be stored in the training data of API providers, leaving users with limited or no control over how their data is retained or used.*

At the heart of this unease lies a perception that LLMs "learn" from the data they touch. Even when providers insist that customer data isn't stored or reused for training, the black-box nature of these systems leaves many decision-makers uneasy. This skepticism is not unfounded especially as the industry watches ongoing legal disputes over models that appear to generate copyrighted or proprietary material without explicit authorization. Each such incident reinforces the fear that sensitive corporate data could one day surface in unintended ways.

For highly regulated sectors like finance, healthcare, and government, this concern isn't theoretical, it's existential. Data privacy is not just a compliance checkbox; it's a question of reputation, accountability, and customer confidence. As a result, many organizations lean toward on-premise or private deployments of LLMs, ensuring that their data never leaves controlled infrastructure. This approach provides a clear privacy advantage, but it also introduces practical challenges: increased infrastructure costs, limited scalability, and the need for specialized expertise to maintain high-performance systems in-house.

Finding the right balance between privacy, performance, and scalability is therefore a central design question in modern AI architecture. The goal is not to choose between innovation and security, but to integrate both through techniques such as data anonymization, controlled fine-tuning, encryption at rest and in transit, and rigorous access governance.

In the chapters ahead, we'll look at how organizations can navigate this balance thoughtfully , building systems that protect what matters most while still unlocking the transformative potential of agentic intelligence.

Restraint

If scalability tests the strength of an architecture, cost tests its discipline. *One of the main reasons large language models (LLMs) haven't yet become mainstream in production environments is simple economics.* Running these systems at scale is expensive often *dramatically* more so than traditional query or analytics engines.

The cost stems from the kind of infrastructure these models demand. LLMs don't run efficiently on conventional CPUs; they rely on specialized graphics processing units (GPUs), purpose-built for parallel computation. These GPUs are powerful but costly, that's today's equivalent of how a few megabytes of RAM once commanded a premium in the early days of computing. As a result, the economics of intelligence remain a central concern in any serious deployment.

CPU	GPU
Central Processing Unit	Graphics Processing Unit
4-8 Cores	100s or 1000s of Cores
Low Latency	High Throughput
Good for Serial Processing	Good for Parallel Processing
Quickly Process Tasks That Require Interactivity	Breaks Jobs Into Separate Tasks To Process Simultaneously
Traditional Programming Are Written For CPU Sequential Execution	Requires Additional Software To Convert CPU Functions to GPU Functions for Parallel Execution

Figure: CPU Vs GPU: There is a huge difference in the processing power of the 2 hardware (courtesy: https://medium.com/@abhishekjainindore24/gpus-vs-cpus-threads-core-speed-75b5732ce389)

Most organizations access LLMs in one of two ways:

The **first** is through **hosted APIs** offered by providers like OpenAI, Anthropic, or Mistral. This option offers ease of use and rapid integration as it doesn't require any hardware maintenance or software update. However, the convenience comes with a recurring cost structure based on the number of tokens, or effectively, the number of model interactions. At first glance, $0.0005 per API call might seem trivial. But at scale, those micro-costs add up quickly. For instance, a system serving 10,000 users for 12 hours a day could easily accumulate $60 per day in usage, translating to nearly $2,000 per month and this is just for inference. Add higher-end models or longer prompts, and the expenses rise further. Appendix C discusses the cost implications in more detail.

The **second approach is self-hosting** which is deploying the model on an organization's own GPUs, either on-premises or in the cloud. This can reduce per-call costs at large volumes but introduces significant upfront investment. A single capable GPU can cost $4,000 or more, and that's before factoring in the engineering expertise required to deploy, scale, and maintain the environment. Most enterprise-grade models, including GPT-5, aren't available for local deployment, which limits flexibility. And even with open models, scalability remains a challenge; a single GPU can only handle so much load before you need to expand horizontally.

Both approaches come with trade-offs. Hosted APIs offer simplicity and scalability but can become prohibitively expensive over time. Self-hosting promises cost control and data ownership but demands capital investment, technical skill, and ongoing maintenance. The right choice depends on an organization's usage patterns, security needs, and long-term strategy.

As adoption grows, hybrid models (Smart Router) are emerging. These are systems that rely on hosted APIs for complex queries while using self-hosted instances to handle simpler ones. In scenarios where consistent performance must be guaranteed, hosted APIs often remain the more reliable choice

In the chapters ahead, we'll look at how such hybrid strategies can help organizations exercise financial *restraint* without limiting the potential of intelligent systems achieving a balance between capability and cost that makes large-scale AI truly sustainable.

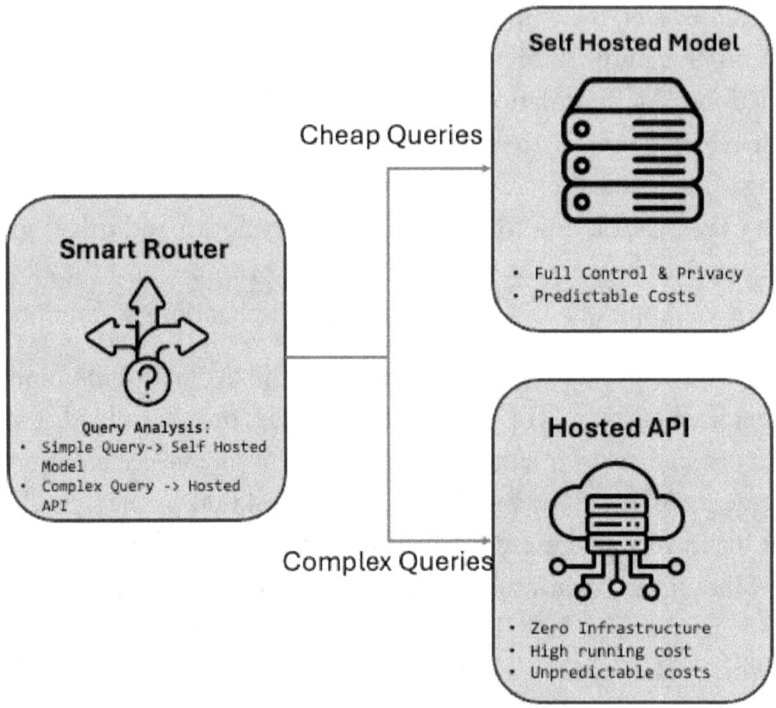

Figure: The smart router analyzes query characteristics to direct simple questions to cost-effective local models while routing complex or creative tasks to more capable hosted APIs, with automatic fallback ensuring reliability.

As we step back from these four dimensions—**Reach**, **Reliability**, **Restraint**, and **Respect**—a common theme begins to emerge. Building intelligent systems isn't just an engineering challenge; it's an exercise in balance. Each "R" represents a tension we must learn to manage rather than eliminate.

Reach *pushes us to scale, but* ***Reliability*** *reminds us to stay consistent.* ***Restraint*** *demands fiscal and operational discipline, while* ***Respect*** *keeps us grounded in ethics, privacy, and trust.*

Together, these principles form the architectural compass for agentic systems. They help ensure that as our models grow more capable, they also grow more responsible and that every layer of intelligence we add is matched by a layer of intentional design. Because intelligence, at scale, is not simply about thinking faster or bigger, it's about thinking *wisely*.

Balancing the 4 R's

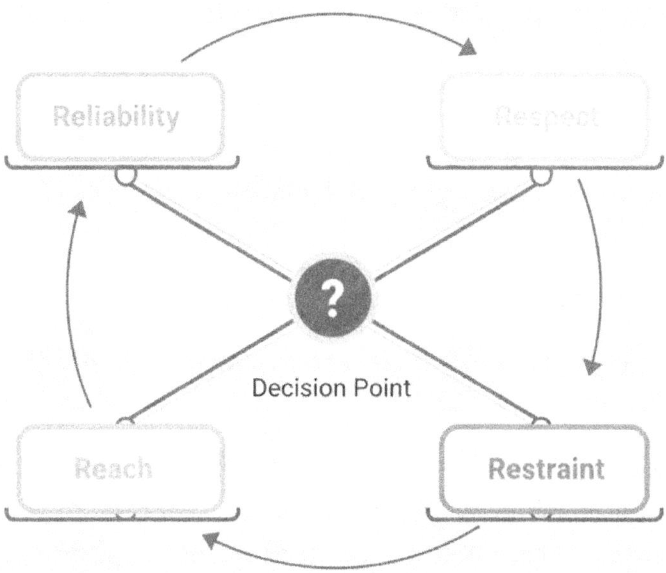

Figure: Any Agentic Architecture has to have a balance between the 4 R

If the 4 R's—Reach, Reliability, Restraint, and Respect—describe *what* a well-engineered agentic system should embody, the design decisions determine *how* we get there. But here lies the challenge: these four principles do not always move in harmony. Pushing one often means pulling another. Expanding *Reach* may stretch *Reliability*; enforcing *Restraint* may limit *Responsiveness*; and ensuring *Respect* for privacy might constrain flexibility. Engineering, in this context, becomes a careful act of balance and an art of trade-offs guided by intent.

There is no perfect equilibrium, no universal recipe that satisfies all four dimensions simultaneously. What exists instead is a series of trade-offs, more precisely, engineering judgments that reflect context, constraints, and intent. Each choice in architecture, data handling, and orchestration represents a subtle negotiation among the 4 R's.

When designing agentic systems that operate over structured data like relational databases, two foundational decisions shape this balance from the very beginning. These choices of how we structure the interaction between the agent and the data, and how much reasoning we delegate to the model versus to traditional systems have profound implications for cost, latency, reliability, and future extensibility.

Design Decisions

In the following section, we explore the key design levers in detail and examine how each decision reshapes the delicate tension between the 4 R's

1. Hosting Strategy for Language Models (LLMs)

A major architectural question is: **Where and how should the LLM be hosted?**

This decision defines the system's *Reach*—its scalability and ability to grow—and deeply influences *Reliability*, *Restraint*, and *Respect*. Broadly, there are three primary strategies, each representing a different point on the 4 R's spectrum.

- **Third-Party API Access (e.g., OpenAI, Anthropic):**

  These services offer the fastest path to production with minimal setup. You can call LLMs via REST APIs and immediately tap into the latest reasoning and generation capabilities without managing any infrastructure. It offers exceptional *Reach*, scaling effortlessly to millions of users, and solid *Reliability* from mature infrastructure. But these strengths come with trade-offs. API calls can become expensive at scale, challenging *Restraint*. Moreover, data must leave your environment for inference, raising questions about *Respect*, especially in privacy-conscious or regulated domains.

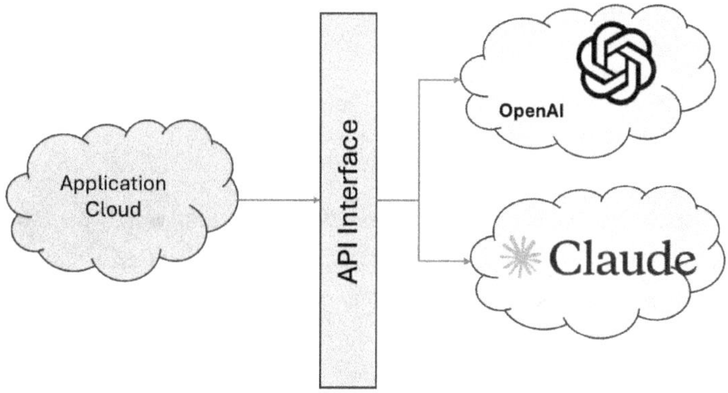

Figure: When applications run in the application cloud, they access APIs hosted by large language model (LLM) providers such as OpenAI or Anthropic on their respective servers. This process involves data moving from the application cloud to the public cloud.

- **Self-Hosted Models via Ollama or Local GPU Runtimes:**

  Running LLMs locally using frameworks like **Ollama** gives full control over data and deployment. This approach strengthens *Respect* by keeping sensitive information within organizational boundaries, and reinforces *Restraint* by minimizing recurring API costs. *Reliability* can also improve when infrastructure is tuned to domain-specific workloads.

  However, this path limits *Reach*. Scaling self-hosted models requires GPU infrastructure and operational expertise. The latest model innovations are also slower to adopt, as you manage updates yourself. This trade-off often makes self-hosting ideal for smaller, controlled workloads where governance and efficiency outweigh raw scalability.

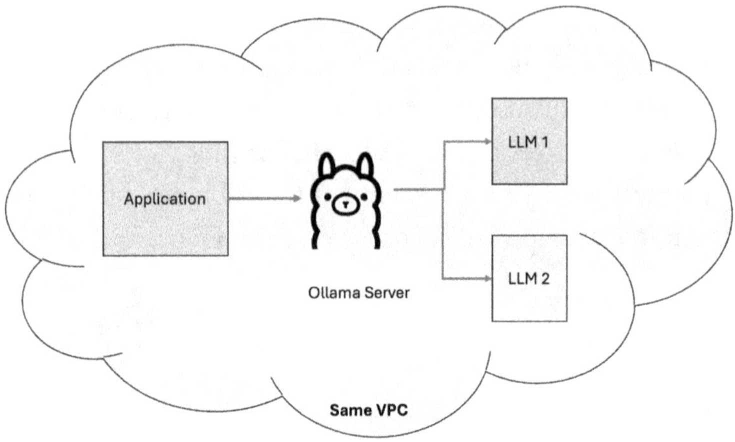

Figure: Ollama running inside a private cloud setup. By deploying Ollama within the same VPC, we can run multiple language models locally without sending any data outside the application environment. Everything stays inside the private cloud, ensuring privacy, security, and full control over how data is processed

- **Using AWS Bedrock or Cloud-Hosted Frameworks:**

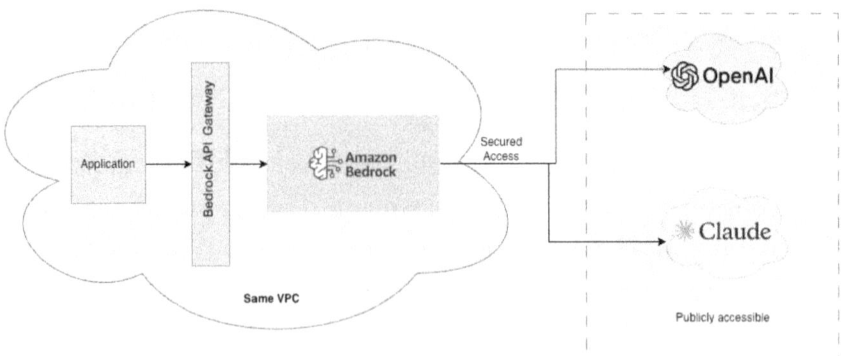

Figure: Shows the interaction between Application, Bedrock and the public APIs. The access to the public APIs is through Bedrock. Bedrock gives the guarantee of the data security , privacy and flexibility to move between the public APIs.

Platforms like **Amazon Bedrock** (See Appendix B for more details) aim to blend convenience with control. They abstract the complexities of hosting, offering access to multiple model providers through a unified interface, tightly integrated with enterprise tools like IAM and VPCs. This strengthens *Reliability* and *Respect* through better observability and compliance integration, while preserving moderate *Reach* via cloud elasticity. However, *Restraint* can still be a concern, as cost structures remain tied to third-party usage. Bedrock inherits some of the same latency and pricing dynamics of the underlying models, demanding careful governance to balance scalability with spend.

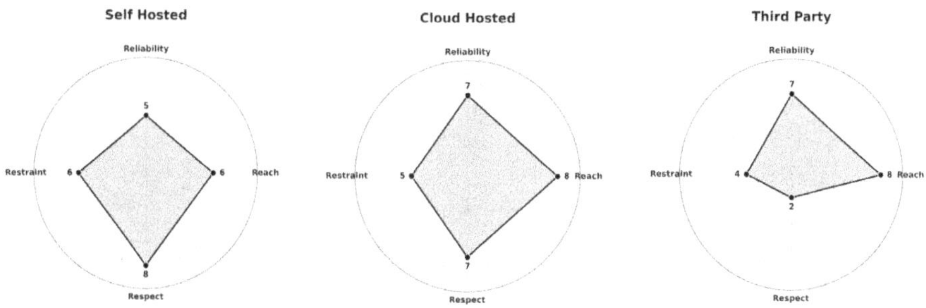

Figure: The above radar graph shows the trade off between the Reach, Reliability, Restraint , Respect for the 3 approaches. The self hosted approach is high on the Respect while Cloud Hosted & Third Party solutions are high on the Reach

Each of these hosting strategies represents a different interpretation of the 4 R's: what they mean in context, and which ones the organization chooses to prioritize

The solution might be an Hybrid approach where depending on the load and the type of query the application might choose to interact with each of these hosting solutions like the smart router approach discussed earlier.

2. Query Strategy (Generation vs. Execution)

Once the model's hosting architecture is decided, the next crucial question is **how the agent retrieves and reasons over structured data (in context of CPG workflows)**. Should it dynamically generate SQL queries, or should it operate on predefined, controlled queries and focus only on interpreting results?

This decision directly influences *Reliability* and *Respect*—how consistent and safe the system's interactions with data will be—while shaping *Reach* and *Restraint* through scalability and efficiency.

- **LLM-Generated SQL:**

  Here, the agent interprets natural language and generates SQL queries dynamically translating prompts like ***"Show me the top 5 SKUs by sales"*** into database operations like

```
SELECT
  sku_id,
  SUM(sale_amount) AS total_sales
FROM sales
GROUP BY sku_id
ORDER BY total_sales DESC
LIMIT 5;
```

  The allure of this approach lies in its flexibility: it extends *Reach*, allowing users to ask any question without predefining logic. Yet flexibility often undermines *Reliability*. As query complexity grows—joins, filters, subqueries—the accuracy and stability of generated SQL degrade. Dynamic generation can also compromise *Respect* by exposing potential vulnerabilities, from unintended data access to injection risks. *Restraint is also affected as the generation might involve multiple LLM calls.* It is a powerful but high-variance approach, suitable for exploratory analytics rather than mission-critical workflows.

- **Predefined Queries + LLM Formatting:**

  A more controlled strategy is to rely on predefined or parameterized SQL queries to fetch structured results, and use the LLM primarily for interpretation, summarization, or explanation.

This approach maximizes *Reliability* and *Respect*, since queries are deterministic and auditable, while still preserving *Reach* through natural language output and contextual insights.

It also embodies *Restraint*: compute usage is predictable, and the LLM's role is focused where it adds true value that is reasoning and communication, not data access. While this design limits open-ended flexibility, it offers a stable, scalable foundation for consistent enterprise-grade workflows such as dashboards, reports, and operational summaries.

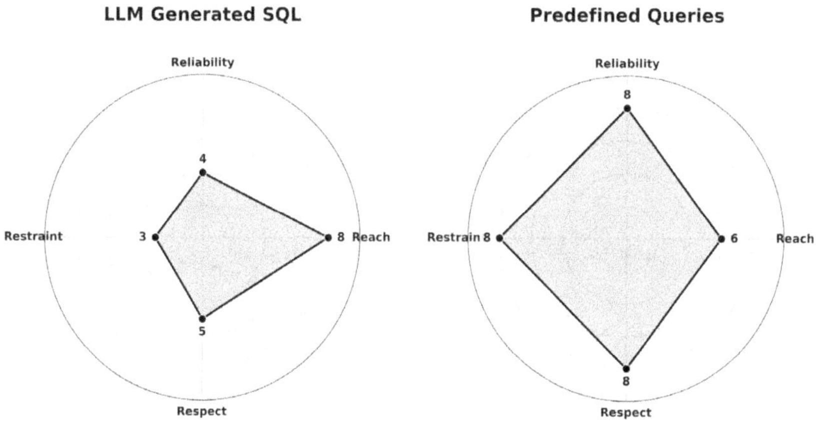

Figure: The radar chart illustrates the trade-offs between ***Reach, Reliability, Restraint,*** *and* ***Respect*** *for two different approaches:* ***LLM-Generated SQL*** *and* ***Predefined SQL****. The LLM-based approach scores high on Reach due to its flexibility in dynamically modifying queries, but it falls short on Reliability because of potential inaccuracies and unpredictability. In contrast, Predefined SQL excels in Reliability and consistency, offering stable and validated outputs, but provides limited Reach since queries cannot be easily adapted or altered on the fly.*

This second approach is particularly well-suited for **fixed workflows,** such as dashboards or end-of-day reports, where the logic is stable but the user experience can benefit from natural language explanations.

Bringing It Together

These two foundational choices: **how the model is hosted** and **how it reasons about data** define the architecture of any agentic system that interacts with structured data. Every variation, from an internal analytics agent to a customer-facing assistant, exists somewhere along these two axes.

Across the chapters that follow, we examine implementations of simple but relevant queries like *"Show the top 5 selling SKUs and their sales and quantities"* under different combinations of these strategies. By observing how performance, cost, and reliability shift across configurations, we'll uncover how the 4 R's manifest in practice, and how thoughtful design can turn trade-offs into enduring strengths.

Here is a pictorial way to summarize the above Design Decisions as we explained above.

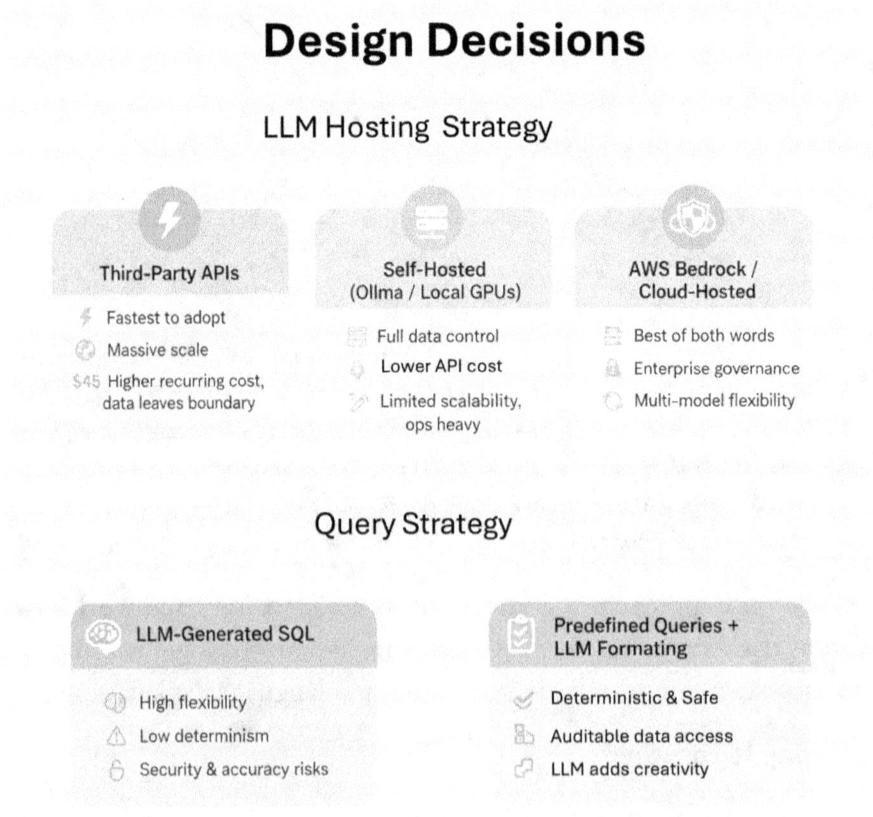

What Makes an Architecture Truly Agentic?

Not every system that uses a large language model is an *agent*. Many AI-powered tools today can answer questions, summarize documents, or run simple automations but that doesn't necessarily make them *agentic*. They're intelligent, yes, but mostly reactive. They respond when spoken to, much like a smart assistant that waits for instructions.

An **agentic system**, in contrast, behaves more like a thoughtful collaborator. It doesn't just react but it *decides*. It can interpret a goal, plan how to achieve it, take the right actions, and know when it's done. In short, it has a sense of purpose.

For an architecture to be truly agentic, three key ingredients must come together. Each one gives the system a distinct kind of intelligence to think, to act, and to adapt.

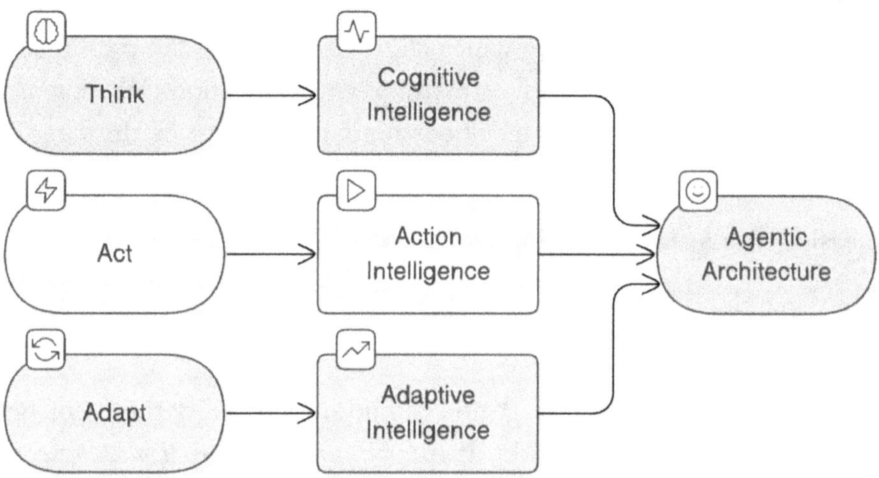

There are **three foundational components** that define an agentic system. These components work together to enable the agent to reason through a task, take meaningful action, and iterate as needed. Below is a deeper look into each of these pillars:

1. Power to Generate Dynamic Content

At the heart of every agent lies its power to **generate** ideas, code, queries, or plans from scratch. This is the agent's creative spark, its ability to turn abstract intent into something concrete and actionable.

This generative intelligence can take many forms:

- Writing a SQL query to "find the top 5 selling products"
- Producing a short Python function to clean a dataset
- Creating an API call to send a notification
- Laying out a step-by-step plan to complete a goal

This is what gives the agent its *mind*. It doesn't wait for a predefined rule, rather it *creates* the rule it needs in the moment. Unlike static scripts or flowcharts, it looks at the current situation and generates logic that fits.

That's what makes agentic systems feel alive: they can adapt. They can take a vague prompt like "Help me understand last quarter's sales" and generate a chain of reasoning which starts from writing the right query, interpreting the results, and formatting an explanation. It's not just about language generation; it's about **logic generation** or thinking in structures that can drive real outcomes.

2. Using Tools and Executing Decisions

Thinking alone doesn't get work done. An agent must also **act** to take the plans it generates and bring them to life.

This is where **tools** come in. A tool can be any capability the agent can use to interact with the world. It can be ***a function, API, database, or system command***.

Through tools, the agent gains its *hands*:

- It can call a function to pull customer data.
- It can use an API to place an order or send an email.
- It can run a script to process information or update a dashboard.

Without tools, even the most intelligent agent is stuck in its own head with all thought and no action. But once it can combine reasoning with real operations, it becomes something more powerful: a system that doesn't just describe what should happen, but **makes it happen**.

This ability to act turns the agent from a "talker" into a "doer."

3. Reasoning, Evaluating, and Knowing When to Stop

The third ingredient and perhaps the most human of all is the **power to reflect**.

Thinking creates ideas; reflection shapes judgment. A truly agentic system doesn't just generate and execute, it **evaluates**. It asks itself: *Did that work? Is the result correct? Do I need to adjust?*

Reflection is what allows the agent to:

- Break complex goals into smaller, logical steps
- Check whether the output of each step makes sense
- Choose to retry or take a different route if something fails
- Recognize when the task is complete and stop gracefully

This self-awareness gives the agent control over its own process. Without it, an AI might keep running in circles, fetching too much data, calling APIs endlessly, or generating unnecessary outputs. With reflection, it can course-correct, conserve resources, and deliver meaningful results.

If generation is the *mind* and tools are the *hands*, reflection is the **conscience**—the part that monitors progress and ensures that actions stay aligned with goals.

A Simple Example: From Thinking to Acting to Reflecting

The Agentic AI Financial Advisor

Figure: Image generated using Gemini

Imagine you're chatting with an AI financial advisor. You tell it, *"I want to invest $100K safely for the next three years. Suggest something better than a fixed deposit but without too much risk."*

First, the agent **thinks.**

It starts by reasoning through your intent, understanding your risk appetite, time horizon, and investment preferences. It recalls concepts from its knowledge base: debt funds, short-term government bonds, balanced mutual funds, and inflation-adjusted returns. Using its internal reasoning (its *parametric memory*), it creates an initial plan, a 60 - 40 allocation between debt and hybrid funds.

Then comes the power to **act.**

Realizing that its stored knowledge may be outdated, it fetches live data pulling current NAVs and yields from APIs like Morningstar or Zerodha, checking interest rate trends, and retrieving the latest inflation projections. It also cross-verifies whether any of the suggested funds have recently underperformed or changed risk categories.

Finally, the agent **reflects.**

It evaluates what it found against your goals. Are the returns realistic for your timeline? Are there better alternatives with lower expense ratios? Is inflation likely to erode real gains? If the answers don't align, it rebalances the portfolio, replacing a high-risk hybrid fund with a safer bond ETF.

Once satisfied, it stops and presents you a personalized, real-time investment plan, complete with reasoning, trade-offs, and even a short natural-language summary:

> *"Based on your risk profile and market conditions, a 70-30 split between Gold Bond ETFs and XYZ Short-Term Funds will give you ~7.2% annualized returns with minimal volatility."*

That full cycle of **thinking (reasoning), acting (tool use),** and **reflecting (validation and correction)** is what makes this AI *agentic.* It doesn't just predict, it *decides, verifies, and improves* before responding.

Essence of being Agentic (Agency)

An agentic system isn't defined by how smart it sounds, but by how intelligently it behaves. It's not just a model that can write; it's a system that can reason, execute, and adapt in pursuit of a goal.

In the broader lens of the **4 R's—Reach, Reliability, Restraint, and Respect**—agentic systems push each principle to its limits:

- They expand **Reach** through autonomy and scalability.
- They demand **Reliability**, because every decision must be consistent and correct.
- They test **Restraint**, since each reflection and action consumes cost and compute.
- And they must embody **Respect**, ensuring that every decision honors privacy, policy, and purpose.

Agentic AI represents a shift from systems that **react** to systems that **reason** and from technology that answers questions to technology that *pursues understanding*.

Measuring Agency: The Scorecard Approach

As we move through the rest of this book, each Agentic AI solution we explore will not just be described, but *evaluated* through the lens of its **agentic behavior**. Because not all architectures are equally "agentic." Some may think deeply but never act; others may act decisively but without reflection.

To make this clearer, every implementation will end with a **Scorecard of Agentic Nature**, a concise assessment of how the design expresses the three core traits we've just discussed: **generation, action**, and **reflection**.

This scorecard helps ground the discussion. It shows not just *what the system does*, but *how agentic* it truly is.

The following bullets are used in the various tables in the chapters that follow:

Bullet Symbol	Meaning
●	Low Values/Unstable/Non Deterministic
◍	Medium Values/Moderate
○	High Value/Stable/Deterministic

Here's what the format will look like for a sample agent:

Agentic Criteria	Status	Explanation
Generative Aspect	Could be better	The LLMs were used to generate the SQL queries but suffer from Hallucination
Action-Oriented Aspect	Present	The agent calls external tools or APIs based on the processing it has done so far.
Planning & Reasoning Aspect	Not Active	The architecture is not reasoning out the various paths it can take to solve the problem

This consistent framework allows us to compare solutions not only by their performance or cost, but by their *depth of agency* and how far they go along the spectrum from **reactive** to **autonomous**.

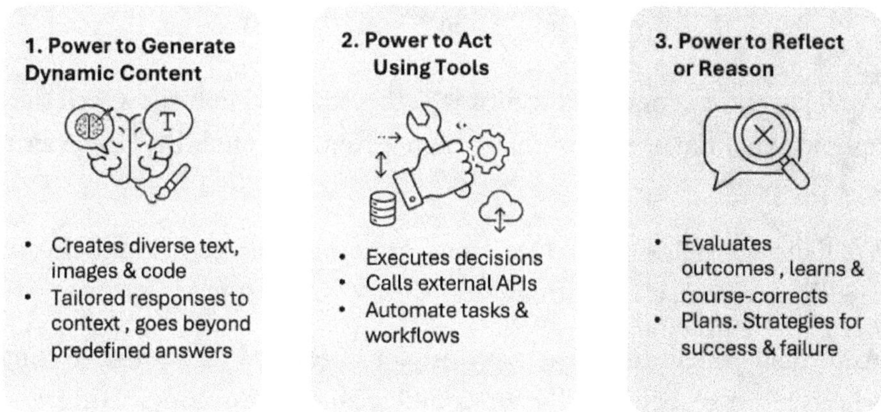

Figure: Easy way to remember the 3 Agentic Traits

Over time, as we examine different combinations of hosting, querying, and reasoning strategies, these scorecards will reveal how architectural choices shape the four dimensions we care about most—**Reach, Reliability, Restraint, and Respect**—and how close each design comes to embodying the true spirit of *agentic intelligence*.

Measuring What Truly Matters

As we move deeper into the world of Agentic AI, it's important to separate ambition from engineering. Every architecture we explore in the coming chapters from the simplest SQL-driven setups to complex self-reflective loops will be evaluated through a consistent lens.

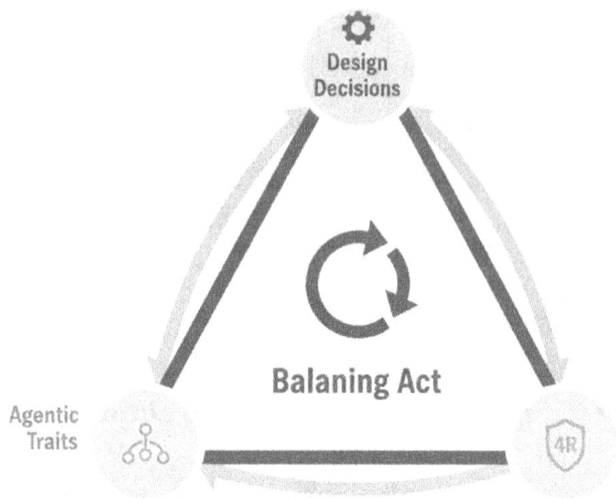

We'll judge them not by how futuristic they appear, but by how well they uphold the **4 R's** of responsible design—**Reach**, **Reliability**, **Restraint**, and **Respect**.

We'll dissect their **Design Decisions**, examining the trade-offs between intelligence, cost, and control.

And finally, we'll assess each against the **Agentic Framework**, testing whether it truly behaves like an agent capable of reasoning, acting, and reflecting or merely mimics one through clever prompting.

Because in the end, building Agentic AI isn't about chasing hype. It's about mastering the architecture of intelligence where every loop, layer, and decision moves us closer to systems that don't just compute, but *comprehend.*

Reference:

1. https://www.ndtv.com/world-news/deloittes-ai-fallout-explained-the-440-000-report-that-backfired-9417098

CHAPTER 04

The SQL-Focused Agent: From Queries to Conversations

Every journey begins with a simple step, or, in our case, a simple SQL query.

When we started experimenting with **Agentic AI**, our first prototypes weren't "intelligent" in the grand, cognitive sense. They didn't plan, reflect, or reason. They just *worked.* Think of it as the "NLP-to-SQL" era or the AI equivalent of learning to crawl before walking.

At its core, this early architecture was designed around a straightforward idea:

> *Let the user ask questions in plain English, and let the agent handle the SQL behind the scenes.*

So, if someone typed:

> "Show me the top 5 selling SKUs for outlet 1234,"

the agent would automatically translate that into:

```
SELECT skuId, SUM(quantity) AS total_qty
FROM sales
WHERE outletId = 1234
GROUP BY skuId
ORDER BY total_qty DESC
LIMIT 5;
```

No manual coding. No database jargon. Just a question and an answer.

It wasn't "cognitive" yet, but it was liberating. For the first time, business users could interact with data conversationally.

It was the **Retrieve–Analyze–Format–Respond** paradigm in its purest form.

How did we build it?

To bring this to life, we used **LangChain**, a popular agentic framework that made it surprisingly easy to connect large language models with databases. LangChain offers a handy component called the **SQLDatabaseToolkit**, which acts as a bridge between natural language and structured queries.

Here's how the architecture looked conceptually:

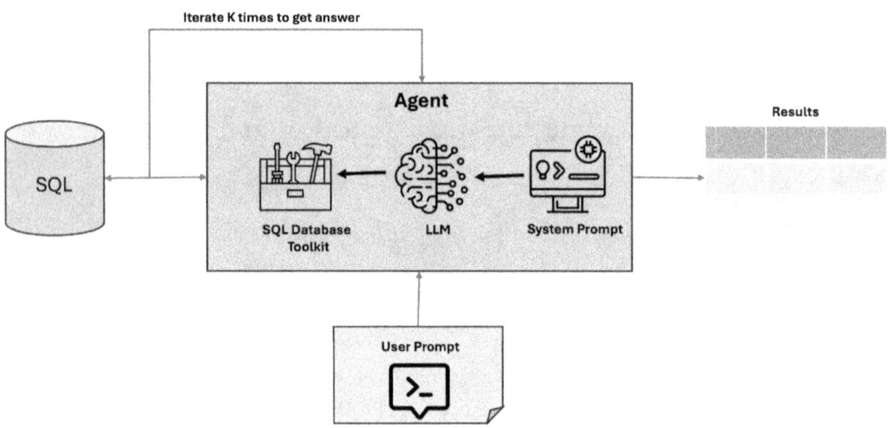

It was a simple three-layer design:

1. **Agent:** This comprises of 3 modules:

    a. **LLM:** provides the functionality for NLP to SQL which means that it will take a NLP based prompt written by the user like "Show me the top 5 selling SKUs for the Outlet 1234". This will be converted to a SQL like statement "select * from sales …"

b. **SQLDatabaseTookit:** This is a Langchain component that allows the LLM to interact with the database and execute the SQL queries

c. **System Prompt:** This is a set of roles and responsibilities of the LLM. This is one of the ways in which you can control the LLM's generation abilities.

Lets see an example of the system prompt and it looks like. Here's a simplified version of the kind of system prompt we used, with each instruction serving a specific purpose:

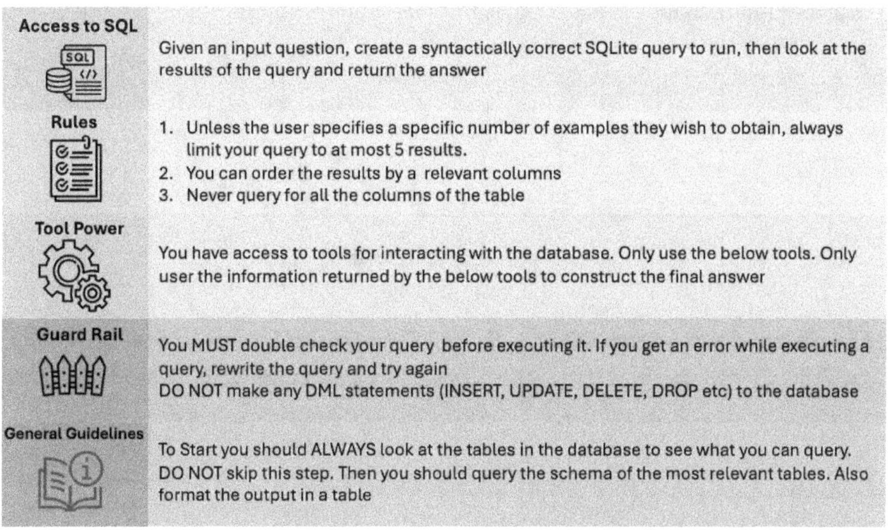

The system prompt will contain the necessary rules, guardrails, tool power to ensure that the LLM is aware of the sqlAgent and will call it once it is done with the NLP to SQL translation.

2. **User Prompt:** This is the prompt that is written by the end user. In other words this is how the user is interacting with the agent. *"Give me the top 5 SKUs"* is a user prompt entered by the user
3. **Database:** This serves as the data source for the LLM to operate on. The architecture resembles a **RAG** setup, where we don't depend on the LLM's parametric knowledge since it has no

awareness of the company's internal data and instead connect it to a database so it can generate answers grounded in that information.

Just as a side note here is a difference between the parametric retrieval and the RAG retrieval

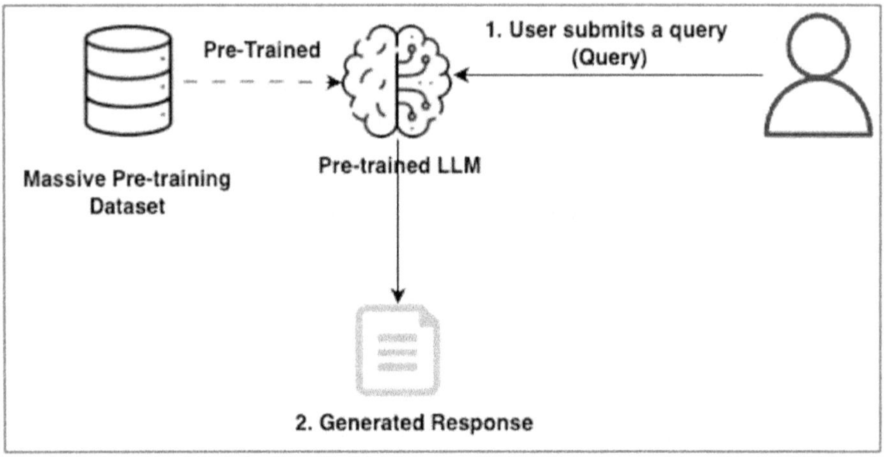

Figure: In case of Parametric Retrieval the LLM is generating the response from its training knowledge. This knowledge is stored in its billions of parameters and hence parametric retrieval

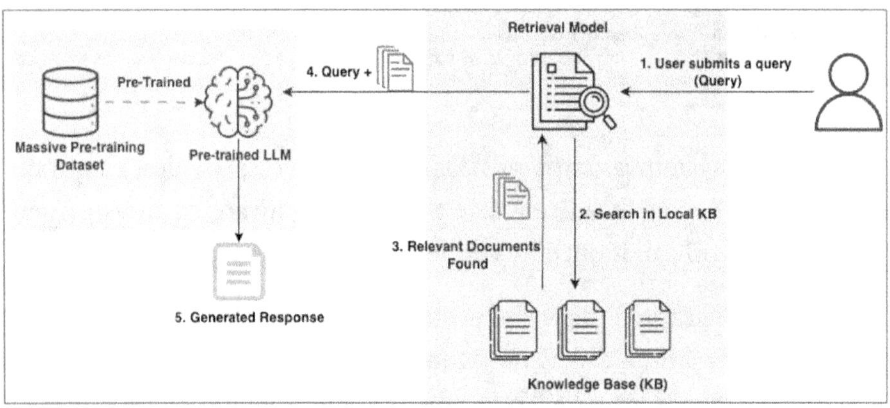

Figure: In case of RAG (Retrieval Augmented Generation), LLM attempts to look up externally for the information apart from its parametric knowledge. The user will send the documents or database along with the query. The task of the LLM here is to act as a powerful search engine which will find out the information and then format it in the required template

The Four Pillars of SQL Agent Architecture

As we started experimenting with our first Agentic AI prototype, we realized that even a simple SQL-driven agent needed structure. It wasn't enough to just convert natural language into a SQL query and print the result. We needed a repeatable design. Something that could scale, stay auditable, and feel human to interact with.

That's when we landed on a simple but powerful framework: the **Retrieve, Analyze, Format, and Respond** paradigm. It soon became the blueprint for how our early agent worked, and it still echoes through every design we've built since.

1.Retrieve

The first stage focuses on acquiring relevant data from a connected SQL database.

Based on the user's natural language input, the agent interprets intent (usually with the help of a language model) and translates it into a structured query or identifies a predefined data retrieval function.

This retrieval process is often powered by either **templated SQL or LLM-generated queries**, depending on the complexity of the request and the sensitivity of the database.

This stage is all about **intent clarity and secure access**. Every query generated can be traced back to a specific user intent making the process both auditable and explainable.

It's the agent's way of asking: *"What exactly do I need to fetch, and from where?"*

LLM is resolving the NLP based query to a SQL query that can be executed in the database using the SQLToolkit.

2. Analyze

Once the data comes back, the agent doesn't stop at retrieval. It moves into the **Analyze** phase, turning raw results into something meaningful.

Here, it looks for patterns, aggregates values, highlights top performers, or compares trends across dimensions like time or region. Sometimes, this is done using prebuilt business logic; other times, the LLM itself summarizes the trends in plain English.

This is the moment when the system stops being a query engine and starts acting like an **analyst** focusing not just on *what* the data says, but *what it means.*

3. Format

Not everyone enjoys reading SQL tables.While analysts may prefer raw rows and columns, most users appreciate clear, concise results they can act on immediately.

In the **Format** phase, the agent takes the analyzed data and refines it for readability converting results into:

- Bullet-point summaries,
- Brief natural-language narratives,
- Charts or visual snippets (when available).

This stage is all about communication. It ensures that insights are not buried under technical details but presented in a way that makes sense to the user. Essentially, the agent asks: *"How can I say this in the simplest, clearest way possible?"*

4. Respond

Finally, in the **Respond** phase, the agent delivers the result back to the user completing the conversational cycle.The output could appear as:

- A chat message,
- A dashboard element, or
- A neatly formatted report section.

By structuring the SQL agent around this **Retrieve–Analyze–Format–Respond** model, the system achieves a careful balance between the precision of backend logic and the fluidity of natural language interaction.

It minimizes the risk of incorrect interpretations while maximizing the value users derive from data. This architecture, while simple in concept, lays the groundwork for scalable, secure, and intelligent SQL query agents that can be extended to support more dynamic workflows in future iterations

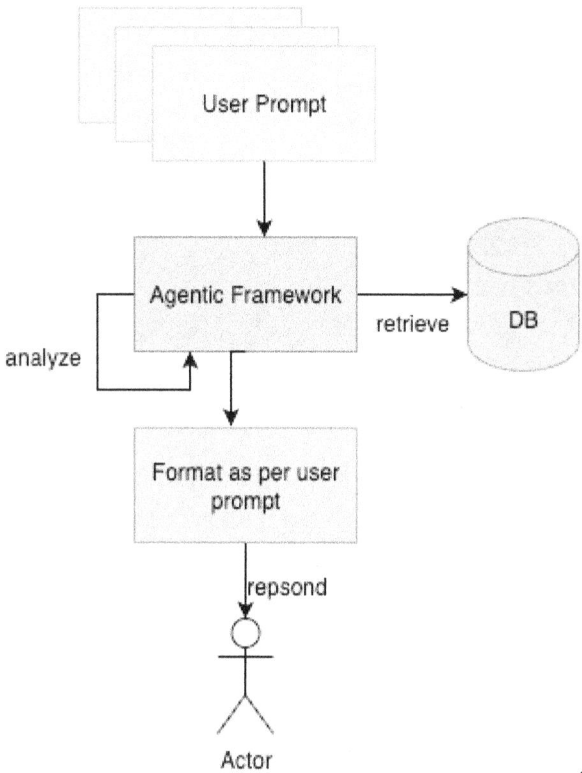

Figure: The diagram summarizes the stages of this agentic architecture.

Illustrative Examples

Let's look at some of the NLP queries that might be sent to this Agent

```
"For each outlets in the beat id 338: find the top 3 SKUs for each outlets ordered by amount in the month of December 2022.Format the result as outlet|SKU1|SKU2|SKU3"
```

Note: Beat is an area of a salesman. A beat consists of many outlets that are visited by the salesman to sell the products.

In this case the formatting has been defined as outlet Id followed by the 3 SKUs. This will follow the same 4 steps as discussed above

First the NLP will be changed to a sql which would look like

```
SELECT outlet_id,
 skunit_id,
 Sum(amount) AS total_amount
 FROM orderdetails
 WHERE beat_id = 338
 AND month = 12
 AND year = 2022
 GROUP BY outlet_id,
 skunit_id
 ORDER BY outlet_id,
 total_amount DESC
```

Then using the DB this data will be retrieved. It will be analyzed to check if all that was needed has been fetched or more queries need to be fired. Formatting will be done as per the user prompt.

Outlet	SKU1	SKU2	SKU3
5853	68		
5861	26	1070	56
5868	399	1071	1070
5870	1071	1070	807
5876	1071	837	1072
15508	401	400	
15516	9	836	837
15592	837	1072	836
15600	401	56	809
15666	1069	840	843
15688	1070	1071	56
15737	26	1071	1070
15778	401	875	1069
15831	399	1070	860
15854	879	144	145

Finally it will be responded back to the user.

Shortcomings of the SQL Agent

For all its simplicity and elegance, this early "NLP-to-SQL" solution came with a fair share of hidden challenges. On paper, it looked perfect. Ask a question in plain English, get structured data back instantly. But as we started deploying it across more complex and real-world databases, the cracks began to appear.

1. The Fragile Art of NLP-to-SQL Translation:

The heart of this approach lies in the translation of natural language into valid SQL. Early on, we tried fine-tuning smaller open-source models like **LLaMA** using supervised fine-tuning (SFT) essentially training them on question–answer pairs where:

> **Question:** *"Show me total sales for outlet 1234 in April."*
>
> **Answer:** `SELECT SUM(amount) FROM sales WHERE outletId=1234 AND month='April';`

One such reference dataset is know_sql (https://huggingface.co/datasets/knowrohit07/know_sql) , and several models fine-tuned using SFT on it can be found at https://huggingface.co/models?dataset=dataset:knowrohit07/know_sql

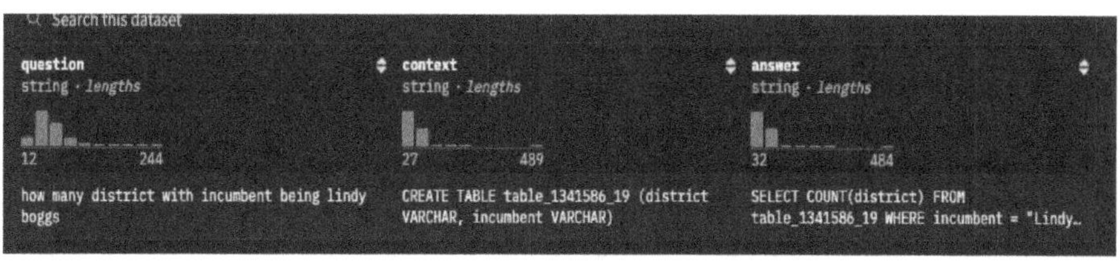

These models were designed to take a user query and a database schema as context, and then generate an appropriate SQL statement. It worked but only in controlled settings.

Following diagram summarizes this approach

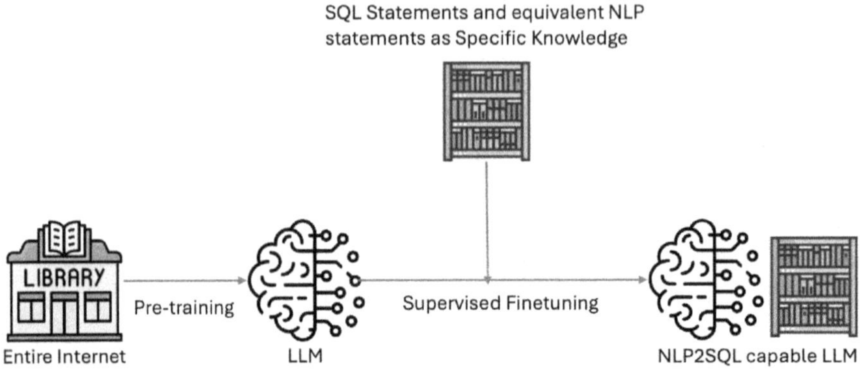

Figure: This diagram illustrates the typical ***fine-tuning process*** *used to enable an LLM to generate SQL queries. We begin with an* ***off-the-shelf, pre-trained model****, the one that has already learned general language patterns from large-scale datasets, often spanning the entire internet. While such a model performs well on everyday text-based tasks, it lacks domain-specific capability for* ***structured query generation****. To equip the model with this new skill, we collect a dataset containing pairs of* ***natural language prompts and their corresponding SQL queries****. Using this dataset, we perform* ***Supervised Fine-Tuning (SFT)****, a process that refines the model's parameters to learn mappings between questions and SQL syntax. The result is an LLM that combines* ***broad world knowledge*** *with* ***specialized understanding of translating natural language into SQL queries****.*

Today's GPT-class models, trained extensively on both **code and SQL**, can handle many of these conversions directly, often producing good results without fine-tuning. However, problems emerge quickly when real-world database schemas come into play.

Most enterprise databases are **not flat tables**. They're deeply normalized, split across multiple related tables (often in **third normal form, or 3NF**) to minimize redundancy. This creates headaches for NLP-to-SQL generation:

- Joins become confusing for the model.
- Subqueries are often missing or malformed.
- Column references can get mismatched or hallucinated.

So while GPT might perform beautifully on textbook examples, it stumbles when facing production-grade schemas.

Example of a complex user prompt could be

```
"LPSC is defined as ratio of the order amount November 2022 compared to December 2022.Find out the LPSC for all the outlets of user 546. Format the results as a table with 2 columns: OutletId , LPSC"
```

This translates to

```
SELECT   o1.outlet_id AS OutletId,
          (Sum(
          CASE
                   WHEN o1.month = 11
                   AND      o1.year = 2022 THEN o1.amount
                   ELSE 0
          END) / Sum(
          CASE
                   WHEN o1.month = 12
                   AND      o1.year = 2022 THEN o1.amount
                   ELSE 1
          END)) AS LPSC
 FROM     orders o1
 WHERE    o1.user_id = 546
 GROUP BY o1.outlet_id
```

Which will give the result as

```
Here are the results for the LPSC (ratio of order amount in November 2022 compared to December 2022) for all the outlets of the user 546:
OutletId | LPSC
13495 |0.3950384
13534 |0.2974070
13537 |0.5201752
16594 |0.5468156
16588 |0.6114620
15529 |0.9801380
16621 |0.6701376
16628 |0.3066635
```

As the prompts become complex the SQL query generation also becomes difficult and will result in erroneous results. The SQL generated might miss out on the subqueries or joins.

2. Data Privacy and Leakage Risks

Another practical concern is **data privacy**. For the model to generate correct SQL, it often needs to "see" the database schema and sometimes even sample data as part of the prompt.

This means that unless the model is self-hosted, your schema (and potentially sensitive data) is being sent to an **external LLM provider**.

Worse, if the generated SQL accidentally pulls the entire dataset, all that data can flow outside your secure environment. In industries like CPG or banking, this is a deal-breaker.

3. Non-Deterministic Behavior

One of the biggest frustrations with NLP-to-SQL generation is **non-determinism**. Ask the same question twice, and you might not get the exact same SQL both times even if both queries technically work.

The model could rewrite the same logic differently: changing the order of joins, altering filter syntax, or swapping aggregation styles.

For e.g. next time when we run the same NLP2SQL the output might be different as this time the SQL generated by the LLM might be different.

```
Here are the results for the LPSC (ratio of order amount
in November 2022 compared to December 2022) for all the
outlets of the user 546:
OutletId | LPSC
13495 |0.6672901
13534 |0.5219034
13537 |0.8610231
16594 |0.9482006
```

```
16588 |0.2541528
15529 |0.1093272
16621 |0.3919421
16628 |0.7201328
```

While this doesn't always affect correctness, it does hurt **repeatability**, which is crucial for production systems where consistency matters more than creativity.

4. The Cost of Inefficiency

Every LLM call costs both **time** and **money**. When the query logic is deterministic meaning the same SQL is run repeatedly with different parameters, it makes little sense to use GPUs and large models just to rebuild the same SQL every time.

In these cases, a **balanced approach** works better: Use the LLM **once** to generate the SQL, store it, and then run it directly as needed. Reserve the LLM for what it's good at—**formatting**, **summarizing**, and **contextualizing** results—rather than repeating mechanical query generation.

5. Time Wasted in Failed SQL Resolutions

Sometimes, the LLM would simply get *stuck* trying to resolve a SQL statement either looping on syntax errors or overcomplicating a simple query. And because SQL execution is supposed to be deterministic (i.e., same query = same result), introducing non-deterministic query creation defeats the purpose.

You end up wasting compute cycles and time trying to "fix" something that was never supposed to break.

In Summary

The **SQL Agent** was an essential first step. It gave us the thrill of watching an LLM talk to a live database and fetch data on demand. But in hindsight, it was **too brittle, too dependent on LLM quality**, and **too risky** for large-scale enterprise use.

It taught us our first big lesson in Agentic AI design:

> *Not every part of intelligence needs to come from the model. Sometimes, structure, control, and determinism are far smarter choices than unbounded generation.*

Evaluation Through the Lens of the 4Rs

Looking back, the SQL Agent may have been our simplest design but it set the tone for everything that followed. When evaluated through the lens of the **4Rs**, we start to see both why it worked so well as a prototype and why it struggled to scale beyond it.

1. Reach

The SQL Agent offered impressive **reach** in its ability to democratize access to data. For the first time, anyone, not just analysts, could ask questions about sales, inventory, or performance using plain language and get instant answers. That was revolutionary.

However, its reach was **horizontal**, not **deep**. The architecture scaled well across users, but not across **complexity**. As soon as questions involved multiple joins, nested filters, or time-based aggregations, the model's performance degraded. It could reach *everyone*, but it couldn't *understand everything*.

- Broad Reach
- Limited Depth

2. Reliability

Reliability was the first major pain point. The system's output depended entirely on the LLM's ability to correctly interpret natural language and generate valid SQL, which, as we quickly learned, is far from deterministic.

The same query could produce different SQL statements on different runs. Worse, small changes in phrasing could completely alter the logic. For a data-driven organization where accuracy is non-negotiable, this was a red flag.

- Useful for exploration
- Risky for production analytics

3. Restraint

In theory, the system was efficient: one model, one query, one result. In practice, it wasn't. Each query required a fresh LLM call, even if it was just a variation of a previous one. And because large models run on GPUs, this meant every casual "what if" question carried a measurable compute cost.

For recurring reports or dashboards, repeatedly invoking an LLM just to build the same SQL made no sense. It was like hiring a consultant every morning to re-invent your Excel formulas.

- Poor cost efficiency
- high redundancy

4. Respect

Respect, in our context, is all about **privacy and data protection**. And here, the SQL Agent fell short. To generate accurate queries, the model often needed access to the entire **database schema**, sometimes even a few rows of actual data. When using hosted LLM APIs, that meant sending potentially sensitive information outside the organization's boundary.

While fine for sandbox environments, this was unacceptable in enterprise settings where **data sovereignty** and **privacy compliance** are paramount.

- Functional in controlled settings
- unsafe for sensitive data.

Summary

4R Principle	Focus Area	Assessment	Remarks
Reach	Scalability & Adaptability	◯ Democratized data access ⬤ Limited complexity handling	Great entry point for casual analytics.
Reliability	Consistency & Accuracy	⬤ High variance in SQL outputs	Too fragile for production
Restraint	Cost & Efficiency	◍ Redundant LLM usage	Needs caching and reuse of SQL
Respect	Privacy & Control	⬤ Schema/data exposure risk	Must be hosted securely on-prem

From POC to Production: Why It Didn't Scale

Like many early agentic experiments, the SQL Agent began as a proof of concept; a sandbox for possibility. It was fast to build, visually impressive, and immediately useful for exploratory analysis. But as soon as we started thinking about **production-scale deployment**, the limitations became impossible to ignore.

Here's why this approach, despite its promise, didn't make the cut for real-world rollout.

1. Unpredictable Behavior, Unacceptable Risk

Production systems demand **predictability**. The SQL Agent, however, was inherently non-deterministic as the same query could yield different SQL translations depending on the phrasing or model state. This meant two users could ask the same question and get two slightly different results.

In a business where data drives decisions, this kind of inconsistency was simply unacceptable. You can't run your quarterly strategy review on "probably correct" numbers.

2. Scaling the Cost Curve

Each user query triggered a new LLM invocation, an expensive proposition when scaled to thousands of concurrent users. Even though the queries themselves were often similar, the model had to re-interpret and regenerate SQL every single time.

What felt cheap in a demo quickly turned into a cost spiral in production. The architecture had no concept of **query caching, reuse, or optimization**, which made it both inefficient and commercially unsustainable.

3. Data Privacy Barriers

In production environments, data security is not an afterthought, it's a prerequisite. The SQL Agent relied on sending database schemas (and occasionally sample data) to the model for context. When using a third-party API, this effectively meant **exporting sensitive internal metadata** to an external system.

For enterprise clients, especially in regulated industries, this was an immediate showstopper. Even if no raw data leaked, the very act of sharing schema details could expose the company's data model and business logic.

4. Poor Extensibility

The architecture wasn't designed for **evolution**. If tomorrow's use case needed joining across data sources or applying post-query analytics (like running a forecasting model on the result), the design couldn't support it easily. It was built to fetch and not to **reason**, **plan**, or **adapt**.

In other words, it was a smart query layer, not an intelligent system.

5. Lack of Cognitive Understanding

Perhaps the most important realization was that the system had **no understanding of the data it was handling**. It could translate natural language into SQL, but it didn't know what the SQL meant. It couldn't reason about the logic, identify anomalies, or question whether the query even made sense.

This absence of cognition became the key insight that pushed us toward the next generation of designs: the architectures that could **think**, **plan**, and **self-correct**.

In Summary

The SQL Agent was an important **milestone**. It proved that large language models could talk to structured data, but it also showed us what was missing:

- Determinism
- Privacy
- Cost efficiency
- True understanding

Those missing pieces became the blueprint for our next architectural leap: the **PADM family** of designs, where the agent wasn't just a translator but a **cognitive participant** in the reasoning process.

Agentic Test: Is this Architecture Agentic?

Before we move on, it's worth asking the question we now apply to every architecture we build, **"Is this system truly agentic?"**

When we put the SQL Agent under that lens, the answer is, **not quite.** It was a great translator, a capable executor, and an important foundation. But an "agent"? Not yet.

Let's see why.

1. Generative Aspect

At its core, the SQL Agent was **partially generative** but only within a narrow band. Its job was to take a user's natural language prompt and turn it into a SQL query. That's generation, yes but of a **fixed, mechanical kind**.

The LLM didn't reason about the question or validate the logic. It simply translated intent into syntax. So while it technically generated something new, it didn't demonstrate creativity, adaptability, or deeper contextual understanding.

Verdict: *Mechanically generative, but not cognitively generative.*

2. Action-Oriented Aspect

Here, the SQL Agent scores better. Once the SQL was generated, the system could automatically execute the query, retrieve results, and send them back to the user, all without human intervention. That's **agentic behavior in action**, albeit within strict limits.

However, it still lacked autonomy.

- If the query failed or produced an error, the system had no fallback mechanism.
- It couldn't retry, repair, or rethink.
- It could *act*, but not *adapt*.

Verdict: *Action-oriented, but without self-direction.*

3. Planning & Reasoning Aspect

This is where the SQL Agent truly showed its early-stage nature. There was no reasoning, no ability to plan multiple steps, infer dependencies, or make judgment calls. If you asked for something complex like *"Compare this quarter's top SKUs with last year's"*, the model didn't "plan" how to achieve it, it just guessed a single SQL query and hoped it worked. It couldn't decompose problems or reason about relationships. It could only execute direct translations.

Verdict: *No reasoning, no multi-step planning.*

Assessment Against Agentic Principles

Pillar	Description	Evaluation
Generative Aspect	Converts natural language into SQL statements. Lacks deep reasoning or creative flexibility	🟤 Limited generation—mechanical, not cognitive
Action-Oriented Aspect	Executes SQL autonomously and returns results. No self-correction or adaptation	○ Strong execution, limited autonomy
Planning & Reasoning Aspect	No planning or reasoning capability; acts as a single-step translator.	● No cognitive reasoning present

From Translation to Cognition

The SQL Agent marked the beginning of our Agentic AI journey. It could listen, translate, and execute, turning natural language into structured queries with impressive accuracy. But it couldn't think, plan, or reflect. It was intelligent in form, not in function.

Still, this was where we first saw the spark. The realization that an agent could act as a bridge between human intent and machine execution. And that single idea became the foundation for everything that followed.

Here is a Radar graph for the 4R and the Agentic test for easy reference.

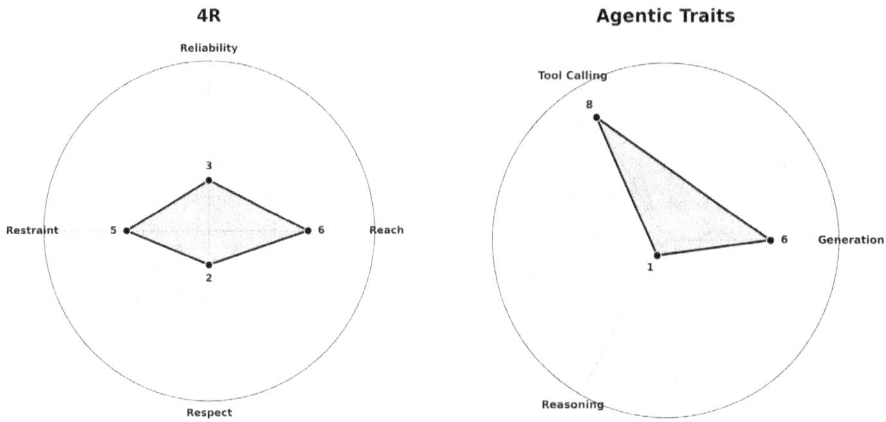

Figure: The 4R Radar graph indicates that the approach has generally poor performance across the Reach, Reliability, Respect, and Restraint dimensions. However regarding Agentic Traits, the approach shows a strength in tool calling, moderate capability in Generation, and a weakness in Reasoning. The poor Reasoning score is attributed to its limited capacity for independent thought to further refine or improve the output.

In the next chapters, we'll take this foundation further, evolving from **translation** to **true cognition** with architectures like **PADM, PADM_FUNCT**, and beyond. If the SQL Agent was our first brick, the next ones are where the structure truly starts to take shape.

CHAPTER 05

A Balanced Agentic Approach: Deterministic Queries with Generative Enrichment

"Order and simplification are the first steps toward mastery."
— Thomas Mann

When we first started experimenting with LLMs for data access, the excitement was all about one thing—asking questions in natural language and getting instant answers from databases.

"Show me the top 5 selling SKUs for outlet 1234."

"Compare sales growth for the last three months."

It felt magical. It was a system that could understand English, generate SQL, and return structured results. But as soon as we moved beyond the initial demos, reality struck. The same prompt that worked beautifully one day failed the next. Some queries ran for too long. Others fetched the wrong data and sometimes, the LLM simply invented SQL clauses that didn't exist in the schema (Hallucination).

These early lessons made one thing clear: **While LLMs are great at understanding language, they are not reliable database engineers.**

The Core Idea

We came up with some improvisations in the NLP-to-SQL approach. Unlike the earlier NLP-to-SQL model, where the LLM tried to dynamically generate and execute queries, this approach separates the concerns:

- The **application** or backend code handles all **data retrieval** through **deterministic, parameterized SQL**. These queries are curated by the data engineers in the conventional way which is to write the SQL queries in their favorite editor.
- The **LLM** focuses purely on **interpretation, summarization, and presentation** of the retrieved results.

So instead of the LLM deciding *what* to query, it only helps explain *what the data means.*

It's a simple shift in responsibility but a powerful one. The database remains the source of truth, while the LLM becomes the storyteller.

Architecture Overview

The architecture can be summarized in four clear stages:

1. **Retrieve**: The system executes **predefined SQL queries or stored procedures** using input parameters (like outlet ID or date range). These queries are deterministic, tested, and optimized ensuring reliability and consistent performance.
2. **Analyze**: Basic calculations or aggregations (e.g., totals, averages, comparisons) are performed in code, not by the LLM. This avoids logical inconsistencies and keeps business logic centralized.
3. **Enrich (via LLM)**: The processed data is sent to an LLM with a carefully designed prompt asking it to summarize, interpret, or narrate the results.

   The LLM might produce text such as:

   "Outlet 1234 recorded ₹5.6M in total sales last month, led by SKU X, which accounted for 35% of the total volume."

4. **Respond**: The final output is formatted and delivered to the user through a chatbot, dashboard, or report. It's accurate, readable, and business-ready.

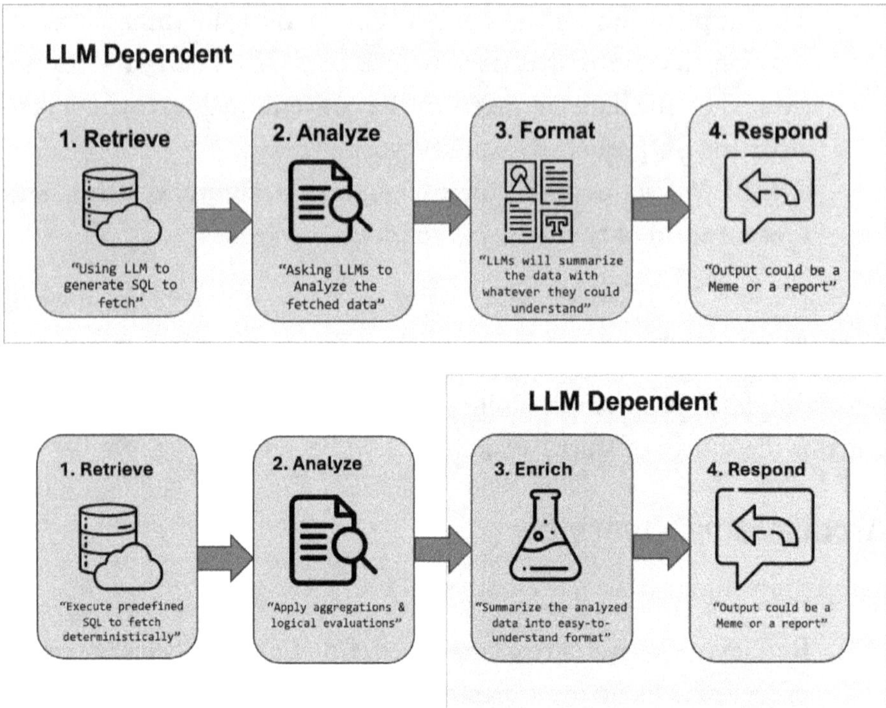

*Figure: From **Retrieve–Analyze–Format–Respond** approach we transformed it to **Retrieve-Analyze-Enrich-Respond.** The LLM is used only for the Summarization and the final output creation while the query and data aggregations are done in conventional way which provides the deterministic output*

This balanced architecture thrives in real-world, large-scale deployments because it **keeps intelligence where it belongs**:

- **Data logic** stays inside the codebase: deterministic, version-controlled, and secure.
- **Language generation** stays with the LLM: flexible, human-like, and adaptive.

It gives enterprises what they actually need:

- **Accuracy**: every number comes from a verified SQL query.
- **Repeatability**: the same input always yields the same output.
- **Efficiency**: only one or two LLM calls per user query.
- **Security** no raw data exposure to the model.

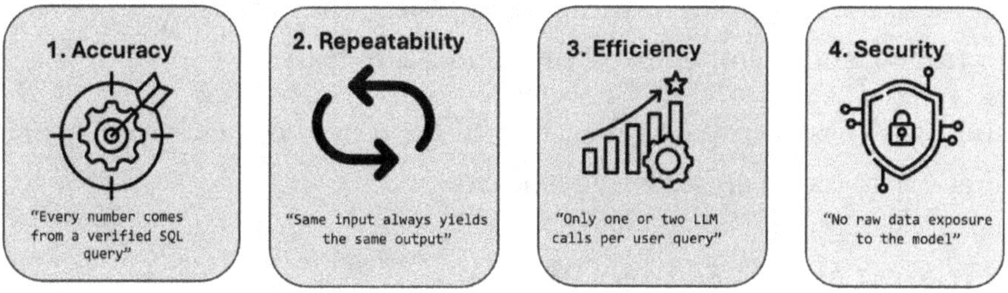

Overview of the Approach

In practice, this balanced approach operates through a simple yet powerful workflow, the one designed to fit seamlessly into existing enterprise systems without the unpredictability of fully autonomous agents.

Everything begins with a **structured input**, typically representing a specific screen, dashboard, or report request.

```
{
 "datetime": "2025-03-21",
 "companyId": 1300,
 "screenName": "EOD_SCREEN",
 "env": "production",
 "outletId": 366047,
 "userId": 186
}
```

Here, the screenName, such as "EOD_SCREEN" (End-of-Day Summary), tells the backend exactly what to do. Based on this value, the system automatically executes a **predefined sequence of SQL queries**, each retrieving a different slice of insight:

- Top-selling SKUs of the day
- Low-stock or out-of-stock alerts
- Outlet performance summaries
- Overall sales and growth metrics

All these queries are **deterministic**, meaning they are written, version-controlled, and maintained by the application team.

The LLM has no role in generating SQL; it only comes into play once all raw data has been securely retrieved.

Bringing the LLM into Play

Once the backend has fetched and aggregated the required data, the results are fed into a **prompt template** designed for narrative enrichment and summarization.

A typical prompt might look like this:

```
you are a sales performance assistant for a retail analytics platform.
Summarize the following data in a conversational and insightful way:
- Highlight key sales trends for the day
- Identify top and struggling SKUs or outlets
- Mention any unusual spikes or drops
- Suggest one action the user could take tomorrow
Data:
{{structured_json_output}}
```

The LLM now transforms raw numbers into a **clear, human-like story**:

```
"Outlet 366047 reported ₹58000 in total sales today, led by SKU-132, which alone contributed 38% of total revenue. However, SKU-214 continues to underperform for the third straight week. You might consider running a localized promotion tomorrow to boost its visibility."
```

This simple division of responsibility between **SQL for accuracy** and **LLM for communication** keeps data integrity intact while delivering user-friendly, context-aware summaries.

Enhanced User Engagement: Adding a Meme Generator

After generating the text summary, the next step takes engagement to another level. The output is passed to a **Meme Generator module**, which converts analytical insights into **visual metaphors** like a mascot or meme representing the "mood" of the data.

Here's how it works:

1. **Sentiment Mapping**: The LLM analyzes the tone of the summary (e.g., celebratory, neutral, or disappointing).
2. **Template Selection**: A mascot image or meme template is selected to reflect that tone (for example, a happy mascot when sales surge, or a stressed one when targets are missed).

3. **Caption Generation**: A short, witty caption is generated from the summary text. This is generally 20-30 words.
4. **Final Composition**: The text and image are combined into a shareable, lightweight visual perfect for dashboards, WhatsApp summaries, or quick team updates.

The result: a daily report that's not only accurate but also **emotionally engaging**.

Instead of a dry *"Sales increased by 8%,"* you get a cheerful mascot saying,

> *"We crushed it today! SKU-132 is on fire 🔥"*

This subtle humanization dramatically improves user engagement and recall. Few examples of the final output: (See the difference between the Mascot. The first one is Happy while the other one is Sad)

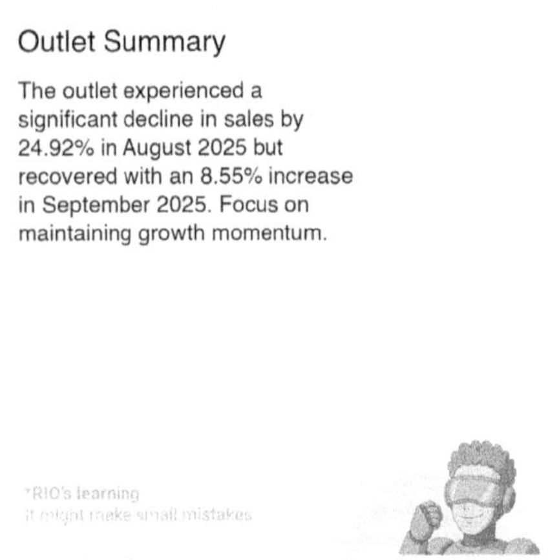

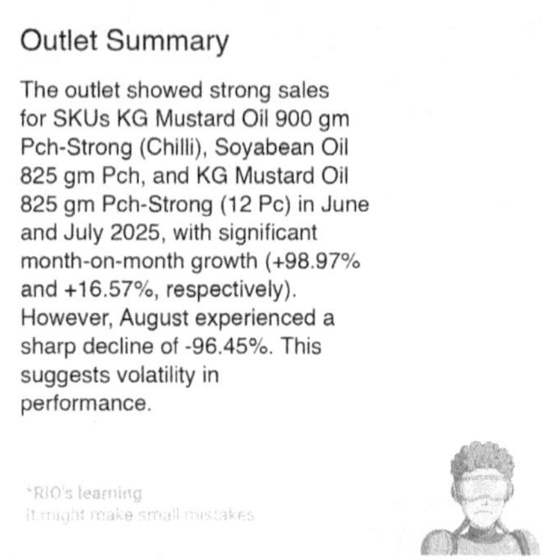

Operational Efficiency & Cost Implications

One of the biggest wins of this approach is cost efficiency. Because the LLM is only invoked **once per output**, after all SQL queries are executed, the total number of LLM calls per report stays low and predictable. In production deployments, this translates to **dramatic cost savings** compared to dynamic agentic models that might make multiple calls per query resolution. This cost-effectiveness, combined with the system's reliability and repeatability, makes it highly suitable for **enterprise-scale rollout** even across millions of outlets or daily transactions.

In Essence

This is **Agentic AI done practically**:

- Deterministic where it matters
- Generative where it adds value
- Engaging enough to make analytics feel human

It's a system that doesn't just deliver reports. It tells stories, celebrates wins, and nudges teams toward better decisions.

Design Decisions

Here are some of the key design decisions embedded in this approach:

Design Area	Decision
Infrastructure	The framework is model-agnostic. It can run on any LLM, including lightweight, self-hosted models such as **phi-4 on Ollama** or **Mistral-instruct**. This makes the system deployable even in cost-sensitive or data-restricted environments without compromising performance.
Query Handling	All SQL logic is **predefined** and resides within the application's backend layer. The LLM is **not involved** in query generation. It only receives structured outputs for summarization. This ensures determinism, security, and full control over data access.
LLM Role	The LLM is used **exclusively for summarization, narrative enrichment, and rephrasing**. It does not alter, compute, or decide; keeping the boundary between deterministic logic and generative presentation crystal clear.
Output Modalities	The system supports multiple output formats: **structured tables, natural-language summaries**, and **meme-style visualizations** for enhanced user engagement. This flexibility allows the same underlying data to serve analytical, conversational, and creative interfaces seamlessly.

Pros and Cons of the Balanced Agentic Approach

This approach represents a practical middle ground, combining the reliability of traditional database systems with the expressive power of modern language models.

It doesn't try to make the AI fully autonomous; instead, it focuses on **making intelligence dependable, predictable, and production-ready**.

Here's a closer look at its strengths and trade-offs:

Pros of the approach

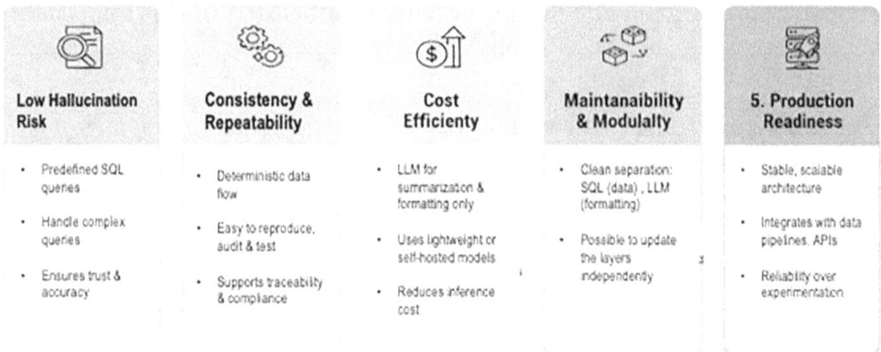

1. Low Hallucination Risk

Because SQL queries are predefined and maintained by developers, there's almost no room for the LLM to fabricate or misinterpret data. The outputs remain grounded in actual, verifiable database results ***ensuring trust and accuracy***.

2. Consistency & Repeatability

Every user, screen, or report follows the same deterministic flow. This makes results easy to reproduce, audit, and test. This is a must for enterprise systems that require ***traceability*** and ***compliance***.

3. Cost Efficiency

Since the LLM is used only for summarization and narrative enhancement (not reasoning or query generation), the system can run efficiently on **lightweight or self-hosted models** like *phi-4* or *Mistral* on Ollama. This dramatically ***reduces inference costs*** while maintaining excellent response quality.

4. Maintainability & Modularity

The design keeps logic cleanly separated: SQL for data retrieval, LLM for presentation. Developers can update one layer without affecting the other, improving ***maintainability*** and ***reducing regression risks***.

5. Production Readiness

The architecture is inherently stable and easy to deploy at scale.It integrates seamlessly with existing data pipelines, APIs, and visualization tools which is ideal for organizations prioritizing ***reliability over experimentation***.

Cons of the Approach

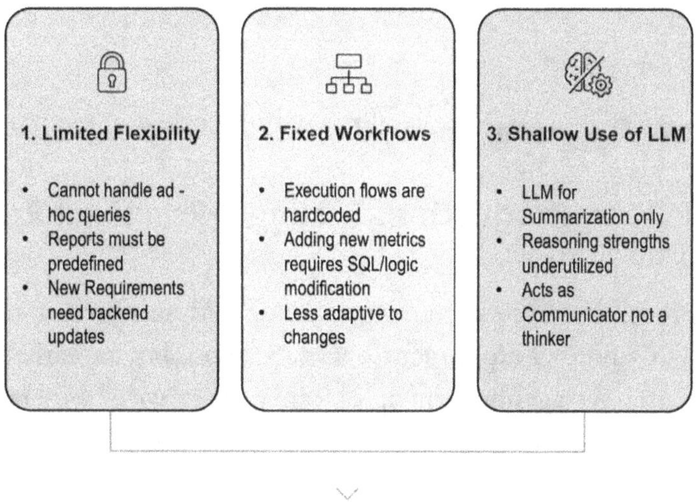

1. Limited Flexibility

The system cannot handle ad-hoc natural language questions. All reports and insights must be predefined, meaning any new requirement needs backend updates.

2. Fixed Workflows

Execution flows are hardcoded. To add new metrics, queries, or screens, developers must modify SQL and redeploy the logic layer. This makes the system less adaptive to rapidly changing analytical needs.

3. Shallow Use of LLM Capabilities

Because the LLM is used only for summarization and formatting, its deeper reasoning and analytical strengths remain underutilized. It acts as a **communicator**, not a **thinker** though that's a fair trade-off for stability and cost control.

In Summary

This architecture lays the foundation for **enterprise-grade, production-ready intelligence** that's stable, predictable, and easy to maintain. It's a design that delivers real business value without the unpredictability or cost of fully autonomous systems.

In simpler terms,

> ***"Let the SQL ensure accuracy. Let the LLM make it human."***

From POC to Production: Scaling a Practical, Reliable Design

This approach was built from the ground up with **production readiness** in mind. It's not an experiment or a lab demo. It's an early, working example of how agentic principles can coexist with the stability of traditional enterprise systems.

Response Time & Execution Architecture

At its core, this design is fast, efficient, and predictable. Data retrieval happens through **pre-validated SQL queries** that already exist in the core Bizom application stack. These queries are battle-tested, optimized, and run well within the acceptable latency thresholds for real-time or near-real-time analytics.

Once the data is fetched, it is handed over to the LLM not for computation but for **formatting and summarization**. This adds only a minor delay of typically **2–3 seconds per formatting call**, depending on the model used and the length of the summary.

Because the LLM isn't generating queries or reasoning across steps, these formatting calls can be **non-blocking** and even **executed in**

parallel, ensuring the user experience remains smooth. In other words, data moves at the speed of SQL; presentation moves at the speed of creativity.

Infrastructure Coupling

The system follows a **loosely coupled design**, allowing each layer viz. database, LLM, and output engine to evolve independently.

- Any **relational database** (PostgreSQL, MySQL, Redshift, etc.) can serve as the data source.
- The **LLM layer** is flexible. It can use lightweight, **self-hosted models** like *Phi-4 on Ollama* or connect to external APIs like *GPT-3.5* via *Bedrock*.

This modularity means the same design can run on-prem, in hybrid setups, or in the cloud without rewriting the architecture. If in future a cheaper or faster model becomes available, it can be swapped in seamlessly.

LLM Dependence & Cost

A key strength of this approach is that **LLM usage is limited and predictable**.The LLM only handles deterministic tasks of formatting, summarization, or light narrative generation, all of which can be managed by small, inexpensive models.

There's no tool discovery, no recursive reasoning, and no chain-of-thought complexity. This keeps costs low and **predictable per screen or report**. Since every output corresponds to a fixed number of LLM calls, organizations can confidently forecast monthly API usage and expenses.

In most cases, lightweight models like *Phi-4*, *Mistral*, or *GPT-3.5* deliver excellent results without the need for costly reasoning-centric models like *GPT-4* or *Claude-3 Opus*.

Platform & Security Constraints

This design also checks all the boxes for **enterprise-grade security**. Unlike fully agentic or Langflow-based solutions (See Appendix A) where the LLM may see raw data or full database schemas, here the LLM only receives **post-processed, aggregated results**.

That means:

- No schema leakage
- No raw data exposure
- No risk of data exfiltration through prompt injection

Additionally, **personally identifiable information (PII)** can be masked before the data reaches the LLM, and re-inserted after summarization. All authentication, authorization, and audit controls remain under the client platform's governance layer, ensuring compliance with enterprise security standards like **SOC2**, **GDPR**, and **ISO 27001**.

Determinism & Repeatability

Perhaps the most important production characteristic: **consistency**. Because all SQL queries are predefined, the same input will always yield the same output data. This **deterministic execution** is critical for auditing, regression testing, and compliance reporting.

While the LLM may slightly vary the phrasing of its summary, the underlying metrics such as sales numbers, SKU rankings, performance insights remain identical across runs. This separation of **data (fixed)** and **language (flexible)** ensures stability without losing personality.

Compared to dynamic, LLM-driven systems like Langflow (where both query and response are generated afresh each time), this design delivers **repeatability, reliability, and trustworthiness**—the three pillars every production deployment depends on.

In Summary

This architecture proves that AI doesn't have to be unpredictable to be powerful. By pairing deterministic data logic with selective LLM enrichment, it achieves the holy grail of production systems—**speed, stability, and storytelling—all in one loop.**

Evaluation Through the Lens of the 4R's

The *Balanced Agentic Approach* was designed not to impress with complexity, but to deliver with consistency. Let's see how it performs when viewed through our four guiding principles —**Reach, Reliability, Restraint, and Respect.**

1. Reach

The architecture was designed with scale as a first-class concern. Because all SQL queries are pre-defined and optimized, the system can easily handle thousands of concurrent requests without straining infrastructure.The LLM is used sparingly and asynchronously, meaning it doesn't bottleneck performance. From daily reports to nationwide deployments, this model scales linearly, a rare feat for AI-driven systems.

Verdict: *High scalability and reach that's ready for large-scale rollout*

2. Reliability

Reliability here comes from one word: **determinism**.The SQL queries are written, reviewed, and version-controlled ensuring consistent and auditable outputs. No LLM ever generates or modifies the queries, which removes the risk of hallucination or logic drift.This design gives confidence not just in the data, but in the process that produced it.

Verdict: *Exceptionally reliable as results are consistent across every run.*

3. Restraint

Restraint in AI design means using intelligence wisely, not excessively. This architecture embodies that principle perfectly. The LLM is called only when it adds clear value for summarization, rephrasing, or formatting and not for computation or reasoning. This selective usage keeps both latency and cost in check. Low-cost, self-hosted models like *Phi-4* or *Gemma* work beautifully, reducing dependency on expensive APIs..

> **Verdict:** *Extremely cost-efficient. Shows smart use of LLM power, not overuse*

4. Respect

Respect for data is built into every layer of this system. The LLM never touches raw or sensitive data. It only sees aggregated, anonymized results. PII fields like outlet IDs or customer references can be masked before processing and restored afterward. All authentication, authorization, and audit trails are handled by the core Bizom platform ensuring full compliance with enterprise security standards.

> **Verdict:** *Privacy-safe and compliant. Built with respect for data boundaries.*

Summary Table

Principle	Definition	Evaluation	Remarks
Reach	Ability to scale efficiently across large deployments	◯ **High** — pre-defined SQL scales linearly	LLMs are offloaded asynchronously, so no performance bottleneck.
Reliability	Consistency and trustworthiness of outputs	◯ **Strong** — deterministic data flow	SQL logic is fixed and versioned; same result every time.
Restraint	Cost control and efficiency in LLM usage	◯ **Excellent** — minimal LLM dependency	LLMs are only used for summaries; predictable and low-cost execution.
Respect	Protection of user data and adherence to privacy norms	◯ **High** — data anonymization built-in	No schema exposure or raw data sharing; fully compliant design

Agentic Test: Is This Architecture Truly Agentic?

Now that we've seen how this design performs against the 4R's, let's put it through another lens: the **Agentic Test**.

As we've discussed earlier, the three pillars of agentic behavior are:

- **Generative Capability:can the system create or infer new steps on its own?**
- **Action Orientation: can it execute tasks autonomously?**
- **Planning & Reasoning: can it think ahead, make decisions, and adapt?**

Let's see how our *Balanced Approach* performs on each.

1. Generative Aspect

In this design, the LLM doesn't generate SQL, plan logic, or make decisions. Its creative power is used selectively to **format outputs**, **summarize structured data**, and sometimes **enhance engagement** through meme captions or narrative phrasing.

This is intentional restraint: the LLM adds a human touch without touching the logic that drives the business.

Verdict: *Present, but restricted to post-processing and narrative enrichment. Focused creativity that adds polish without compromising predictability.*

2. Action-Oriented Aspect

The system is *not* action-driven by the LLM. All actions: data fetching, aggregation, computation, and logic execution are performed entirely by the backend application.

The LLM is invoked **after** all that is complete, purely for presentation and interpretation.

Unlike later PADM architectures, where the agent autonomously decides which tool to call or what to do next, here the LLM doesn't initiate or control any process.

This deliberate exclusion ensures total determinism and auditability (no black-box actions, no surprises).

Verdict: *Absent, all actions are pre-executed outside the LLM's control. The LLM never drives behavior; it only describes outcomes.*

3. Planning & Reasoning Aspect

Because all workflows are predefined in the backend, there's no dynamic task decomposition or multi-step reasoning. The LLM doesn't decide which SQL to run, how to group data, or what sequence to follow. The only mild form of reasoning it performs is in the **meme selection process**—inferring tone or sentiment from text and matching it with an appropriate visual.

It's more "presentation reasoning" than "problem-solving reasoning." This keeps the architecture predictable, though it limits its ability to adapt to unexpected situations.

Verdict: *Very limited reasoning, mostly sentiment or tone-based. Enough to feel intelligent, not enough to be autonomous.*

Assessment Against Agentic Principles

Agentic Pillar	Description	Evaluation
Generative Aspect	LLM generates summaries, captions, and narratives but not queries or plans	◍ Present but narrow
Action-Oriented Aspect	Execution handled fully by backend; LLM performs no active control.	● Absent — passive architecture
Planning & Reasoning Aspect	No dynamic planning; only basic reasoning for meme sentiment or summarization.	● Minimal reasoning

Looking Ahead

While this *BalancedApproach* marked a major leap in making AI practical and production-ready, it also revealed a deeper question:

Could an agent go beyond presenting insights and actually **think, plan, and adapt** on its own?

The deterministic SQL architecture gave us reliability and trust, but it lacked the spark of autonomy. It could summarize beautifully, but it couldn't reason about *why* certain patterns appeared, or *how* to act on them.

Here is the Radar graph to remember the strengths and weaknesses of this approach

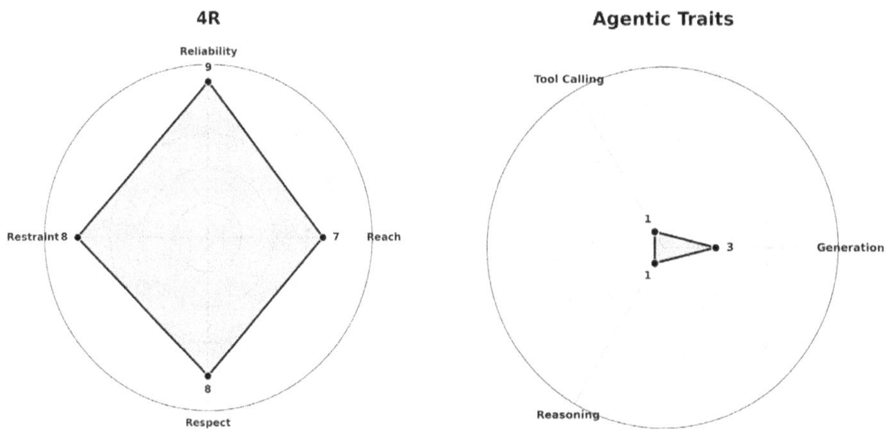

Figure: The 4R Radar graph illustrates that the approach performs strongly across Reach, Reliability, Respect, and Restraint. However, in terms of Agentic Traits, it scores lower on Reasoning and Tool Calling since these functions are handled through predefined SQL queries rather than dynamic decision-making.

That gap led us to explore the next frontier: architectures where the agent doesn't just format information, but **interprets**, **decides**, and **learns** through interaction.

In the next chapters, we'll build on this foundation and introduce the **PADM family** of architectures, the designs that attempt to make AI truly agentic, bringing reasoning, memory, and feedback into a unified cognitive loop.

> *"If this chapter was about control, the next one is about cognition. How an agent begins to think for itself."*

CHAPTER 06

From Language to Action: The Journey to the Model Context Protocol

"We shape our tools, and thereafter our tools shape us."
— Marshall McLuhan

The early 2020s marked a turning point in artificial intelligence with the arrival of large language models (LLMs). For the first time, systems could generate fluent text, structured reasoning, and even executable code from natural language prompts. Businesses quickly embraced these capabilities, integrating LLMs into chat interfaces, content pipelines, and decision-support tools.

The results were impressive, at least on the surface. Models could compose emails, draft policies, or write SQL queries that appeared intelligent and contextually aware. Yet a critical limitation soon became clear: these systems were not acting; they were *simulating* action.

An LLM could describe how to book a flight, but it couldn't actually make the booking. It could explain an API call, but not execute it. It had no persistent memory, no world model, and no mechanism to verify outcomes. In short, early LLMs were remarkable communicators but passive systems confined to **text generation** rather than **task completion**.

This realization led to a new engineering challenge: **how to give language models agency**. Researchers and developers began extending LLMs with the ability to perceive state, make decisions, and interact with external systems bridging the gap between *conversation* and *computation*. This shift required more than fine-tuning; it demanded new architectural layers for reasoning, control flow, and integration.

At the center of this transformation lies the **Model Context Protocol (MCP)**, a lightweight yet powerful interface that allows LLMs to discover, access, and invoke external tools safely. MCP provides the connective tissue between language and action, enabling models to move beyond static reasoning toward dynamic, goal-driven execution.

This chapter explores that evolution from the first wave of text-only intelligence to the emergence of **Agentic AI** systems capable of acting autonomously within real-world constraints. We'll examine how architectures built on protocols like MCP redefine what it means for a model to *understand*, *decide*, and *do*.

Let's examine different phases of evolution of LLM based use cases

Phase 1: The Struggles of Foundational LLMs

Early large language models (LLMs) were a major leap in natural language understanding, capable of generating human-like text based on training data. However, they struggled with following instructions. Their responses were based on pattern prediction, not task execution.

Example:

- *User*: "Who is the president of the USA?"
- *LLM*: "The most influential person in the world"

Here, the model produced a generic statement rather than a direct answer.

Similarly:

- *User*: "Write an email stating that I will be on leave today."
- *LLM*: "And then send it to my manager."

Instead of generating the email, it inferred a next action showing it couldn't interpret or execute direct instructions reliably.

Phase 2: Supervised Fine-Tuning (SFT) and RLHF

To fix this, researchers introduced **Supervised Fine-Tuning (SFT)** and **Reinforcement Learning from Human Feedback (RLHF)**.

- **SFT** trained models on datasets where inputs were paired with clear, human-written outputs.
- **RLHF** took it further. Humans evaluated multiple model responses, helping fine-tune the model toward preferred answers

As a result, instruction-following improved drastically.

Example (Improved):

- *User*: "Write an email stating that I will be on leave today."
- *LLM*

```
Subject: Leave Notification
Dear [Manager's Name],
I wanted to inform you that I will be on leave today.
Please let me know if you need any further details.
Best regards, [Your Name].
```

Still, models had limitations. Users expected factual and real-time responses such as:

- "What's the square root of 14.52321"
- "What's the current GDP of India?"

LLMs struggled because:

- They aren't calculators. Precise math is outside their native capabilities.
- They rely on pre-training, meaning no real-time awareness of current data.

Phase 3: Function Calling to Extend Model Capabilities

To overcome this, **function calling** was introduced. Instead of answering with only its training data or the parametric memory, the model could now **invoke external tools** for real-time tasks or data retrieval.

Example:

- *User*: "What is the square root of 14.5232?"
- *LLM (with function call)*: "The square root of 14.5232 is approximately 3.81."
- *User*: "What is the current GDP of India?"
- *LLM (with function call)*: "As of 2025, the estimated GDP of India is $3.7 trillion."

This allowed LLMs to provide **accurate, real-time, and context-aware answers**. But users didn't stop there. They wanted the AI to take real-world actions.

Phase 4: The Rise of Agentic AI

The next leap was **agentic AI**: models that don't just provide answers but perform **actions** across applications:

- Send emails
- Schedule calendar events
- Message on platforms like Slack or Telegram
- Conduct transactions or bookings

Early implementations were application-specific, integrating with one service at a time (e.g., Gmail, Zoom, Stripe). But this revealed serious issues:

1. **Diverse tech stacks**: Apps use different languages (e.g., Python, JavaScript, Go).
2. **Inconsistent APIs**: Each has unique formats, rate limits, and logic.
3. **Complex authentication**: From API keys to OAuth, each service required unique handling.
4. **Poor scalability**: Building and maintaining one-off integrations for thousands of apps was inefficient and brittle.

A new solution standardized and scalable solution was clearly needed.

Phase 5: The Emergence of Model Context Protocol (MCP)

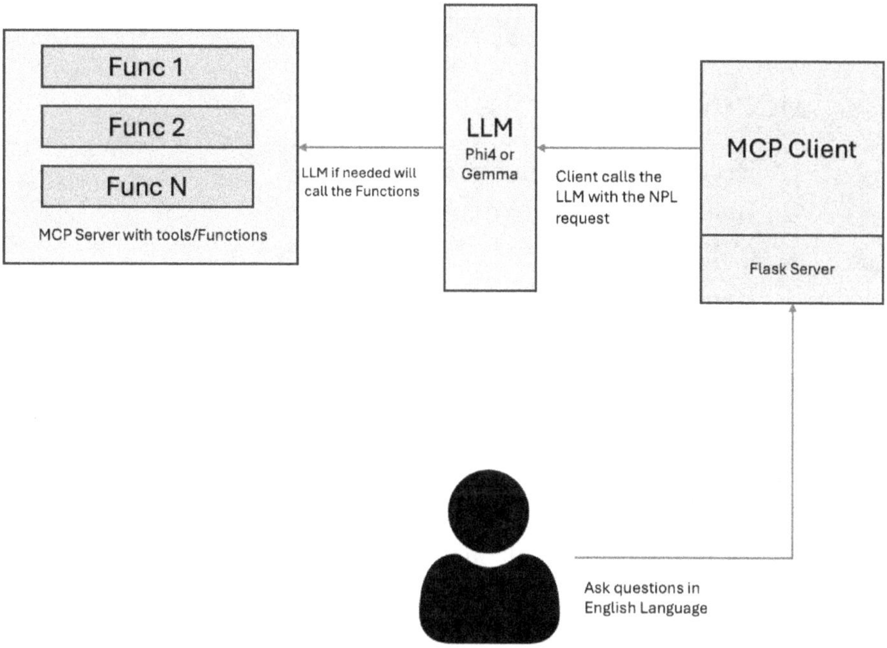

Figure: Shows a typical flow of a user request getting served using the MCP server. The LLM will call the functions exposed using the MCP server

This led to the development of the **Model Context Protocol (MCP)**, a standardized way for LLMs to communicate with any external application or service.

Rather than hardcoding integrations for each use case, **MCP defines a universal interface**, allowing any compliant application to be used by any capable model.

With MCP:

- LLMs can invoke **any tool** or service or functions, regardless of the app's underlying tech.
- Developers no longer need to create custom logic for each app.
- A model can **dynamically understand and use** services just by reading their usage metadata or schema.

Example:

- *User*: "Schedule a Zoom meeting with my team tomorrow at 10 AM"
- MCP-enabled LLM:

    1. Recognizes scheduling intent
    2. Invokes a standard scheduling API
    3. Calls Zoom API
    4. Returns: "Your Zoom meeting is scheduled for 10 AM tomorrow. Link: [link]"

This is a paradigm shift. The LLM isn't just understanding text; it's **interpreting context, identifying required tools, executing actions, and confirming success** autonomously.

This follows the architectural diagram of Agents that we had earlier discussed in the chapter1

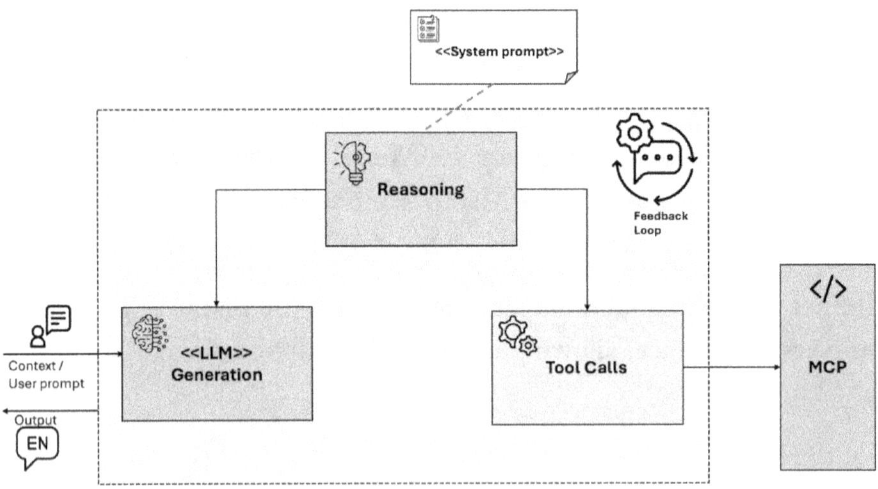

Where LLM along with the reasoning element could figure out the need for the tool call and also understand when the required data to generate the output has been obtained so that it can show the final output to the user.

The following figure summarizes the phases of evolution.

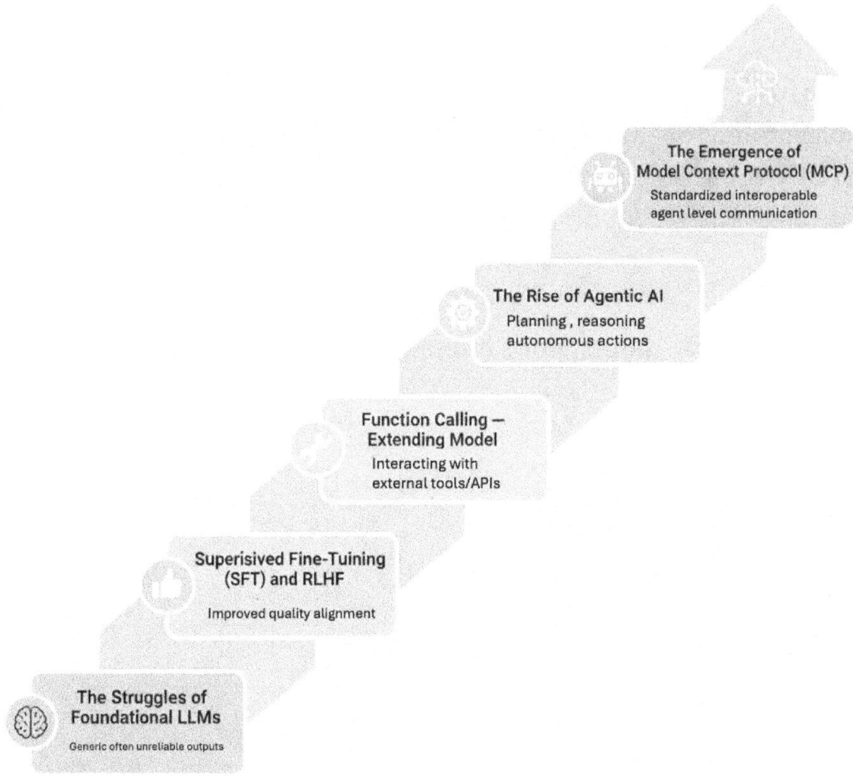

MCP as the Core of AI Ecosystems

The journey from pattern-matching text generators to action-taking agents culminates with MCP as the backbone. MCP turns LLMs into **adaptive agents** that can operate across ecosystems without being tied to one-off integrations or middleware. Instead of needing handcrafted frameworks, the protocol becomes a universal bridge between AI and the digital world.

In this new world:

- APIs expose standardized MCP interfaces.
- LLMs understand and use them out of the box.
- AI ecosystems become truly plug-and-play.

MCP marks the transition from reactive AI to autonomous, tool-using intelligence. It's not just an enhancement, it's the foundation for the next era of AI.

Since MCP is the core of Agentic AI we will try to put a more simplified explanation. To simplify the concept of the **Model Context Protocol (MCP),** think of it as a discovery and interaction protocol for tools, very much like REST, but designed specifically for use by LLMs.

The key difference?

In MCP, **it's the model, not a human developer, that makes the calls.**

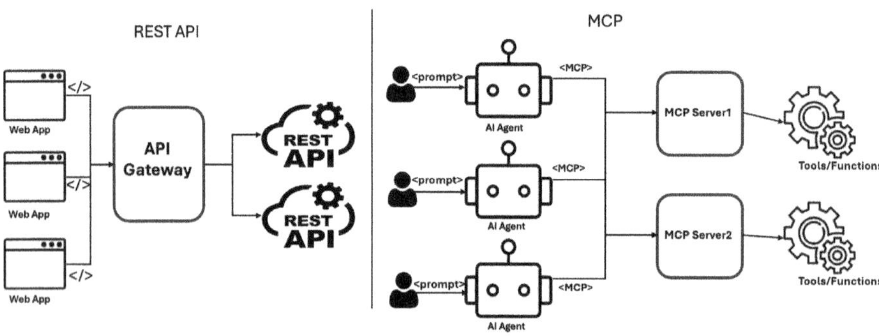

Figure: REST APIs execute decisions that were made at design time. MCP enables decisions to be made at run time. In the former, API calls are coded explicitly into the application flow; in the latter, tool calls are generated dynamically by AI agents based on intent, context, and intermediate reasoning. This shift from hard-coded execution to agent-driven orchestration is the most important difference between the two approaches.

In a traditional REST API–based approach, requests are explicitly coded into the application, either hard-wired into the UI or driven by predefined conditional logic. The application decides in advance which API to call and when.

In contrast, with MCP, the decision is deferred to the AI agent. The agent determines, at runtime, which tools to invoke and in what sequence based on the context and the goal at hand. This distinction is fundamental: REST API interactions are *predefined by developers*, whereas MCP interactions are *generated dynamically by the agent itself.*

MCP enables a model or agent to discover and interact with external tools in a dynamic and standardized way. Using MCP's registry functions, an AI agent can determine which tools are available to it at runtime.

Tool Discovery with MCP

At the core of this process is a registry pull.

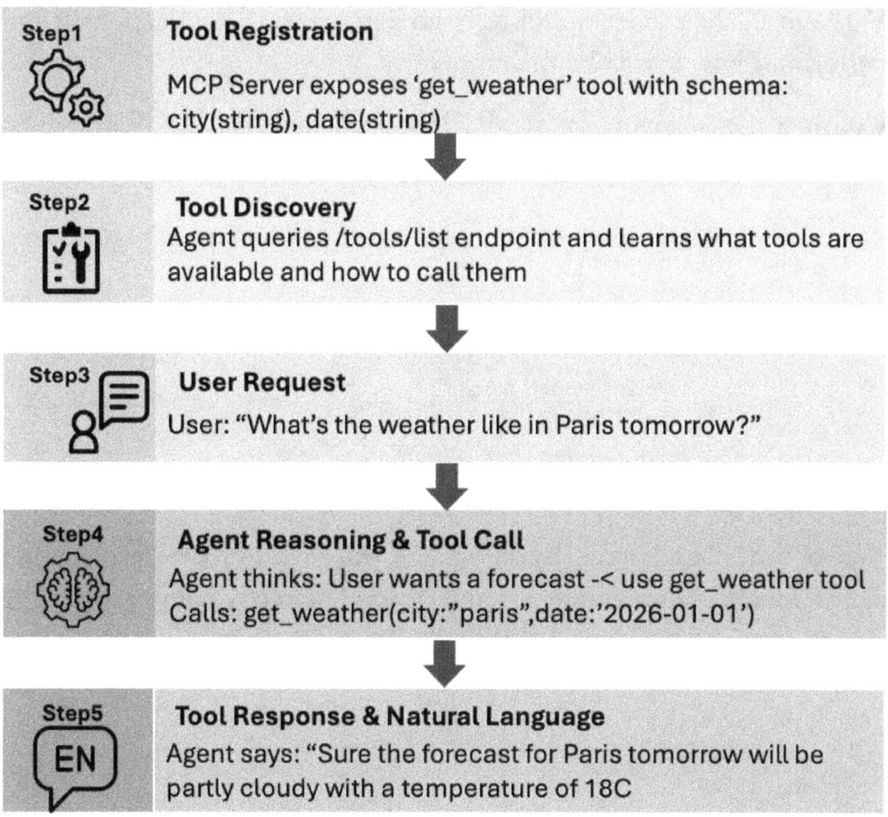

Figure: The above flow lists down how agents discover and use MCP tools automatically

```
self.tools = await self.mcp.list_tools()
```

This is a **one-time, full discovery call** that retrieves a list of all available tools, along with their usage schemas and parameters. It gives the agent everything it needs to:

1. Call a tool:
2. await session.call_tool("tool_name", input)
3. Inspect input/output types for compatibility or planning
4. Filter and select tools dynamically during multi-step reasoning
5. Reference the tool's docstring or usage description for guidance

This registry acts as the **source of truth** during an agent's execution. Without it, the model would have no context for which actions it can perform or how to invoke them properly.

Consider the following set of MCP tools available in a MCP server

```
@mcp.tool()
def multiply(input: MultiplyInput) -> MultiplyOutput:
    """Multiply two integers. Usage: input={"input": {"a": 6, "b": 7}} result = await
mcp.call_tool('multiply', input)"""
    print("CALLED: multiply(MultiplyInput) -> MultiplyOutput")
    return MultiplyOutput(result=input.a * input.b)

@mcp.tool()
def divide(input: DivideInput) -> DivideOutput:
    """Divide one number by another. Usage: input={"input": {"a": 20, "b": 4}} result = await
mcp.call_tool('divide', input)"""
    print("CALLED: divide(DivideInput) -> DivideOutput")
    return DivideOutput(result=input.a / input.b)
```

When the tool list is asked by the agent it will get (Notice the explanation of the functions/tools multiply and divide is directly coming from the docstring present in their definition)

```
multiply-Multiply two integers. Usage: input={"input": {"a": 6, "b": 7}}
result = await mcp.call_tool('multiply', input)

divide-Divide one number by another. Usage: input={"input": {"a": 20, "b":
4}} result = await mcp.call_tool('divide', input)
```

As you can see, the protocol doesn't just expose the tool names, it also provides metadata and usage formats that make autonomous use by a model possible. This brings us to a critical point: **every function exposed to an LLM via MCP must be properly documented.**

Since the agent relies on tool names, descriptions, and parameter schemas to decide when and how to use a tool, poorly defined tools can lead to failure or unexpected behavior. Good documentation becomes a runtime requirement.

Under the hood the way it works is that the LLM is reading this documentation that is supposedly written in English to understand the usage of the tool or function. When the user requests any task from LLM , it refers to this documentation to decide which tool will help in solving the problem.

Let's look at a function and its documentation

```
async def get_sales_for_particular_outlet(inputData:OutletSpecificInput) ->
floatOutput:
    """
    <Description>
            Retrieves the total sales happening at a specific outlet.This
function takes the outlet ID and company ID as input and returns the sales
amount for the specified outlet. It is designed to work with a single
outlet only, not a list of outlets.
            Args:
                inputData (OutletSpecificInput):
                    An input object containing:
                    - outlet_id (int): Unique identifier for the outlet.
                    - company_id (int): Unique identifier for the company.
                    - query_date (str): the query date

            Returns:
                floatOutput:
                    An object containing:
                    - result (float): Total sales amount for the specified
outlet.

           Example Usage:
                input = {"inputData": {"company_id": 800, "outlet_id":
1234,"query_date":"2025-06-18"}}
                get_sales_for_particular_outlet(input)

        </Description>
"""
///body of the function
Return value
```

The documentation should ideally include:

1. A detailed description of what is the intent of this tool
2. The arguments it takes and their data type
3. Return values
4. An example to show the input and output

The documentation is the part of the tool listing that will be provided to the Agents. If sufficient information about the tool is provided the LLMs can take the proper decision on which tools to use.

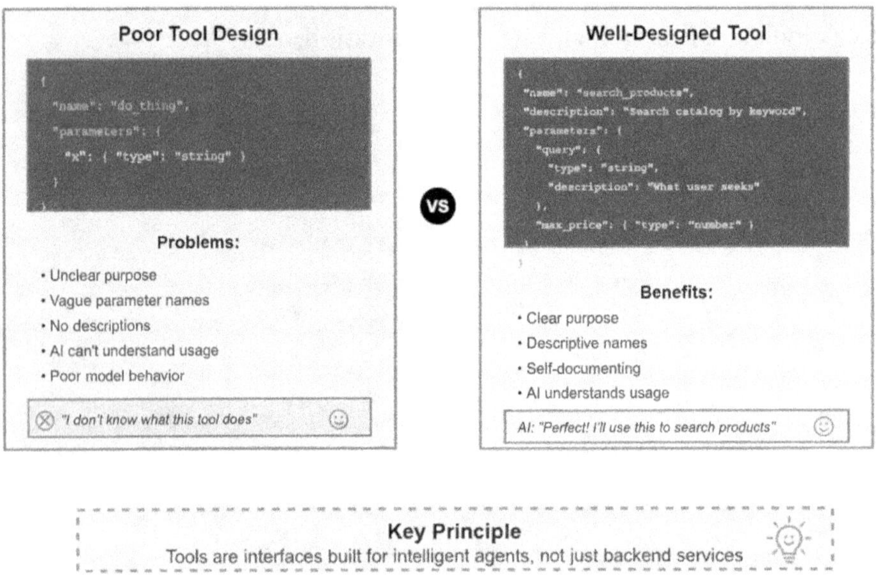

Figure: A Comparison of a Poor Tool Design Versus Good Tool Design. Notice the Documentation and the type information in the code

How to make an existing function as a MCP tool

It is actually very simple to make an existing function as a MCP tool. There are essentially 7 steps to do. Lets see this step by step

Step 1: Add the decorator @mcp.tool() on a function that you want to expose as MCP tool

```
@mcp.tool()
async def get_sales_for_particular_outlet(inputData:OutletSpecificInput) ->
floatOutput:
```

Step 2: Make the function asynchronous by adding the keyword **async.**

```
@mcp.tool()
async def get_sales_for_particular_outlet(inputData:OutletSpecificInput) ->
floatOutput:
```

Step 3: Introduce strict type for the input arguments and the output values using Pydantic or similar data type validation libraries

```
@mcp.tool()
async def get_sales_for_particular_outlet(inputData:OutletSpecificInput) ->
floatOutput:
```

We need to basically define the classes inputData and floatOutput as

```
class intOutput(BaseModel):
   result: int


class floatOutput(BaseModel):
   result: float
```

Step 4: Add the documentation to the tool

```
@mcp.tool()
async def get_sales_for_particular_outlet(inputData:OutletSpecificInput) ->
floatOutput:
    """
    <Module Name="Outlet" Type="Function">
        <Description>
            Retrieves the total sales happening at a specific outlet.This
function takes the outlet ID and company ID as input and returns the sales
amount for the specified outlet. It is designed to work with a single
outlet only, not a list of outlets.
            Args:
                inputData (OutletSpecificInput):
                    An input object containing:
                    - outlet_id (int): Unique identifier for the outlet.
                    - company_id (int): Unique identifier for the company.
                    - query_date (str): the query date


            Returns:
                floatOutput:
                    An object containing:
                    - result (float): Total sales amount for the specified
outlet.

           Example Usage:
                input = {"inputData": {"company_id": 800, "outlet_id":
1234,"query_date":"2025-06-18"}}
                get_sales_for_particular_outlet(input)

        </Description>
    </Module>
    """
```

Step 5: Read the input arguments

```
outlet_id=inputData.outlet_id
dbId=inputData.company_id
queryDate=inputData.query_date
```

Step 6: Pass these arguments to the legacy function

```
dfRes= await get_total_sales_for_outlets(cfg.ENV,
                                         queryDate,
                                         outlet_id,
                                         dbId
                                         )
```

Step 7: Return the result coming from the legacy function after converting to the Pydantic data type

```
return floatOutput(result=dfRes.iloc[0]['total_amount'])
```

Here is the full function

```
//step1
@mcp.tool()
//step2 & step3
async def get_sales_for_particular_outlet(inputData:OutletSpecificInput) ->
floatOutput:
//step4
    """
    <Module Name="Outlet" Type="Function">
        <Description>
            Retrieves the total sales happening at a specific outlet.This
function takes the outlet ID and company ID as input and returns the sales
amount for the specified outlet. It is designed to work with a single
outlet only, not a list of outlets.
            Args:
                inputData (OutletSpecificInput):
                    An input object containing:
                    - outlet_id (int): Unique identifier for the outlet.
                    - company_id (int): Unique identifier for the company.
                    - query_date (str): the query date



            Returns:
                floatOutput:
                    An object containing:
                    - result (float): Total sales amount for the specified
outlet.

           Example Usage:
                input = {"inputData": {"company_id": 800, "outlet_id":
1234,"query_date":"2025-06-18"}}
                get_sales_for_particular_outlet(input)

        </Description>
    </Module>
    """
```

```
//step5
        outlet_id=inputData.outlet_id
        dbId=inputData.company_id
        queryDate=inputData.query_date
//step6
        dfRes= await get_total_sales_for_outlets(cfg.ENV,
                                        queryDate,
                                        outlet_id,
                                        dbId
                                        )
//step7
         return floatOutput(result=dfRes.iloc[0]['total_amount'])
```

By following these steps, it becomes possible to transform almost any existing functionality into an **MCP tool**, enabling language models to automatically discover and invoke those functions as part of their reasoning process.

Conclusion

The explanation here has focused deliberately on the **practitioner's view**, a hands-on guide to using MCP in real scenarios. But the framework itself goes much deeper. For those interested in exploring its full scope, the official specification provides detailed guidance and evolving standards[1].

We believe that the **Model Context Protocol (MCP)** represents one of the most significant architectural milestones in advancing *LLM autonomy*. It offers a clear, standardized way for models to understand and interact with the world beyond text.

In the agentic architectures discussed in the next few chapters, we'll see the MCP pattern in action, serving as the connective tissue that allows agents to **call external tools automatically**, bridging the gap between *thinking* and *doing*.

Reference

1. https://modelcontextprotocol.io/specification/2025-06-18/server/tools

CHAPTER 07

From Summarizers to Cognitive Agents: Designing Multi-Layered AI Systems

"True intelligence isn't just knowing what to do — it's knowing when, how, and why to do it."

So far, most AI "agents" built on top of large language models have been clever. They can summarize documents, translate text, generate SQL queries, or extract structured data from unstructured sources. These are valuable capabilities, but they mostly operate at the surface performing what could be called *reactive pattern-matching*.

In other words, the model receives a prompt, processes it, and returns an answer. The response might sound intelligent, but the system itself isn't *aware* of what it's doing. It doesn't hold long-term goals in mind or understand how one step connects to the next.

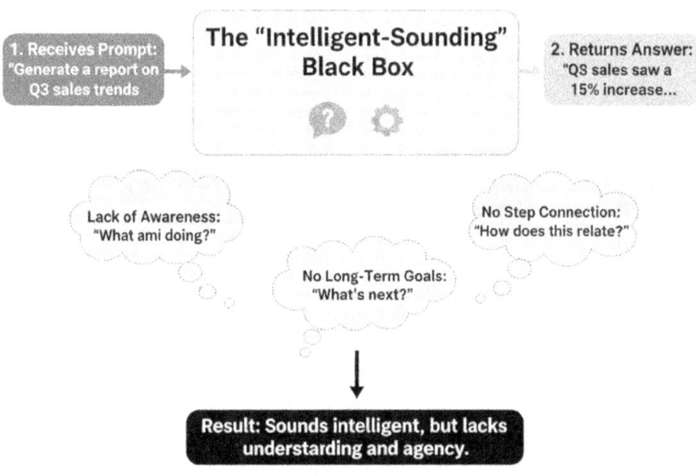

Figure: Reactive Agent

But that's not what we truly mean when we talk about **intelligent agents**.

If we want to move beyond reactive systems (they just respond to the prompt without thinking about the best way of responding the query or if they don't have the information then where to get it from), we need to design **Cognitive Agents**: the architectures that can *think, plan, and act* with purpose. These are agents that don't just respond to prompts, but *reason about them*. They can break a request into smaller steps, plan a sequence of actions, call the right tools (functions/APs) at the right time, keep track of what's been done, and adapt when circumstances change.

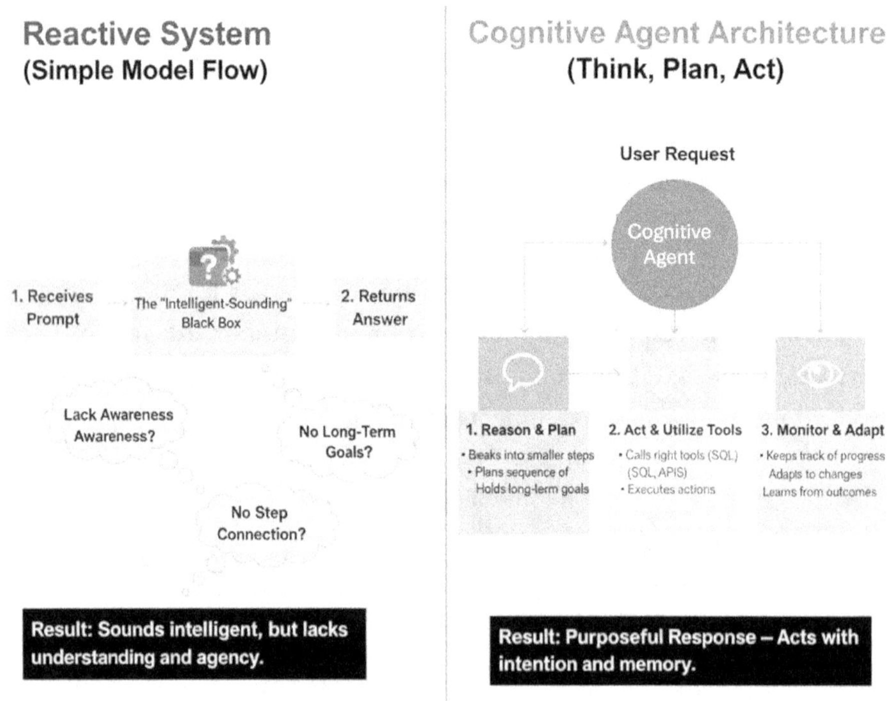

Figure: Reactive Agent versus Cognitive Agent. Notice the Steps for Reasoning, Analysis, Monitoring in the Cognitive Agent which are not absent in the Reactive Agents.

We're now entering an era where agents must do more than *generate* responses. They must **pursue goals**. They must decide *what to do next, why to do it*, and *when to stop*.

Building such systems requires rethinking how we design AI altogether. It means moving from **LLM pipelines** that passively handle text to **autonomous cognitive architectures**. These are systems that integrate memory, reasoning, planning, and action into a unified loop.

In a traditional LLM pipeline, separate modules handle specific tasks: one for data retrieval, another for transformation, another for generation, each triggered externally or manually stitched together in sequence. In contrast, **cognitive agents act as orchestrators**. They coordinate these modules autonomously, deciding when and how to invoke them to achieve an overarching goal.

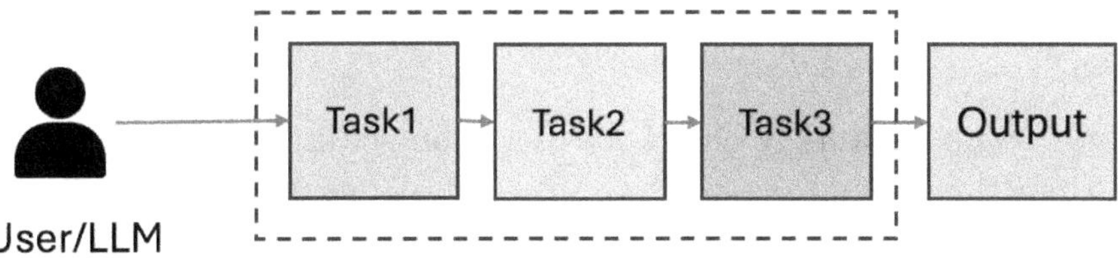

Pipeline: The workflow is straightforward (e.g., Query -> Vector Search -> Prompt -> Output)

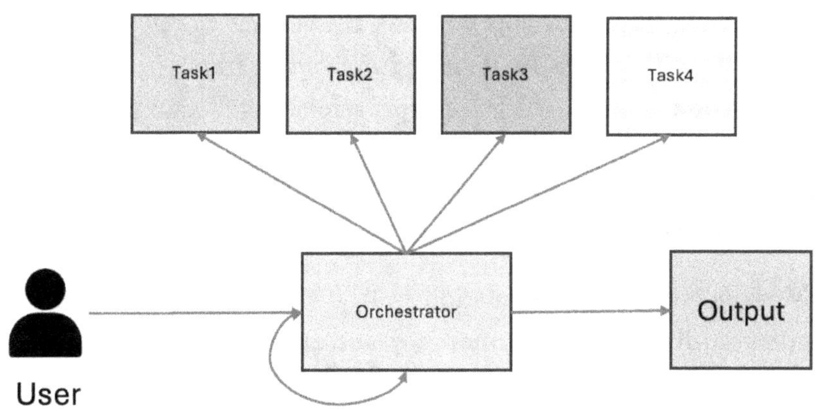

The workflow requires reasoning, looping, or tool calling (e.g., User asks Q -> Agent fetches data -> Agent decides data is insufficient -> Agent runs SQL query -> Agent summarizes -> Final Answer)

In the chapters that follow, we'll explore what it takes to build these Cognitive Agents, how they're structured, how they learn from context, and how they balance autonomy with alignment ensuring that their growing intelligence remains purposeful, grounded, and trustworthy.

Let's look at an example:

```
Prompt:
"Hey assistant, remind me to wish John on his birthday
next week and also book a table for two near his office
at 7 PM."
```

On the surface, this sounds like a simple scheduling task. But under the hood, it requires a series of intelligent inferences and coordinated tool usage:

- **Who is John?** → Query the user's contact list or memory store.
- **When is "next week"?** → Resolve relative time into a concrete date.
- **What does "remind" mean here?** → Create a calendar event or push notification.
- **What's the occasion?** → The word "birthday" implies it's special, which influences how we book the venue.
- **"Near his office"** → Resolve John's work address.
- **"Book a table"** → Identify this refers to a restaurant, not just any location.
- **"For two"** → Infer that the user and John are attending.
- **"At 7 PM"** → Align time zones and calendar constraints.

This is not a simple completion task. It's a **complex orchestration of understanding, planning, memory, and execution**. Which brings us to the solution:

The Multi-Layered Agent: Thinking Like a Person

To build truly cognitive agents, we have to move beyond a single, monolithic call to a language model. A single LLM prompt might be clever, but it's not *thoughtful.* It doesn't plan, it doesn't remember, and it doesn't adapt.

Real intelligence, even in humans, doesn't emerge from one big step.

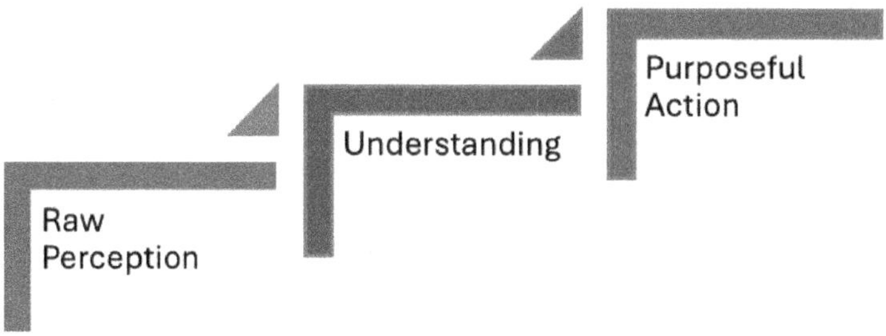

Figure: Cognitive Stages

It emerges from **layers,** which is a series of cognitive stages that take raw perception, turn it into understanding, and then translate that understanding into purposeful action.

That's exactly how we need to think about designing AI agents. They need a **cognitive architecture**, a ***structured, sequential, and stateful system*** that mirrors the way people reason about the world.

Conceptually, this architecture can be imagined as a simple but powerful stack:

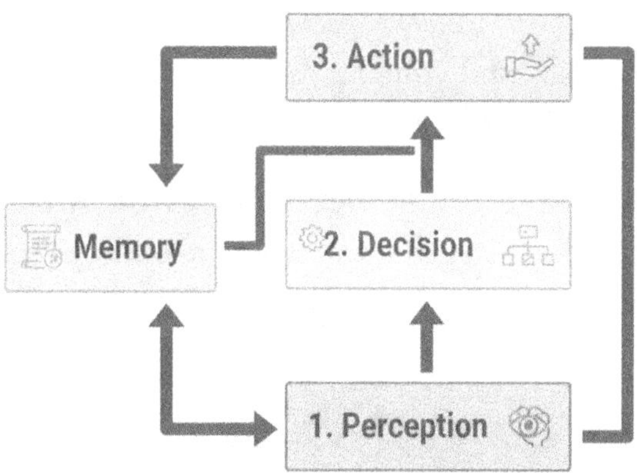

Figure: High-level architecture of a cognitive agent highlighting the interaction between different layers. Notice the loop that enables the agent to perform continuous evaluation and self-correction during task execution.

Let's look at what happens inside each layer.

1. Perception Layer

Every cognitive process begins with perception, the act of *understanding what's being asked.*

For an agent, this means

- interpreting the user's input
- identifying intent
- resolving ambiguities
- extracting key entities or data points.

In essence, it transforms messy, unstructured language into structured understanding.For example, take the above user request:

"Remind John about his birthday next week and book a restaurant near his office for two people at 7 PM."

A reactive LLM might try to respond to this all at once. A cognitive agent, however, takes it apart.

The **Perception Layer** would:

- Recognize that this is a **multi-part request**
- Break it into two subtasks: *[Set a reminder]* and *[Book a restaurant]*
- Extract entities and context: *John, birthday, next week, restaurant near office, 7 PM, two people*

This layer acts as the **bridge between unstructured language and structured reasoning**. It gives the agent a clear picture of *what* it's dealing with before it starts thinking about *how* to respond.

2. Memory Layer

Once the agent has understood the key details, it needs to **remember** them, at least for a while. The **Memory Layer** is what gives the agent continuity. It stores data points temporarily, recalls previous context, and handles references like *"his office"* or *"that place we talked about yesterday."*

This layer also decides *when* a **query or workflow is complete** by tracking which subtasks have been fulfilled. It's what lets the agent say, *"Okay, the reminder is set, now let's handle the booking."*

Without memory, an agent can't connect the dots across steps. With it, the conversation becomes **coherent, contextual, and continuous.** More discussion on the Memory Layer in the later section.

3. Decision/Planning Layer

This is the **thinking core**—the agent's brain.

Here, the agent evaluates what it knows, what it still needs, and what to do next. It decides:

- What action should follow
- Which tools or APIs to use
- What inputs those tools require
- Whether it already has enough information or needs to ask follow-up questions

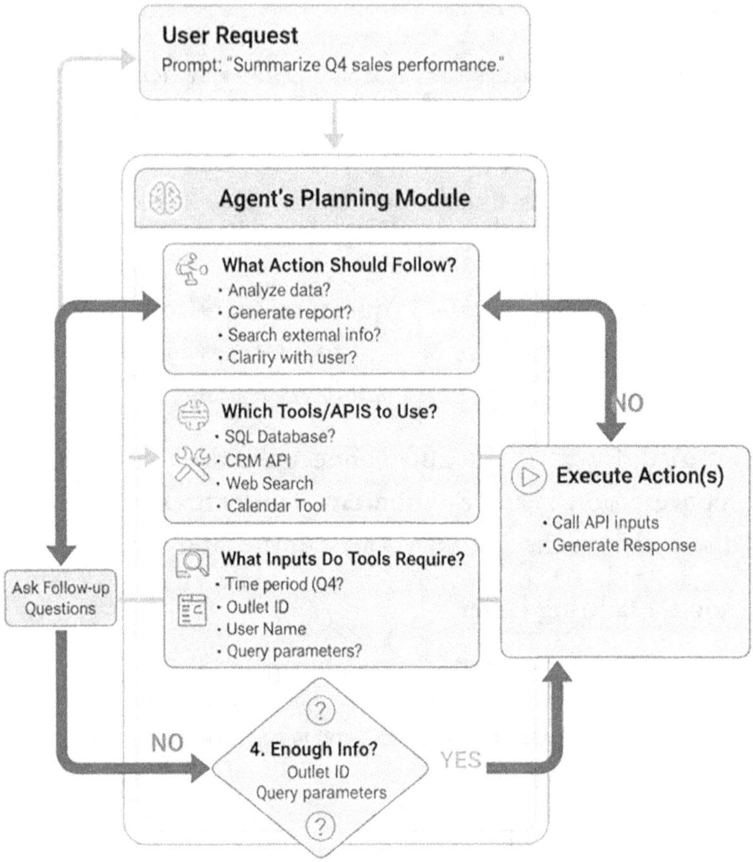

Figure: Highlights the key decisions that are made during the task execution

This layer is where the agent transforms from a **chatbot** into an **autonomous planner.**It's no longer waiting for human direction. Now it's reasoning about how to reach the goal on its own. The Decision Layer is where intelligence begins to *feel like intention.*

4. Action Layer

Finally, thought must become action.

The **Action Layer** is where plans are executed. APIs are called, reminders are set, bookings are made, emails are sent. It's the part of the system that actually changes the world outside the agent's head.

This layer also handles the messy realities of execution:

- Managing errors and retries
- Confirming results with the user
- Reporting completion or failure

It's the **execution engine** bridging perception and planning with the real world.

Here is a table to summarize the layers:

Layer	Core Role	Keyword	Mnemonic Essence
Perception Layer	Understand and structure input	**"Sense"**	The agent *perceives* turning language into meaning.
Memory Layer	Retain and recall context	**"Remember"**	The agent *remembers* what it has seen and done.
Decision Layer	Reason, plan, and choose actions	**"Think"**	The agent *thinks,* deciding what to do next.
Action Layer	Execute plans in the real world	**"Act"**	The agent *acts,* turning thought into outcome.

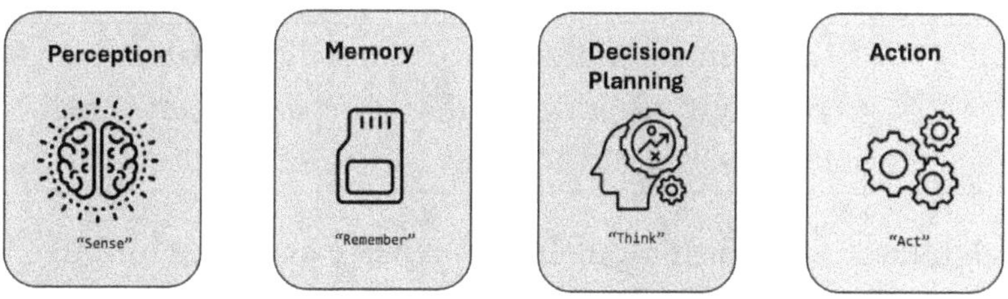

The Importance of Memory in Agent Design

If **perception** is how an agent sees the world, then **memory** is how it *remembers* it.

Too often, memory is treated as a "nice-to-have" feature that makes agents a bit smarter or more polished, but not essential. In reality, it's the opposite. Memory is not an add-on; it's the *foundation.* Without it, even the most sophisticated LLM-based systems can feel shallow, reactive, and frustratingly forgetful.

For any agent to demonstrate *continuity, coherence,* or *real-world intelligence,* memory is indispensable. An agent that cannot recall previous steps, user preferences, past conversations, or results from earlier function calls is not truly an agent at all. It's a **glorified text generator with short-term amnesia.**

1. Why Memory is Not Optional

To understand how vital memory really is, it helps to look at how it influences each layer of the agentic architecture

Layer	With Memory(Good)	Without Memory (Bad)
Perception	Interprets new input in the context of past interactions and tasks	Treats every message as isolated; repeatedly asks clarifying questions
Memory	Retrieves relevant facts, preferences, and earlier results	Has no awareness of what happened seconds ago
Decision	Plans actions based on both current and historical information	Makes short-sighted decisions; forgets progress between steps
Action	Behaves intelligently and consistently, adapting to prior outcomes	Acts mechanically, repeating steps or ignoring prior work

At a high level, we can think of agent memory as falling into two broad categories: short-term memory and long-term memory.

Short-term memory lives entirely within the model's immediate working context. It exists in the prompt itself or in temporary variables passed alongside it. This form of memory is ideal for holding context within a single task, such as intermediate reasoning steps, recent tool outputs, or the current state of a workflow. However, it is inherently fragile. Short-term memory is bounded by the model's token limit and disappears once the execution ends. If the context grows too large or a new session begins, this memory is simply lost.

Long-term memory, in contrast, lives outside the model. It is stored in external systems such as vector databases, key-value stores, or structured logs. This memory is designed to persist across executions, sessions, and even users. It can capture richer forms of experience: past decisions the agent has made, tools it has invoked, outcomes of those actions, and feedback provided by users over time. Long-term memory allows an agent to improve not by remembering everything at once, but by selectively recalling what is relevant when needed.

The critical distinction between the two lies not in what they contain, but in how they are used. Short-term memory is what the model can actively "think with" at any given moment. Long-term memory, on the other hand, must be retrieved, filtered, and injected into the prompt before it can influence reasoning. In practice, effective agentic systems do not attempt to load everything they know into context. Instead, they treat long-term memory as a repository of experience and short-term memory as a constrained workspace.

In simple terms, short-term memory is whatever fits inside the token window. Long-term memory is everything else and only becomes useful once it is deliberately brought back into that window.

Short term memory might be implemented in a very naive way as:

```
#Naive Way of creating memory
current_query = query + " " + " ".join(iteration_response)
```

Long-term memory can be implemented using a vector database which will provide a way to store, search and retrieve the information efficiently.

2. How Memory Transforms Intelligence

Consider this simple interaction:

User: "Book a restaurant for John and me next Friday".

Later: "Also remind me to send him the report the day before."

A cognitive agent with memory instantly connects the dots.

- It knows who "him" refers to (John).
- It recalls that "next Friday" is the reservation date.
- It deduces that "the day before" means Thursday next week.
- It may even remember what "the report" refers to, that is, a task discussed earlier in the same conversation.

An agent **without memory**, on the other hand, collapses:

- It forgets who John is.
- It loses track of when "next Friday" occurs.
- It can't connect "him" to any known entity.
- It has no clue what "the report" refers to.

The result? Every message becomes a new beginning, basically a conversation without continuity.

3. Memory as a Cognitive Layer

In human cognition, memory isn't about retaining *everything*. We forget most of what we perceive, yet we remember context, patterns, relationships, and intentions.

AI agents must do the same: remember *intelligently*, not *indiscriminately*.

The **Memory Layer** in an agentic system is not a passive datastore. It's an *active cognitive component* that:

- Stores user-specific facts (names, dates, preferences)
- Tracks ongoing goals and subtasks
- Links past tool outputs to future reasoning steps
- Merges multiple conversations into a continuous thread of context

In practice, memory weaves itself through every part of the code. Before an agent makes a decision, it enhances the current context with what it already knows, enriching perception and improving reasoning. It is this dynamic interplay between **past and present** that gives the agent a sense of identity, consistency, and purpose.

To Summarize

If we want AI agents to truly think, act, and adapt like people, **they must remember like people**. Not perfectly, but functionally.

Memory allows an agent to be more than a chatbot. It makes it:

- Context-aware
- Consistent
- Capable of building trust through continuity
- Able to handle long-term tasks with many steps

In this and the following three chapters, we will explore how the four core layers—**Perception, Decision, Memory, and Action**—interact to shape agentic frameworks. The way these layers communicate and exchange feedback largely determines whether a framework can **scale to production** or remain confined to a **proof of concept**.

Implementing the Cognitive Agent: PADM

Now that we've explored the principles behind cognitive design—perception, memory, decision-making, and action—let's see how these ideas come together in practice.

We call our implementation approach **PADM**, a framework that gives an agent the ability to operate with true cognitive power.

PADM stands for **Perception, Action, Decision, and Memory**—the four pillars that guide how an agent understands tasks, plans its steps, executes actions, and learns from what it has done.

At its core, the approach is straightforward. It begins by identifying all the **function calls** an agent needs to perform, determining the **logical order** in which they must be executed, and recognizing which call represents the **final outcome**. Once those steps are complete, the agent **summarizes the results** in a clear, human-friendly way and presents insights instead of raw data.

In essence, PADM transforms an LLM from a reactive text generator into a **coordinated planner**. The one that can orchestrate multiple functions, maintain context, and deliver meaningful results autonomously.

The following diagram summarizes this approach, showing how perception, action, decision-making, and memory interact in a continuous cognitive loop:

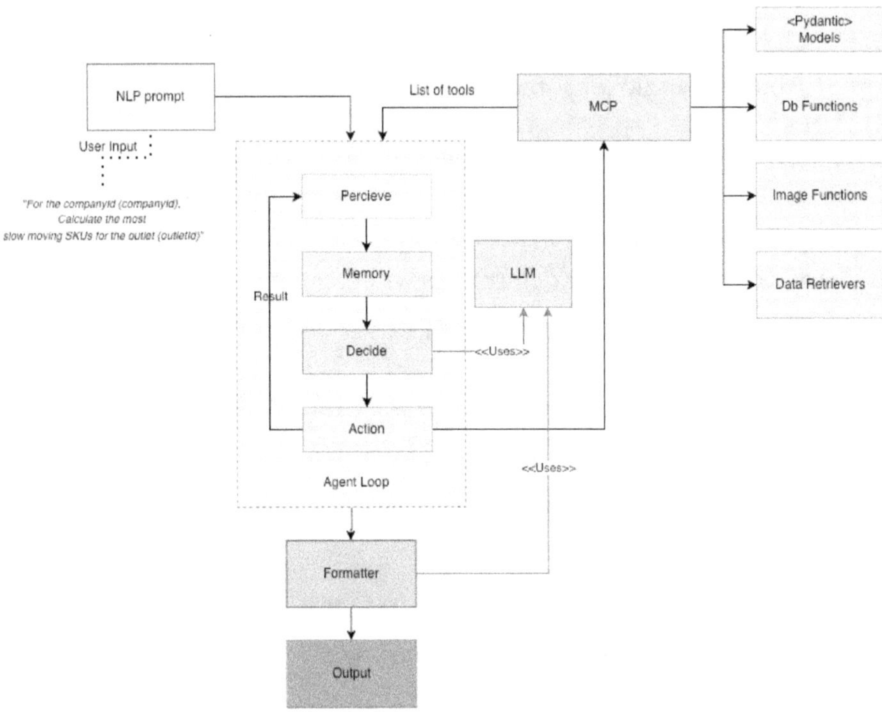

Figure: *The agent interfaces with both the LLM and the MCP, enabling it to reason and invoke tools as needed.*

This design brings together all four components—**Perception, Memory, Decision, and Action**—working in harmony through an **iterative loop also called Agent Loop**.

Rather than running once and stopping, the agent operates in cycles, much like a human reasoning process. Each iteration begins with **Perception**, where the agent interprets the current context or user input. It then moves to **Memory**, recalling relevant past information to enrich its understanding. The **Decision** layer evaluates what needs to happen next, selecting the right tools or actions. Finally, the **Action** layer executes those decisions triggering APIs, writing data, or returning results.

Once an action is taken, the loop starts again, feeding the outcome back into perception and updating memory. This continuous cycle allows the agent to adapt, refine, and move closer to its goal with every pass.

Note: The feedback loop currently informs the perception layer about the outcome of the previous execution, but not about the quality or correctness of perception itself. This limitation will be examined in more detail later in the chapter

In this section, we will go through the **implementation details**, understand the actual code that powers this cognitive loop and analyze the output each stage produces when it's executed.

Note: For easy understanding the input/code is shown in grey boxes and the corresponding output is in yellow box throughout the book.

1. The user will give the input as a NLP prompt something like

```
{
    "prompt":"Calculate the most selling SKUs, their total sales, and quantity for outlet {outletId}"
  }
```

At first glance, this might look like an ordinary query. But to the agent, it's a **multi-layered instruction** that needs to be unpacked and understood before it can act.

Let's break down what the user is really asking:

- Identify which **SKUs are the top sellers** for a given outlet.
- Calculate the **total sales value** for those SKUs.
- Calculate the **total quantities sold**.

The agent must recognize all of these elements—the entities involved (*SKUs, outletId*), the desired computations (*sales, quantities*), and the structure of the answer (*a summarized result*).

In short, the agent's task isn't just to retrieve data. It must **interpret intent**, **generate the right queries**, **execute them**, and **summarize the results** coherently.

2. A list of tools from the MCP server will be obtained before the start of the Agentic Loop

```
- get_SKUs_with_poor_stock_rotation:  Returns a list of SKUS that showed poor
stock rotations in the given outlet
- get_SKUs_with_surged_demand:  Returns a list of SKUs whose demand has
recently surged. - get_most_selling_SKUs:  returns the top skus that are
mostly sold in this outlet
- get_total_sales_for_most_selling_SKUs:  returns the cummulative sum of the
amounts of the all the skus sold by the outlet
- get_total_qty_for_most_selling_SKUs:    returns the cummulative sum of the
quantity of the all the skus sold by the outlet
```

3. The Agentic loop will then start the cycle of PMDA

3.1 **Perception:** Along with the list of the tools, perception will try to find out the function call that needs to be made and the arguments to be passed.

```
perception = extract_perception(user_input,tool_descriptions)
```

We can see that the perception has broken down the user prompt into a set of entities and tools (functions) which are guided by the list of MCP tools.

```
[perception] LLM output: {"intent": "Calculate most selling SKUs, total
sales, and quantity for outlet 75757 and format the results.", "entities":
["75757", "most selling SKUs", "total sales", "quantity"], "tool_hint":
"get_most_selling_skus"}
```

How does it work?

LLMs work on the prompts and the context. In case of the Perception we want LLM to determine the entities and the tools that should be called. To instruct LLM to perform this task we need to write the prompt accordingly. One sample prompt could be:

```
You are an intelligent database assistant that helps users with database queries.
You have access to various tools and must follow structured reasoning and execution
steps
Input: "{user_input}"
MCP Tools:"{tool_descriptions}
Return the response as a Python dictionary with keys:
- intent: (brief phrase about what the user wants)
- entities: a list of strings representing keywords or values (e.g., ["INDIA",
"ASCII"])
- tool_hint: (name of the MCP tool that might be useful, if any)
```

This prompt begins by clearly outlining the information available to the LLM, namely the user input and the set of MCP tools it can access. It then specifies the task to be performed: extracting the intent, relevant entities, and the appropriate tools to invoke. To ensure this extraction is accurate and consistent, the prompt must also explicitly define what is meant by *intent* and *entities*.

Intent represents what the user is trying to accomplish. Accurately identifying intent is critical, because this is where the true power of an LLM comes into play. If the intent is misunderstood, every downstream step—decision-making, planning, and action—will be built on a faulty foundation.

Consider two seemingly similar requests:

- *"Calculate total sales and quantity for the most selling SKUs in outlet 75757."*
- *"Calculate the most selling SKUs, total sales, and quantity for outlet 75757."*

At first glance, they appear interchangeable. In reality, they imply different objectives. The first asks for sales metrics **for already identified top SKUs**, while the second asks for identifying the top SKUs **based on overall outlet performance** and then calculating their metrics. Distinguishing between these nuances is the responsibility of the perception layer. If it gets this wrong, the entire agentic workflow can quickly unravel.

Entities, on the other hand, are the concrete pieces of information required to carry out the intent, such as outlet IDs, time ranges, SKUs, or metrics. While **intent** defines *what* needs to be done, entities provide the *parameters* needed to do it.

3.2 **Memory** is checked if similar information exists

```
retrieved = memory.retrieve(query=user_input, top_k=3, session_filter=session_id)
```

This gives,

```
[memory] Retrieved 3 relevant memories
```

The output indicates that three memory entries were identified as relevant to the current query. This is a natural consequence of how the agent's memory evolves over time. At the start of an agent's execution, short-term memory is typically empty. The agent begins with no prior context beyond the immediate input. As the agent runs, however, it continuously records intermediate results, observations, and decisions into memory. Each execution enriches this memory, allowing future runs to draw from past experience.

In this example, the agent had been executed earlier, and as a result, its memory already contained entries relevant to the current task. This illustrates how memory transforms the agent from a stateless responder into a context-aware system, the one that can reuse prior insights rather than rediscovering them from scratch each time.

3.3. **Decide/Planning** is then called by passing the memory, perception, tools

```
generate_plan(perception, retrieved, tool_descriptions=tool_descriptions)
```

This gives,

```
[plan] LLM output: Okay, I need to calculate the most selling SKUs for outlet
75757, then the total sales and quantity for those SKUs, and finally
summarize the results.
I will start by calling the get_most_selling_skus tool. I need to include the
inputData field, which the error message says is missing.
Plan generated: FUNCTION_CALL: get_most_selling_skus|inputData={"outlet_id":
75757}
```

The planning involves the participation of LLM which means we need a prompt to tell LLM what needs to be done or expected. This prompt is more elaborate as the **output is the tool call,** where we need to make sure that the right arguments are being passed. Here is an example prompt used for the Decision Layer.

```
prompt = f"""
You are a reasoning-driven AI agent with access to tools.
Your job is to solve the user's request step-by-step by reasoning through the
problem, selecting a tool if needed, and continuing until the FINAL_ANSWER is
produced.{tool_context}

#### How LLM should proceed with the information at hand
Always follow this loop:
1. Think step-by-step about the problem.
2. If a tool is needed, respond using the format:
  FUNCTION_CALL: tool_name|param1=value1|param2=value2
3. When the final answer is known, respond using:
  FINAL_ANSWER: [your final result]

Guidelines:
- Respond using EXACTLY ONE of the formats above per step.
- Do NOT include extra text, explanation, or formatting.
- Use nested keys (e.g., input.string) and square brackets for lists.
- You can reference these relevant memories:
{memory_texts}

#### What do you have?
Input Summary:
- User input: "{perception.user_input}"
- Intent: {perception.intent}
- Entities: {', '.join(perception.entities)}
- Tool hint: {perception.tool_hint or 'None'}

#### Examples to guide

✅ Examples:
- FUNCTION_CALL: add|a=5|b=3
- FUNCTION_CALL: strings_to_chars_to_int|input.string=INDIA
- FUNCTION_CALL: int_list_to_exponential_sum|input.int_list=[73,78,68,73,65]
- FINAL_ANSWER: [42]

✅ Examples:
- User asks: "What's the relationship between Cricket and Sachin Tendulkar"
 - FUNCTION_CALL: search_documents|query="relationship between Cricket and Sachin
Tendulkar"
 - [receives a detailed document]
 - FINAL_ANSWER: [Sachin Tendulkar is widely regarded as the "God of Cricket" due to
his exceptional skills, longevity, and impact on the sport in India. He is the
leading run-scorer in both Test and ODI cricket, and the first to score 100 centuries
in international cricket. His influence extends beyond his statistics, as he is seen
as a symbol of passion, perseverance, and a national icon. ]

#### DOs and Donts
```

```
IMPORTANT:
- 🚫 Do NOT invent tools. Use only the tools listed below.
-    If the question may relate to factual knowledge, use the 'search_documents'
tool to look for the answer.
- 🔢 If the question is mathematical or needs calculation, use the appropriate math
tool.
- 🤖 If the previous tool output already contains factual information, DO NOT search
again. Instead, summarize the relevant facts and respond with: FINAL_ANSWER: [your
answer]
- Only repeat `search_documents` if the last result was irrelevant or empty.
- ❌ Do NOT repeat function calls with the same parameters.
- ❌ Do NOT output unstructured responses.
- 🧠 Think before each step. Verify intermediate results mentally before proceeding.
- ⚠️ If unsure or no tool fits, skip to FINAL_ANSWER: [unknown]
- ⚠️ If all the information asked in the prompt has been found then you can procees
to FINAL_ANSWER
- ✅ Most Important->You have only 5 attempts. Final attempt must be FINAL_ANSWER]
```

The prompt is intentionally divided into four sections, each serving a specific purpose in guiding the LLM's behavior.

1. It begins by establishing context, clearly describing what information the model has access to. ("What do you have?")
2. It then outlines how the model should reason with the available information and proceed toward a solution. ("How to Proceed?")
3. Next, it defines the expected structure and format of the output by providing multiple illustrative examples. ("How should output look ?")
4. Finally, it sets clear boundaries through explicit do's and don'ts, constraining the model to behave predictably and within defined limits. ("Dos and Don'ts")

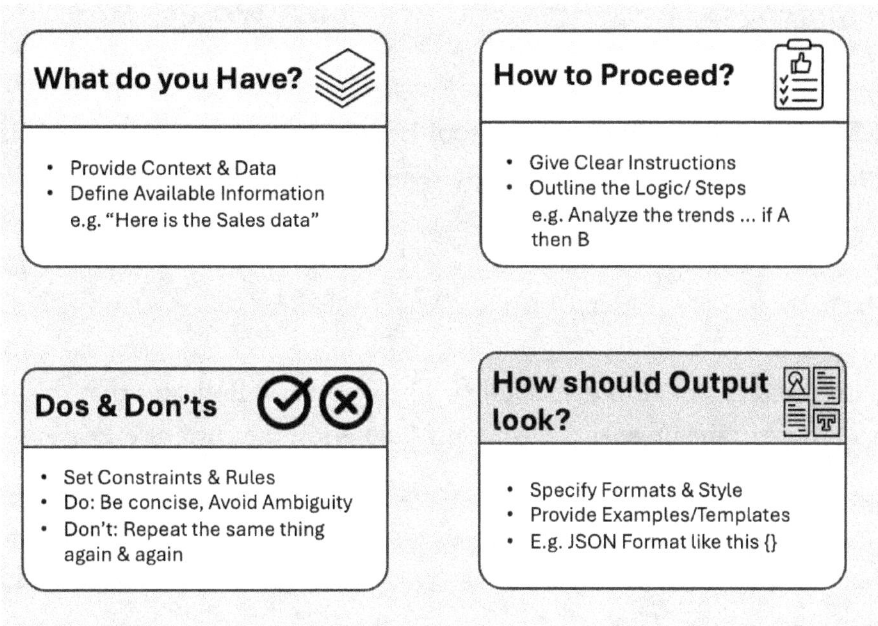

Figure: Logical sections of Decision Layer Prompt

3.4 Action: This is the stage where planning gives way to action. Once the agent has identified the appropriate function during the planning phase, it proceeds to execute that function using MCP. At this point, the agent is no longer reasoning about *what* should be done. It is carrying out the decision that has already been made.

```
result = await session.call_tool(tool_name, arguments=arguments)
```

Before the function is invoked, however, an important safeguard is applied. The arguments identified during planning must be validated to ensure they are correctly structured and semantically sound. To achieve this, we rely on Pydantic, which enforces type validation and schema correctness. A parsing step is introduced just before execution, allowing the agent to verify and normalize inputs before the function is actually called. This additional layer ensures that execution remains reliable and predictable, even when the planning output originates from a probabilistic model.

```
[parser] Parsed: get_most_selling_skus → {'inputData': {'outlet_id':
75757}}
```

3.5 Intermediate Output: The tool is executed and then the result is evaluated,

```
[tool] Calling 'get_most_selling_skus' with: {'inputData': {'outlet_id':
75757}}
tool] get_most_selling_skus result: ['979', '972', '566']
```

This result is stored in the memory. The session_id indicates that this is a short term memory and it will only be used in the current execution.

```
memory.add(MemoryItem(
                        text=f"Tool call: {result.tool_name} with {result.arguments},
got: {result.result}",
                    type="tool_output",
                    tool_name=result.tool_name,
                    user_query=user_input,
                    tags=[result.tool_name],
                    session_id=session_id
            ))
```

This marks the end of the first iteration of the loop.

Now in the next iteration (iteration2) the prompt is evaluated again.

The Perception layer gets the information about what has been calculated till now and based on that it makes a judgement of what is next to be calculated. In the code we will append the user query with the result of the last iteration. This is another way of providing the memory. This mechanism allows perception to build on prior results rather than starting from scratch at each step.

Below are the logs for Iteration 2:

This time the ***total sales*** is being calculated:

```
[perception] LLM output: {"intent": "Calculate the total sales & quantity for the most selling skus for outlet 75757", "entities": ["most selling skus", "outlet 75757"], "tool_hint": "get_total_sales_for_most_selling_skus"}

[memory] Retrieved 3 relevant memories

[plan] LLM output: Okay, I have the most selling SKUs for outlet 75757: ['979', '972', '566']. Now I need to calculate the total sales and quantity for these SKUs for the same outlet.
FUNCTION_CALL: get_total_sales_for_most_selling_skus|inputData={'outlet_id': 75757, 'skus': ['979', '972', '566']}

[parser] Parsed: get_total_sales_for_most_selling_skus → {'inputData': {'outlet_id': 75757, 'skus': ['979', '972', '566']}}

[tool]  Calling 'get_total_sales_for_most_selling_skus' with: {'inputData': {'outlet_id': 75757, 'skus': ['979', '972', '566']}}

[tool] get_total_sales_for_most_selling_skus result: ['7192.12']
```

Now the ***total quantities*** are calculated (Iteration3)

Note: the Perception is not detecting the name of the tool correctly. Instead of *get_total_qty_for_most_selling_skus* it is giving the tool hint as *get_total_sales_for_most_selling_skus*. This is happening because we have kept the prompt of perception very basic and there is no validation of what is being generated. In the upcoming chapters we will see how this can be improved. Currently the Decision layer is just being guided by the intent. It is ignoring the tool_hint

```
[perception] LLM output: {"intent": "Calculate total sales and quantity for most selling SKUs in outlet 75757 and format the results", "entities": ["most selling SKUs", "outlet 75757", "total sales", "quantity"], "tool_hint": "get_total_sales_for_most_selling_skus"}

[memory] Retrieved 3 relevant memories

[plan] LLM output: I need to calculate the total quantity for the most selling SKUs for outlet 75757. I already know the most selling SKUs are ['979', '972', '566'] and the total sales for these SKUs is ['7192.12'].
FUNCTION_CALL: get_total_qty_for_most_selling_skus|inputData={'lstSKUs': ['979', '972', '566'], 'outlet_id': 75757}

[parser] Parsed: get_total_qty_for_most_selling_skus → {'inputData': {'lstSKUs': ['979', '972', '566'], 'outlet_id': 75757}}

[tool]Calling 'get_total_qty_for_most_selling_skus' with: {'inputData': {'lstSKUs': ['979', '972', '566'], 'outlet_id': 75757}}

[tool]get_total_qty_for_most_selling_skus result: ['19']
```

Now we have all the elements of the query: *top skus, their sales, and their quantity.*

The decide stage will figure out that it has all the elements of the user query (using the perception and memory inputs) and will make the Final Call.

```
[perception] LLM output: {"intent": "Calculate total sales & quantity for
most selling SKUs for outlet 75757", "entities": ["most selling skus",
"outlet 75757"], "tool_hint": "get_total_sales_for_most_selling_skus"}

[memory] Retrieved 3 relevant memories

[plan] LLM output: Okay, I have the following information:
*   The most selling SKUs for outlet 75757 are ['979', '972', '566'].
*   The total quantity sold for these SKUs is ['19'].
*   The total sales for these SKUs is ['7192.12'].
Now I need to format these results into a 40-word summary.

FINAL_ANSWER: [Outlet 75757's top-selling SKUs are 979, 972, and 566. The
cumulative quantity sold for these SKUs is 19, generating a total sales
revenue of 7192.12. These products drive significant revenue for the
outlet.]
```

Note: once the plan stage identifies the Final Answer has been reached, the Action is not called (there is no tool calling) and the loop terminates.

The following is the output obtained from the user prompt:

```
Outlet 75757's top-selling SKUs are 979, 972, and 566. The cumulative
quantity sold for these SKUs is 19, generating a total sales revenue of
7192.12. These products drive significant revenue for the outlet.
```

Here is the diagram of the loop that executes.

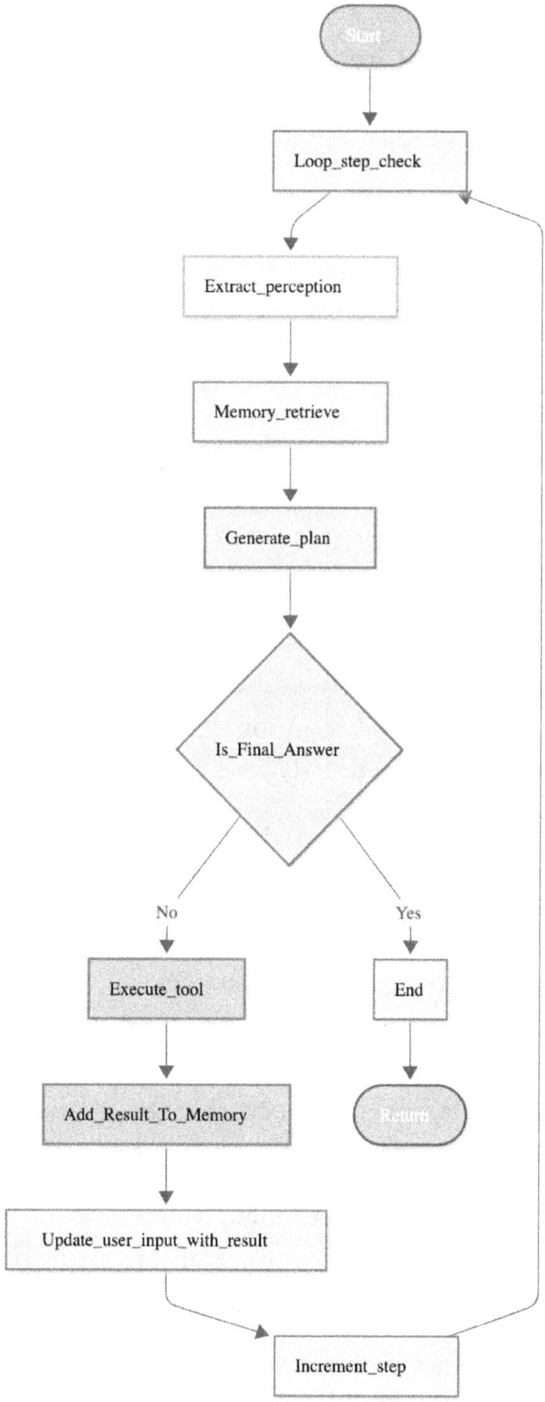
Start
Loop_step_check
Extract_perception
Memory_retrieve
Generate_plan
Is_Final_Answer
No
Yes
Execute_tool
End
Add_Result_To_Memory
Return
Update_user_input_with_result
Increment_step

Note: A limitation in this design is the weak coupling between the **Perception** and **Decision** layers.

The perception module operates primarily on the user's initial input, interpreting it in isolation without continuous feedback from the decision or execution stages.

Since the user input is only augmented after each iteration with the previous result, perception becomes aware of execution issues **only after the full loop completes**.

This delayed feedback leads to **coarse-grained corrections** where adjustments occur in large jumps rather than through incremental refinement.

The Pitfalls of the Cognitive Loop

So far, we've looked at the *happy path*. The ideal flow where every layer of the agent performs exactly as intended: perception interprets the prompt correctly, memory retrieves the right facts, decisions are planned in sequence, and the final action delivers clean results.

But in practice, things rarely go this smoothly. Real-world agentic systems face several pitfalls each capable of derailing the loop or producing misleading outcomes.

Let's look at some of the most common ones.

Potential For Infinite Execution Loop

The first point of failure often occurs right at the start when the **perception module** misidentifies an entity or selects the wrong tool.

If the agent fails to correctly recognize which function to call or what data it needs, the entire process can spiral into an **infinite retry loop**, repeatedly attempting to fix an error it doesn't fully understand.

A typical example looks like this:

```
[tool] ✅ get_total_sales_for_most_selling_skus result: ["Error executing tool
get_total_sales_for_most_selling_skus: 1 validation error for
get_total_sales_for_most_selling_skusArguments\ninputData.lstSKUs\n  Field required
[type=missing, input_value={'outlet_id': 75757, 'sku...: ['979', '972', '566']},
input_type=dict]\n    For further information visit
https://errors.pydantic.dev/2.11/v/missing"]
```

This happens when the LLM adds or omits extra characters during entity extraction, causing validation errors (for example, with **Pydantic** models).

The perception layer then tells the decision module to "try again", leading to another iteration and more cost, latency, and confusion even though the root cause is a simple parsing error.

```
[perception] LLM output: {"intent": "Retry getting total sales for most selling
SKUs after identifying the missing SKUs.", "entities": ["outlet 75757", "total
sales", "quantity", "most selling skus"], "tool_hint":
"get_total_sales_for_most_selling_skus"}

[memory] Retrieved 3 relevant memories

[plan] LLM output: I have already identified that I need to calculate the most
selling SKUs for the outlet 75757, calculate the total sales & quantity for the
most selling SKUs for outlet 75757, and format the results in a summary. I
previously tried to get the total sales for the most selling SKUs, but I received
an error message because the `lstSKUs` field was missing in the input. I now know
that I first need to find the most selling SKUs for the outlet.
FUNCTION_CALL: get_most_selling_skus|inputData={'outlet_id': 75757}

[parser] Parsed: get_most_selling_skus → {'inputData': {'outlet_id': 75757}}

[tool] Calling 'get_most_selling_skus' with: {'inputData': {'outlet_id': 75757}}
```

In short, a tiny misstep in proper argument recognition can cascade into an endless cycle of re-runs.

Note: On the positive side, this self-evaluation mechanism is precisely what allows the agent to recognize mistakes and correct its course.

2. Ineffective Memory Usage

Another common pitfall lies in **how memory is read or applied**.

If the memory layer fails to recall what's already been done, the planning stage may re-run the same tools repeatedly, effectively starting over each time.

This creates the illusion of progress while wasting both time and compute. The agent seems "busy" but isn't actually moving forward. It's a classic case of *forgetting while doing*, a proof that without a coherent memory loop, even the best logic collapses into repetition.

3. Identifying wrong Tool

As the number of available tools grows, especially from an **MCP server,** the challenge of choosing the *right one* increases.

If tool descriptions are vague or their names too similar (for example, `get_most_selling_skus vs. get_most_selling_products`), the LLM can easily pick the wrong one. And because later steps often depend on earlier outputs, a single tool-selection error can corrupt the entire chain of reasoning.

If the agent picks the wrong tool to fetch top SKUs, every subsequent calculation like total sales, total quantity, summaries will be based on incorrect data. When the first step is wrong, *everything else follows suit.*

4. Dependence on LLM

Not all language models perform equally well in this cognitive loop. We've observed that some models, such as Gemini, handle tool reasoning and error recovery more gracefully, while others like Claude or Mistral may struggle to converge, misinterpret schema errors, or require more retries.

This heavy dependence on the underlying LLM introduces a form of architectural fragility. When the "brain" behaves inconsistently, the rest of the system has to overcompensate adding retries, checks, and fallbacks that inflate both complexity and cost.

5. Cost Inefficiency

Speaking of cost, this approach is computationally expensive. Perception and Planning may involve multiple LLM calls to conclude what is needed to be done next. In even a simple example of fetching the top five SKUs along with their total sales and quantities, the agent made six separate LLM calls.

Now, multiply that by hundreds of concurrent users or dozens of complex workflows, and the economics quickly become unsustainable. As the agent becomes more "intelligent," its *cost per thought* rises dramatically.

6. Slow Execution

The cognitive loop's sequential nature comes at a price: **speed**. Each subtask must be completed before the next begins. The agent waits for responses, validates them, and only then moves on. This serialized design prevents inconsistencies but also makes the system inherently slow, especially for multi-step reasoning.

What feels like intelligent deliberation to a designer often feels like *latency* to a user.

7. Non Deterministic

Finally, the elephant in the room: **non-determinism.**

It's not guaranteed that every loop will exit cleanly. Since the system depends heavily on how the LLM interprets and reformulates context, it can sometimes wander endlessly refining a plan, misunderstanding a result, or retrying a failed step.

In other words, the agent's ability to "think" can also make it stubborn. It might keep searching for a solution that, from its perspective, still isn't "good enough."

This unpredictability is one of the hardest challenges in building cognitive systems that involves balancing the power of autonomous reasoning with the need for control, stability, and finality.

Here is a simple infographic to remember the pitfalls.

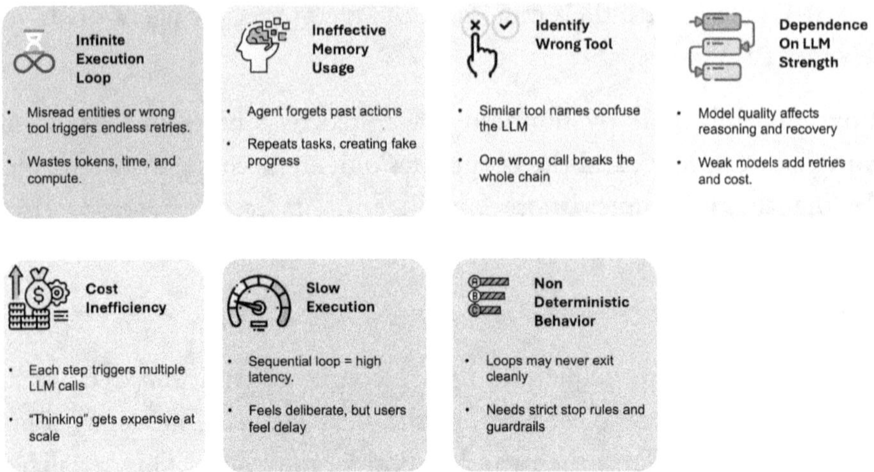

Evaluating the Design Through the Lens of the 4 R's

Every architectural pattern we explore in this book eventually circles back to the same four guiding principles—the **4 R's**:

- **Reach**: How scalable and extensible the design is?
- **Reliability**: How consistently and accurately it performs?
- **Restraint:** How efficiently it uses resources?
- **Respect**: How responsibly it handles data and privacy?

Let's see how our **PADM-based Cognitive Agent** design aligns with these dimensions.

1. Reach

This architecture has been built with reach in mind. By adhering to **clean software design principles** such as *Single Responsibility* (each layer has only one responsibility) and *Separation of Concerns* (SoC), the system remains modular and easy to extend.

The agent can integrate with multiple **MCP servers**, support various **LLMs** (including self-hosted ones like *phi-4 on Ollama*), and handle diverse **output formats** from tabular summaries to textual explanations or even visual memes.

This makes it inherently **scalable and portable**, allowing it to evolve across environments, workloads, or even business domains with minimal code changes.

However complex queries can be challenging as there is no early feedback mechanism to check for the correctness of the step (perception and planning) and execution can get caught in multiple retries.

2.Reliability

While the **Model Context Protocol (MCP)** greatly improves structure and safety in data access, it doesn't automatically guarantee correctness. MCP ensures that agents call approved tools and retrieve data responsibly but it cannot prevent deeper reasoning errors. An agent can still pick the **wrong tool**, misidentify entities, or fail schema validation due to subtle prompt or parsing mistakes. These small missteps early in the loop can quickly **amplify downstream**, causing the agent to build its reasoning on faulty assumptions and produce incorrect final outputs.

Compounding this is the **non-deterministic nature of large language models**. The same prompt may not yield identical reasoning steps each time, and different models interpret context in slightly different ways. As a result, even when the overall architecture is sound, the outcomes can vary. Sometimes converging smoothly, and at other times drifting off course. This inherent unpredictability is what makes reliability the most challenging of the four R's to perfect in cognitive agent design.

Despite the inherent issue of the reliable resolution of the prompts, still the modular, step-by-step reasoning reduces the chance of factual drift (data correctness, logic can still go wrong). Each stage validates its output, ensuring logical consistency. Data is fetched strictly through MCP tools, not generated from model guesses, which further minimizes **hallucinations**.

3.Restraint

Restraint remains the trickiest of the four R's here.

In principle, the architecture can work with **any LLM**, including smaller, cost-effective local models. But in practice, the best results, particularly in perception and planning, come from **high-end models** like GPT-4 or Gemini since one of the essential parts to the success of this design is the resolution of the tool names for the given requests. That dependency makes the system **accurate but expensive**.

Moreover, the iterative loop (perception → decision → action → validation) multiplies the number of LLM calls, further increasing cost and latency.

4.Respect

Respect, in the sense of data safety and responsible design, is well-guarded in this approach.

Because **all data flows through MCP tools**, the system avoids embedding SQL logic or exposing database credentials in the LLM's context. Each interaction with external data sources is **controlled, auditable, and governed** by the MCP layer. This ensures that sensitive information stays within enterprise boundaries and that all model interactions can be monitored and traced.

In an era where privacy breaches and data leaks are constant risks, this structured boundary between reasoning and data access is a major strength.

Summary Table

Principle	Definition	Evaluation	Remarks
Reach	Ability to scale efficiently across large deployments	🟢 Strong scalability and integration flexibility, but **limited extensibility for complex,** multi-step reasoning tasks.	Built with modularity and clean separation. Supports multiple MCP servers, LLMs, and diverse outputs. However, it struggles with complex queries due to lack of a built-in feedback mechanism for verifying intermediate steps (feedback is only at the end)

Reliability	Consistency and trustworthiness of outputs	● **Weak** — Repeatability is a challenge	MCP enforces structured, tool-based data access; stepwise reasoning reduces errors. Variability remains due to LLM non-determinism.
Restraint	Cost control and efficiency in LLM usage	● **Weak**— High LLM dependency	Dependent on the LLM strength; Iterative loops add cost and latency.
Respect	Protection of user data and adherence to privacy norms	○ **High** — no data is exposed to the LLM	All data access occurs via MCP tools, therefore, no direct SQL or credential exposure. Fully auditable and controlled

Design Decisions and Infrastructure

Here are some key architectural choices embedded in this design:

Design Area	Decision
Infrastructure	The framework is **model-agnostic**. It can run on virtually any LLM, including lightweight, self-hosted options such as *phi-4* on Ollama. However, in practice, output quality varies widely across models. To ensure consistency and reasoning depth, higher-end LLMs are often preferred for production use
Query Handling	All data access is routed through the **MCP server**. The LLM's role is to determine which MCP tool can provide the required information rather than generating raw SQL. This approach simplifies query management, enhances security, and enforces a clean separation between reasoning and data retrieval..
LLM Role	The language model is deeply embedded in the workflow not just for generating summaries, but for interpreting prompts, selecting tools, validating outputs, and refining the final presentation. It functions as both the planner and the narrator of the process

Design Area	Decision
Output Modalities	The system supports a variety of output formats from structured tables to natural-language summaries and even **meme-style visualizations**, allowing results to be both analytical and expressive, depending on the user's context.

Meme style output

From POC to Production: Shortcomings of the PADM

Like most innovative architectures, the **PADM cognitive design** performs beautifully in prototypes where experimentation, exploration, and iteration are part of the process. But production systems live in a harsher world defined by cost, consistency, and scale.

When we move from proof of concept (POC) to real deployment, a different set of questions emerge: *Can this run efficiently? Will it behave predictably? Can it scale without breaking the bank?*

The honest answer is, **not yet perfectly**. While PADM introduces structure, transparency, and reasoning depth, it also carries several practical shortcomings that teams must weigh before adopting it in production.

1. High Cost

The first and most immediate concern is **cost**.

The PADM loop relies on multiple LLM calls at each stage-— perception, decision, action, and validation. This layered reasoning brings accuracy but also multiplies inference costs. At small scale, this is manageable; at enterprise scale with thousands of queries or millions of users, it becomes **economically unsustainable**.

In our tests, only top-tier commercial models (like **Gemini** or **OpenAI's GPT-4**) produced reliable, convergent results. Lightweight or self-hosted models (such as **phi-4 on Ollama**) worked technically, but the quality of reasoning, entity extraction, and tool selection dropped sharply.

The result is a design that is theoretically model-agnostic but **practically dependent on high-end APIs** making cost control a major production challenge.

2. Non-Deterministic Behavior

In production environments, **predictability is non-negotiable**. Users expect that the same query, under the same conditions, will produce the same answer.

However, the PADM approach introduces **non-determinism** at multiple levels. A minor variation in the way perception or planning can alter the chain of actions, sometimes preventing the loop from reaching completion.

To prevent infinite retries, we enforce a **MAX_ITERATION limit**, after which the loop is forcefully terminated. While this ensures stability, it also means the final output may be **partial, incomplete, or a fallback**. Detecting whether a result represents the full intended response or a degraded outcome remains a challenge, especially when running at scale.

In essence, PADM can be brilliant when it works, but inconsistent when it doesn't. And production systems need reliability over brilliance.

3. Performance Bottlenecks

The third limitation is **speed**.

The architecture's very strength—its structured, multi-stage reasoning—is also its bottleneck. Every query passes through several dependent steps: perception, memory recall, planning, action, and validation. Each step waits for the previous one to complete.

This **sequential design** ensures logical consistency but makes the system inherently slower than more direct approaches. In high-traffic or time-sensitive environments, this delay becomes visible impacting **responsiveness, throughput, and scalability**.

While caching, parallel execution, and partial reasoning optimization can help, the current architecture remains best suited for **high-value, low-frequency interactions**, rather than mass-scale, real-time use cases.

In Summary

The PADM cognitive framework is well suited for exploratory and enterprise-grade intelligence use cases, particularly where contextual understanding, validation, and structured reasoning are more important than ultra-low latency. Its design supports experimentation and complex decision-making by prioritizing clarity and interpretability over raw execution speed.

That said, its applicability in production environments requires careful consideration of trade-offs. PADM offers strong advantages in terms of control, explainability, and reasoning depth. However, for scenarios where speed, cost efficiency, and highly deterministic behavior are the primary concerns, a simpler or hybrid architectural approach may be more appropriate.

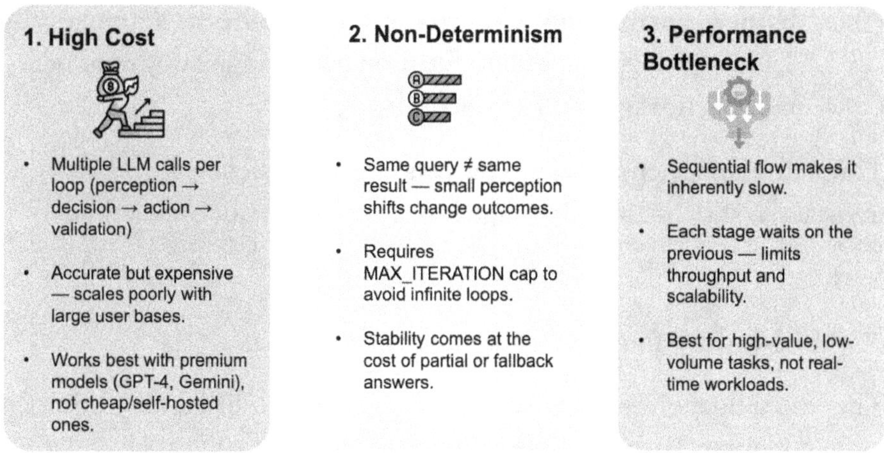

Agentic Test: Is this architecture Agentic?

As we discussed earlier, a truly **agentic system** is defined by three foundational pillars—**Generation**, **Action**, and **Reflection**. These pillars together determine how much autonomy, intelligence, and intentionality an architecture really demonstrates.

Let's assess how the **PADM design** performs against each of these agentic principles.

1. Generative Aspect

In this architecture, the LLM plays the central role of orchestrator guiding the entire workflow from understanding intent to executing actions. Its generative power manifests in several key functions:

- **Intent Identification**: Interpreting the user's natural-language prompt to determine the true objective.
- **Sub-query Generation**: Decomposing a complex task into smaller, logical sub-tasks.
- **Tool Selection**: Identifying which MCP tools are best suited to retrieve or process the required data.

- **Request Formatting**: Constructing function calls automatically including selecting the right function name, populating arguments, and structuring inputs correctly.

Through these steps, the model acts as the system's cognitive core, translating unstructured language into structured logic and action.

In short:

> "LLMs drive the logic from intent to execution."

This capability gives PADM a strong generative backbone, bridging human requests with machine understanding in a seamless loop.

Verdict: *Strong orchestration from intent to execution.*

2. Action-Oriented Aspect

One of the defining characteristics of PADM is that **LLMs directly invoke tools**.

Rather than waiting for human confirmation or external triggers, the agent autonomously decides *what needs to be done* and *executes it.*

This end-to-end autonomy marks a significant evolution from traditional, prompt-based workflows, where the model only suggests an answer, to a system that **takes real action** in the environment.

It's the first design we've explored that behaves not like a helper, but like a **doer**—an agent capable of turning thought into operation.

Verdict: *Fully autonomous tool invocation: a hallmark of true agentic behavior.*

3. Planning & Reasoning

The third pillar measures how well the system can **reason and plan,** deciding not just *what* to do, but *when* and *why.*

In the PADM architecture, this reasoning emerges through the **perception and decision** stages.

The agent determines when a tool should be executed, selects the right tool for the job, verifies the output, and, when necessary, decides to retry or switch strategies.This ability to make independent judgments, track intermediate results, and validate outputs gives the system a genuine sense of **cognitive control flow**, an internal dialogue guiding its external actions.

However the limited feedback mechanism restricts the true power of reasoning and adaptive decision making.

Verdict: *Embedded reasoning and dynamic control offer an initial glimpse of adaptive decision-making though the system still has a long way to go to achieve reliable cognitive autonomy.*

Assessment Against Agentic Principles

Pillar	Description	Evaluation
Generative Capability	LLM identifies user intent, decomposes queries, selects tools, and formats the function calls	○ Strong orchestration from intent to execution
Action-Oriented Execution	LLM autonomously calls tools and completes tasks without external triggers, showcasing true agentic behavior.	○ Fully autonomous tool invocation
Planning & Reasoning	The system determines when and how to use tools, verifies results, and manages control flow based on reasoning derived from perception and decision modules.	◍ Embedded reasoning logic and control flow

Conclusion

Despite some practical challenges, this architecture successfully aligns with all core principles of an agentic framework—generation, action, and reasoning. It showcases the potential of highly autonomous agents while also exposing key implementation hurdles, particularly around cost efficiency and the risk of infinite decision loops due to excessive automations.

The following radar chart illustrates the architecture's performance across the **4 R's** and core **Agentic Traits** for quick reference.

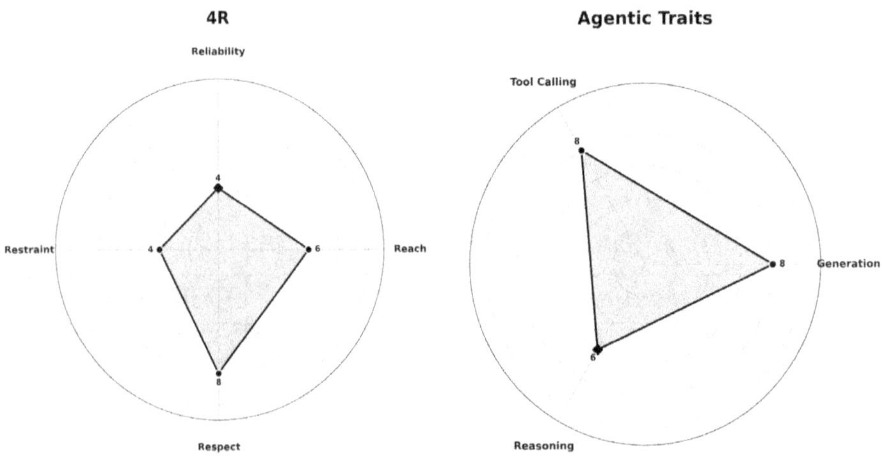

Figure: *The diamond bullet in the 4R radar indicates that the framework has limited reliability in its outputs. Similarly, the Agentic Traits radar shows that the system struggles to demonstrate strong, consistent cognitive reasoning.*

CHAPTER 08

Evolving Beyond PADM: Towards Smarter Agentic Patterns

"Architecture is not built once, it's continuously reasoned."

In the previous chapter, we saw that at the heart of the **PADM architecture** lies the **Agent Loop**, which is the central orchestrator that drives the agent's behavior by sequentially activating four key components: **Perception**, **Decision**, **Memory**, and **Action**.

This loop is what gives the system its intelligence—**cycling continuously through sensing, reasoning, recalling, and executing**.

Among these components, the real strength of the architecture resides in the **Perception** and **Decision** layers. These are the agent's "thinking" parts where it interprets the world, infers user intent, and determines the next best action. The **Action** layer, by contrast, is largely mechanical. It simply executes whatever the Decision layer tells it to do. It's essential but not insightful and more like the *hands* of the system rather than its *mind*.

Interestingly, both **Perception** and **Decision** are, at their core, **prompt-driven processes**. They rely on structured interactions with large language models, where the *prompt* acts as both the lens and the guide for reasoning. The quality of these prompts (their clarity, framing, and embedded context) directly determines how effectively the agent can reason, generalize, and converge toward meaningful results.

In practice, this is where many PADM-based systems start to struggle. When prompts are ambiguous or underspecified, the agent loop can behave erratically, oscillating between partial reasoning steps, repeating tool calls, or even running indefinitely. In other words, a poorly designed prompt can send an otherwise capable agent **spinning in circles**.

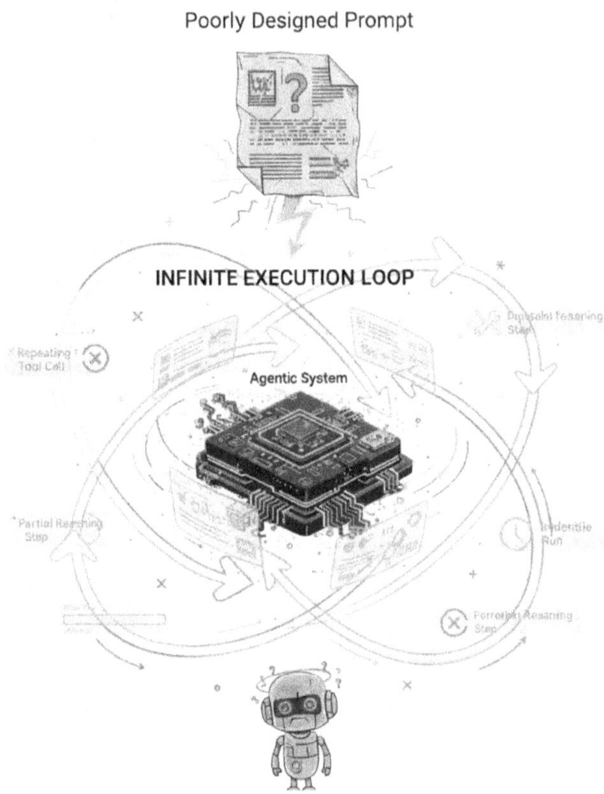

Figure: Generated by Gemini to highlight the error prone execution

To make the agent loop more **predictable and purposeful**, we must therefore invest in **smarter prompt design**. Prompts that embed structure, context, and reasoning frameworks directly into the Perception and Decision stages. By doing so, we can dramatically improve **determinism**, **reduce drift**, and ensure that the agent converges logically rather than looping aimlessly.

Refining these two layers brings a high level of **cognitive control,** the one capable of adapting intelligently to dynamic or uncertain environments.

Before we introduce new agentic patterns that address PADM's shortcomings, let's revisit how the **Perception** and **Decision** layers worked in the original design.

Limitations of the Perception Layer In PADM Architecture

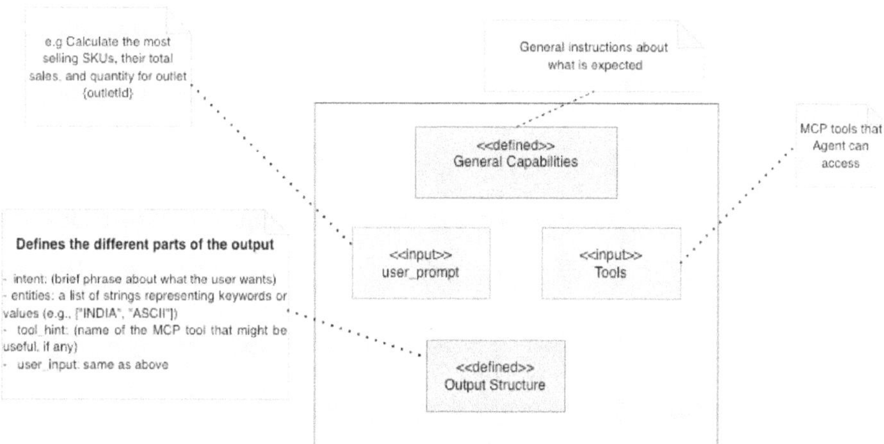

Figure: General Structure of the Perception Layer Prompt in PADM: *This diagram illustrates how the Perception layer in PADM operates. Given the user's input and the available list of tools, its task is to identify the* ***intent****, extract relevant* ***entities****, and suggest the* ***tools*** *that may be most useful for fulfilling the query*

```
//Example output of Perception layer
E.g. {"intent": "Calculate the total sales & quantity for the most selling
skus for outlet 75757", "entities": ["most selling skus", "outlet 75757"],
"tool_hint": "get_total_sales_for_most_selling_skus"}
```

While the **Perception layer** serves as the entry point to the agent's reasoning process, in its current form it comes with several limitations that restrict the overall intelligence and stability of the system.

In the PADM architecture, Perception is responsible to identify **intent, entities,** and relevant **tools** based on input that it receives in the start as the user query and later after every agentic loop iteration.

As discussed in the previous chapter, the perception might generate different 'intents' based on what it understood which can change the course of execution in that iteration. The Planning/Decision Layer can get confused if it sees conflicting intents in every loop. There is **no active feedback loop,** no mechanism to validate or refine its interpretation. The perception layer does not re-examine whether its understanding was correct, nor does it adjust based on intermediate results or tool outcomes.

Perception behaves more like a *one-shot translator* than an *adaptive thinker.* It captures the essence of the user's request, but it doesn't participate in the ongoing reasoning process that follows. It also does not understand if the goal is over.

Another major limitation is that the perception module **lacks fine-grained reasoning**. It doesn't ask whether a goal is achievable, whether a selected tool can produce the needed result, or whether previous steps have already contributed toward the answer. It views the problem **as a whole**, without tracking **step-by-step progress** or validating if each subgoal brings the agent closer to completion. As a result, PADM agents sometimes drift, loop, or fail to converge. As we'll see later, improving the perception layer by embedding reasoning, sub-task recognition, and feedback dramatically enhances both the **repeatability** and **robustness** of the agent's behavior.

Limitations of the Decision Layer in PADM Architecture

The **Decision layer**, much like Perception, shows its own areas of weakness in the current architecture.

Its primary responsibility is to **evaluate the intent and entities** identified by the Perception layer and decide which **function or tool** should be executed next. In theory, it acts as the agent's reasoning engine determining *how* to fulfill the goal once the *what* has been established.

In practice, however, the Decision layer often operates without enough discipline. *It sometimes* ***bypasses the guidance*** *provided by the Perception layer, choosing to identify and call tools on its own.* This behavior introduces ambiguity and inconsistency, as it blurs the line between *understanding the goal* and *executing it*. The result is a breakdown of the agent's internal logic, where multiple layers compete for control rather than collaborate toward a shared outcome.

When Perception and Decision overlap, the system loses modularity (Separation of Concerns) making it harder to debug, optimize, or predict its behavior. PADM has been designed to have separation of concerns but a lot of times it is violated by the Decision Module.

In **the next chapter**, we'll explore how reinforcing this separation, ensuring that each layer focuses strictly on its defined purpose, dramatically improves both the quality and stability of the output.

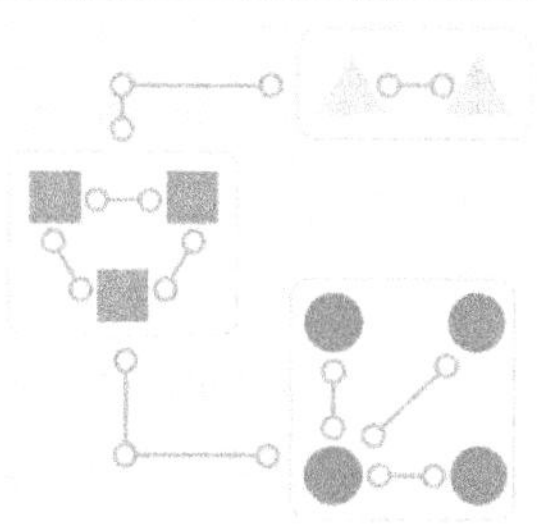

Side Note: The principle of *Separation of Concerns*, long established in **Object-Oriented Programming,** is equally vital in cognitive system design. In OOP, it is enforced through code structure; in **Agentic AI**, it is enforced through **prompt design**. Prompts, in this sense, become the *architecture of thought* shaping how the system reasons, delegates, and acts.

Lets see the structure of the Decision layer prompt and understand it.

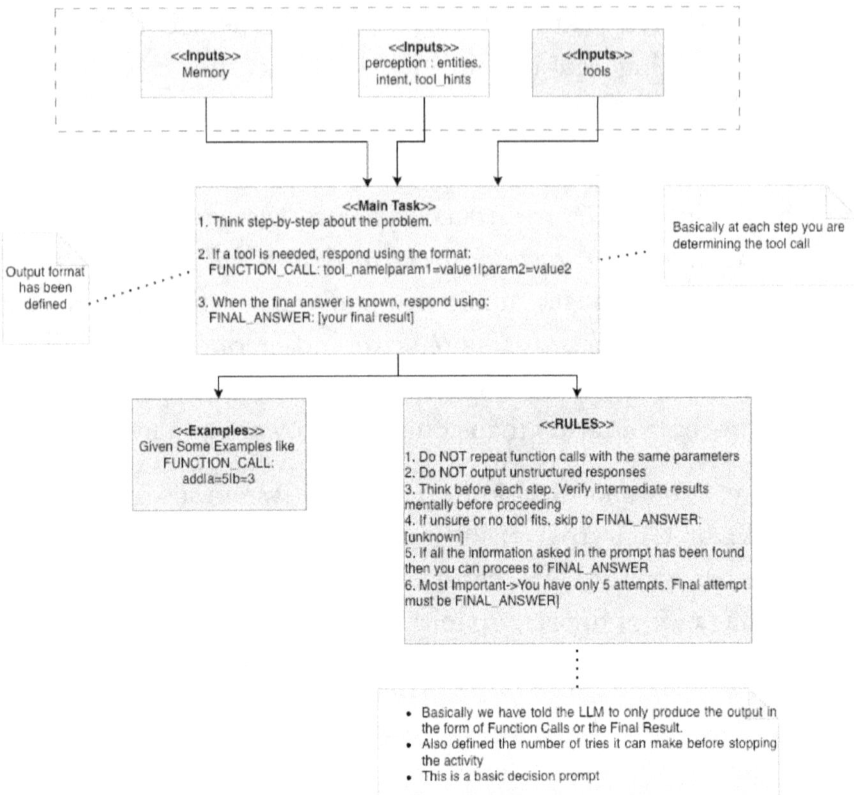

Figure: General Structure of the PADM Decision Prompt: *Given the Perception layer output, memory & tool list find out the actual function call and all the parameters to be passed in that function call. The prompt instructs the LLM to think step by step so that it breaks the complex task into sub tasks and that way chances of identifying the right function/tool are high. There is a list of Dos and Don'ts as well that helps the LLM to know the boundaries. The examples really help in understanding what is expected.*

Note: *The Perception output is just a suggestion, the Decision layer is free to do its own evaluation of the user input.*

At its core, the Decision layer's main task is straightforward: to formulate the correct tool call in the desired format and execute it.

```
E.g. FUNCTION_CALL: get_total_qty_for_most_selling_skus|inputData={'LstSKUs':
['979', '972', '566'], 'outlet_id': 75757}
```

When everything works as expected, this process feels seamless and elegant. The agent identifies the correct intent, selects the right tool, formats the parameters correctly, and executes the function to produce the desired output.

But this smooth "happy flow" is fragile.The entire chain can break if even one part, such as entity extraction, parameter identification, or data typing, fails to align perfectly.

Currently, there is **no feedback loop or reflection mechanism** to verify whether the tool result was actually correct.

If the tool call fails or produces an invalid result, the agent has no internal means to evaluate *why*. It cannot determine whether the problem was with **parameter values from previous calculation or a deeper logical error.**

This issue is compounded by the use of **strict validation frameworks** like *Pydantic*, which enforce precise data types and schema conformity. While this ensures structural correctness, it also makes the system brittle. A small deviation in input structure or type can cause the entire function call to fail and the loop to execute again.

The **Memory module** helps to some extent. It keeps track of progress, allowing the Decision layer to know whether a goal has been achieved or if further steps are needed. However, Memory in this architecture is **exposed only to the Decision layer**, not to Perception.That means it can track *whether* the goal has been reached, but not *why* the goal might have failed, limiting its diagnostic power.

One of the rationales for this design is simplicity. By isolating Perception to focus solely on interpreting the user's input without being influenced by an intermediate execution state, the system avoids entangling understanding with outcomes. Memory, in this view, serves a narrower purpose. It captures execution results so the Decision layer can determine whether further action is needed. From this perspective, feeding memory back into Perception may appear unnecessary, since responsibility for progress and correction resides with Decision, not with input interpretation.

While this separation keeps responsibilities clean, it also introduces a blind spot that becomes increasingly visible as tasks grow more complex. We will revisit this trade-off later in the book and explore how tighter feedback between Perception and Memory can enable more precise and timely corrections without sacrificing architectural clarity.

This setup represents the **simplest possible arrangement** of cognitive layers: easy to implement, easy to explain, but **highly uncertain** in behavior. It lacks the robustness and adaptability needed for real-world agentic performance.

To understand this better, let's now look at the **Agentic Loop**, the mechanism that stitches these four cognitive modules together into a functioning system.

Understanding the Agentic Loop

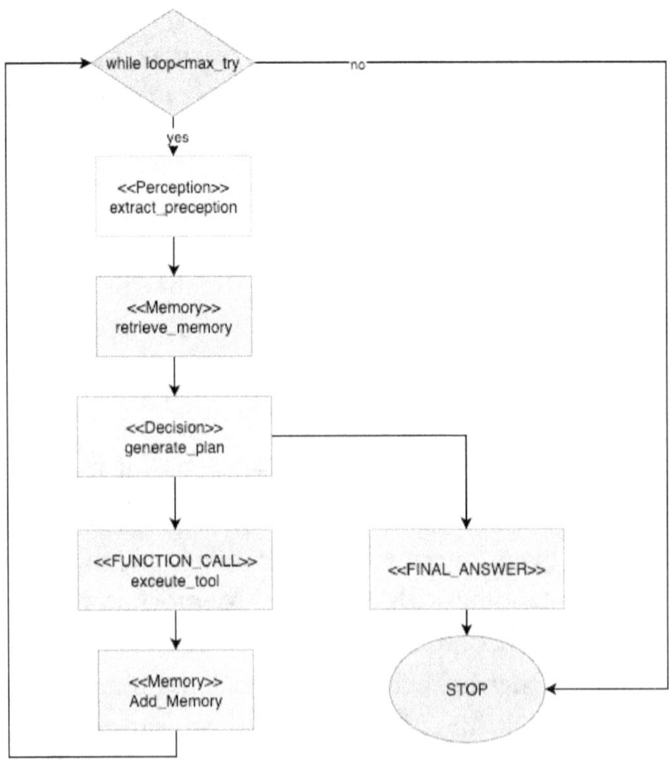

Figure: PADM Architecture Agentic Loop

The **Agentic Loop** serves as the backbone of the PADM architecture. It keeps the system thinking, acting, and iterating until a result is reached.

At a high level, the loop continues running until one of two conditions is met:

- the **maximum number of turns (Max_Turns)** is reached, or
- a defined **stop condition** confirms that the goal has been achieved.

Whichever comes first ends the loop. However, this mechanism has an important caveat: if either the **Perception** or **Decision** logic goes off track, for example, by repeatedly generating the wrong function call, the stop condition may never be triggered. In such cases, the loop can continue indefinitely (or MAX_TURN), wasting multiple LLM calls without meaningful progress.

Here's how the cycle typically unfolds:

1. **Perception Phase:**

   The loop begins with the Perception layer identifying the key entities, intent, and parameters from the user's query.

2. **Memory Retrieval:**

   The system retrieves relevant context from Memory including previously executed function calls and their results. This allows the agent to understand what's already been attempted.

3. **Decision Phase:**

   Using both the perception and the retrieved memory, the Decision layer generates a **plan,** essentially determining the *next function call* to execute.

4. **Action Phase:**

   The Action module executes the selected function or tool, captures the result, and appends it back into Memory for future iterations.

5. **Iteration:**

   The loop then cycles again feeding the new result into the next round of reasoning.

While the architecture appears balanced, in practice, the **Decision** and **Memory** modules dominate the loop. The **Perception layer** plays a relatively limited role, often acting as a lightweight extractor rather than a deep interpreter of context. As a result, much of the reasoning and control flow ends up concentrated in the Decision module—a design choice that makes the loop simple, but also **fragile and non-adaptive**.

In the next section, we'll explore how this Agentic Loop can evolve introducing **enhanced patterns** that make perception more intelligent, decision-making more structured, and the overall loop far more stable and predictable.

Everything is a Function at the end of the day: PADM_FUNCT

As we examined the behavior of the PADM architecture more closely, we realized something fundamental:

At its core, the **user's prompt** is simply a description of a set of **functions that need to be executed in sequence** to fulfill a goal.

In our earlier design (PADM), the agent's task was to *discover* those hidden functions within the natural language prompt one at a time and then execute them sequentially. After each function call, the **Memory** was used to check whether the desired outcome had been achieved or whether additional actions were still required.

While this worked in theory, in practice it proved to be both **slow and error-prone**.The agent spent significant time in **tool discovery and verification**, constantly looping through perception and decision steps to figure out what to do next. Each iteration consumed multiple LLM calls, increasing both latency and cost, while also multiplying opportunities for misinterpretation.

The original prompt guiding the **planning step** looked like this:

"Generate a plan (tool call or final answer) using the LLM based on structured perception and memory."

This meant the LLM was instructed to produce **only one function call at a time**. The system would then execute that tool, review the output, and decide whether further action was needed.

It was a cautious, stepwise approach but also **inefficient and fragile**. At each function level chances of failure are there and hence multiple points of failure.

To improve this, we evolved the planning stage into a more **holistic reasoning step**. Instead of asking the model to think in fragments, we ask it to **design a complete execution plan upfront** identifying all the tools that may be required and sequencing them intelligently.

The new planning prompt looks like this:

"You are a reasoning-driven AI agent responsible for generating a simple, structured execution plan using **only** the tools currently available to you."

This small change in wording introduces a major shift in behavior. It empowers the LLM to reason about the **entire workflow** in one pass, *generating a structured plan that lists all necessary function calls, their dependencies, and their order of execution.*

The LLM will generate a solve() ***function that is a collection of the MCP tools in a specific order based on how the user prompt has been interpreted***

In other words, the model moves from reactively discovering the next step to proactively planning the full path to the goal.

The result is a design that is not only faster and more efficient but also more **deterministic.** This is a crucial quality for any agent meant to operate reliably at scale.

```
E.g. for "Calculate the most selling SKUs for the outlet 75757. Then calculate the
total sales & quantity for the most selling skus for outlet 75757"

LLM output:
```python
import json
async def solve():
    # FUNCTION_CALL: 1
    """get_most_selling_SKUs:
    returns the top skus that are mostly sold in this outlet"""
    input = {"inputData": {"company_id":123,"outlet_id": 75757}}
    result1 = await mcp.call_tool('get_most_selling_SKUs', input)
    most_selling_skus = json.loads(result1.content[0].text)["result"]

    # FUNCTION_CALL: 2
    """Get the total sales of the SKUs"""
    input = {"inputData": {"company_id":123,"outlet_id":
75757,"lstSKUs":most_selling_skus }}
    result2 = await mcp.call_tool('get_total_sales_for_most_selling_SKUs', input)
    total_sales = json.loads(result2.content[0].text)["result"]


    # FUNCTION_CALL: 3
    """Get the total sales of the SKUs"""
    input = {"inputData": {"company_id":123,"outlet_id":
75757,"lstSKUs":most_selling_skus }}
    result3 = await mcp.call_tool('get_total_qty_for_most_selling_SKUs', input)
    total_qty = json.loads(result3.content[0].text)["result"]


    return f"FINAL_ANSWER: Most selling SKUs: {most_selling_skus} and the total
sales of the SKUs is {total_sales} and the total qty sold is {total_qty}"
```
```

The main advantage of this new approach is **efficiency**. By enabling the Decision layer to generate the **entire execution plan in a single LLM call**, we eliminate the repeated reasoning cycles that made the original PADM loop costly and slow.

In the earlier design, the **planning stage (Decision Layer)** was limited in scope. Its only task was to decide *which* function to call next. For example

```
FUNCTION_CALL: get_most_selling_skus | inputData = {"outlet_id": 75757}
```

Once this plan was produced, the **Action layer** would execute the function, validate the output, and then return control back to the Decision layer, which would once again invoke the LLM to determine the next step. This repetitive cycle meant multiple LLM invocations for even simple workflows, making the process both expensive and error-prone.

In contrast, the **PADM_FUNCT** approach brings far more intelligence into the **planning stage**. Here, the Decision layer doesn't just decide *what* to do but also designs *how* to do it.

The model creates a **complete execution plan,** i.e. solve() which specifies:

- **Which tools** need to be invoked
- **The order** in which those tools should be executed
- **The parameters** required for each tool call
- **How the output of each step** feeds into and informs subsequent steps

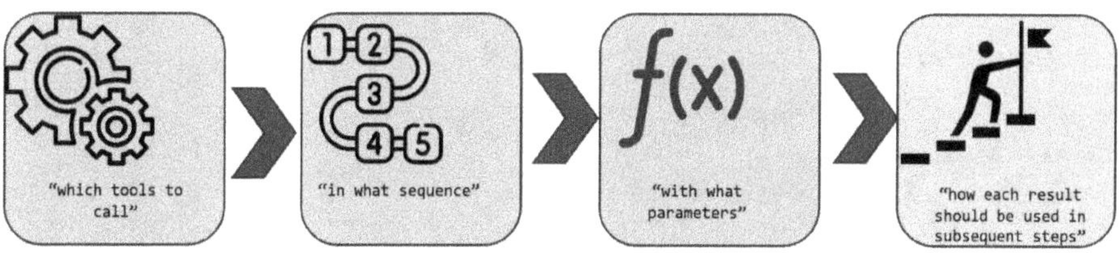

All of this happens in a **single reasoning pass.** This integrated approach reduces the number of LLM calls dramatically while improving determinism and consistency in the overall workflow.

Another advantage of this approach is that the generated solve() execution plan can be easily audited later to verify whether the agent addressed the entire query or missed any parts

The **Action layer** now acts as a lightweight **Python staging environment** responsible only for executing the pre-defined plan, step by step, and returning the final consolidated result. It no longer needs to reason or decide; it simply performs.

Meanwhile, the **Perception layer** plays a much reduced role in this new architecture. Since tool discovery and resolution happen upfront, there is little need for stepwise perception during execution.

This design marks an important evolution from *adaptive iteration (step by step decision)* to *structured cognition*. By allowing the Decision layer to plan comprehensively, the agent moves from being reactive and exploratory to being **purposeful and efficient**.

In the following sections, we'll explore how this change reshapes the **Perception**, **Decision**, and **Agentic Loop** layers in more detail and how it helps the system achieve faster convergence and more stable reasoning.

Perception Layer in PADM_FUNCT

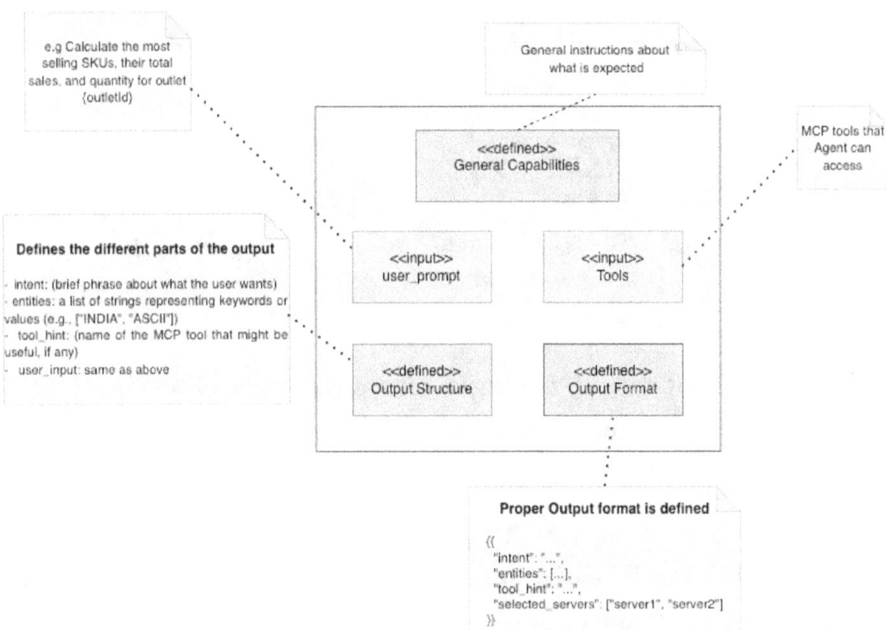

Figure: General Structure of the Perception Layer Prompt for PADM-FUNCT. *This diagram illustrates that the prompt structure of Perception in PADM-FUNCT closely resembles that of PADM with some additional specifications about the output formats. Defining the output format forces the LLM to work properly as it needs to fill the information asked for.*

Much like in the original PADM approach, the **Perception layer** in **PADM_FUNCT** still focuses on understanding the user's complete query rather than decomposing it into smaller subtasks. Its purpose remains to interpret the natural language input and extract the key elements that define what needs to be achieved.

> **Side Note**: LLMs tend to perform better when complex tasks are decomposed into smaller, simpler subtasks. Each subtask can be processed independently through the model, and the individual outputs can then be aggregated to form the final result. This is something we will leverage in the upcoming frameworks.

The key difference lies in how the output of the perception stage is formalized. Rather than producing loosely defined entities or informal tool hints, perception now generates a precise, structured representation of the user's intent, relevant entities, and expected outcomes. This clarity gives the Decision layer a far stronger foundation, enabling it to construct a coherent and deterministic execution plan in the next stage.

Conceptually, perception remains aligned with the original PADM approach, but it now communicates in a cleaner, more structured language, significantly reducing ambiguity and error propagation downstream.

The perception prompt in this setup looks something like this:

```
- Identify the INTENT of the user's query. ## this means explore the entire
  query in a single pass
- Extract important ENTITIES (e.g., company names, numbers, concepts).
- Suggest a TOOL_HINT if you can guess a useful tool (optional).
- Pick the most relevant MCP server IDs from the catalog above.
```

Decision Layer in PADM_FUNCT

The **Decision layer** in **PADM_FUNCT** represents a major evolution from the earlier PADM design. In PADM, the Decision stage was responsible for generating a **single function call** at a time. For example:

```
FUNCTION_CALL: get_most_selling_skus | inputData = {"outlet_id": 75757}
```

It would then pass this to the Action layer, which executed the call, validated the result, and handed control back for the next step.

In **PADM_FUNCT**, the Decision layer goes several steps further. Instead of producing just one function call, it now generates an entire **Python code block**, which is a self-contained execution plan that includes all the function calls required to fulfill the user's query.

This means the Decision module not only identifies *what* needs to be done, but also defines *how it will be done,* like sequencing the tools, linking their inputs and outputs, and preparing the full flow for execution.

The resulting code can be run **in a single shot**, allowing the Action layer to simply execute it as a Python script and return the final result. This eliminates the need for multiple LLM calls, reduces latency, and makes the entire process significantly more deterministic.

In essence, the Decision layer has evolved from being a **planner** to being a **code generator** transforming natural language intent directly into executable logic.

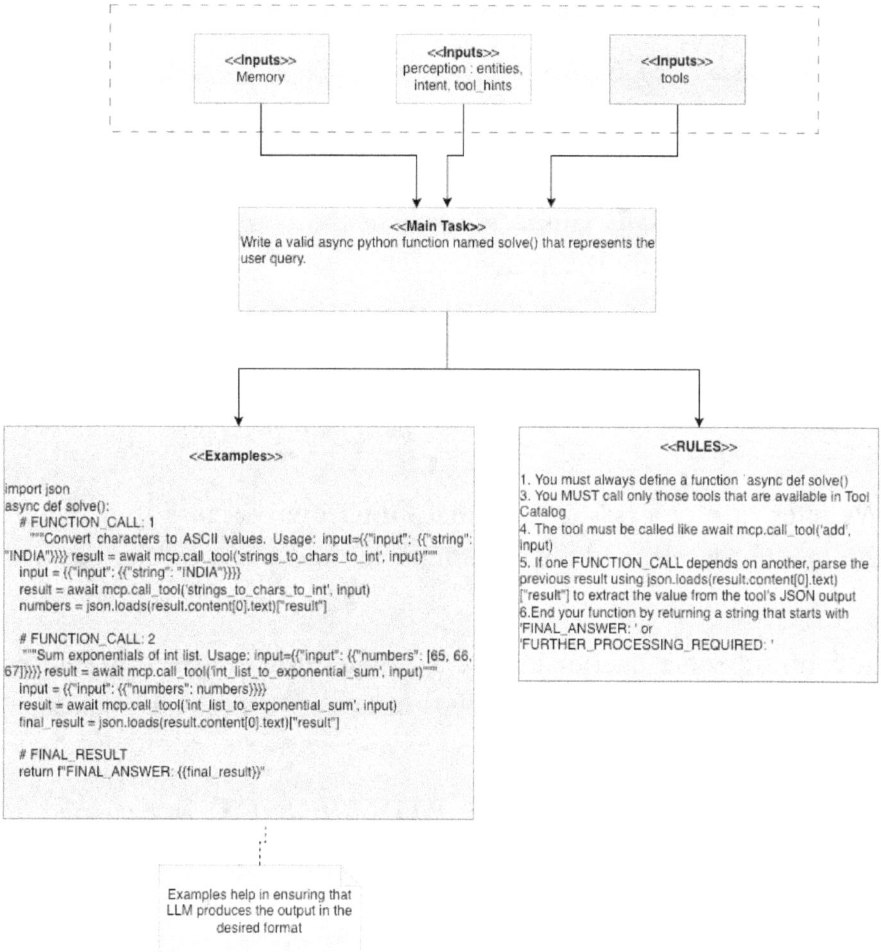

***Figure: General structure of Decision Prompt in PADM-FUNCT:** The most important piece is that it suggests generating a python program rather than a function. There are also lots of examples to understand the chaining functions, independent functions.*

A key strength of the updated **Decision prompt** is its ability to handle **function chaining.** The cases where multiple tools must be executed in a specific sequence because each depends on the results of the previous one.

For example, consider a query like:

> *"Get the top 5 SKUs and their sales."*

Here, the agent cannot compute sales directly. It must first **identify the top 5 SKUs**, and only then **calculate their corresponding sales**. These tasks are **sequentially connected**, where the output of one function becomes the input for the next.

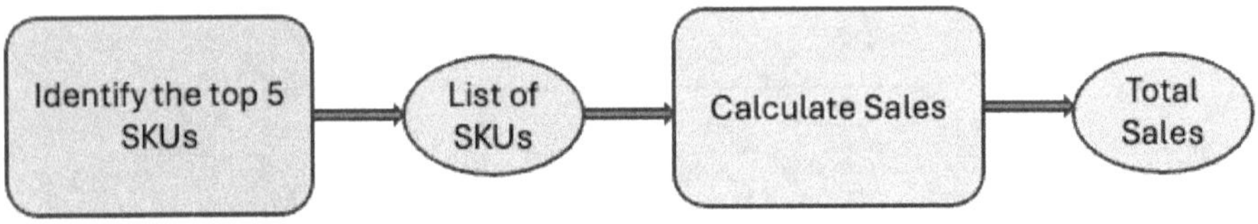

We refer to such cases as **Chained Functions**, because they require the model to reason about dependencies and parse results between steps.

In contrast, some queries involve a **Single Function Call**, where no intermediate results are needed. For instance, *"Get the total number of SKUs sold today."*

The new Decision prompt in **PADM_FUNCT** is designed to recognize and handle both patterns intelligently. It generates execution plans that not only list the right tools but also structure them correctly ensuring that **chained functions** are executed in order, with proper data handoff, while **single calls** are handled directly and efficiently. This capability marks an important step toward deeper reasoning: the model no longer just lists what to do, now it understands *how the parts fit together*.

The Decision prompt shown below is intentionally comprehensive. By combining strict rules with rich examples, it prepares the agent to handle a broad spectrum of real-world scenarios rather than just idealized cases.

```
prompt = f"""
You are a reasoning-driven AI agent responsible for generating a simple, structured
execution plan using ONLY the tools currently available to you.

🔧 Tool Catalog:
{tool_descriptions}

🧠 User Query:
"{user_input}"

🎯 Goal:
Write a valid async Python function named `solve()` that solves the user query
using exactly ONE FUNCTION_CALL.

📏 STRICT RULES:
- Plan exactly ONE FUNCTION_CALL only.
- You must always define a function `async def solve():`
- Each tool call must follow the Usage docstring format exactly.
- You MUST call only those tools that are available in Tool Catalog.
- Call a tool using its tool name string, not function variable.
  E.g., await mcp.call_tool('add', input)
  (NOT await mcp.call_tool(add, input))
- Before each tool call, paste the full tool docstring enclosed in triple quotes
(""").
- Call the tool exactly as per its function signature: tool(input)
- If one FUNCTION_CALL depends on another, parse the previous result using
json.loads(result.content[0].text)["result"] to extract the value from the tool's
JSON output.
- ❗ Important: Never inline json.loads(...) inside f"" strings. Always assign it to
a variable first (e.g., parsed = json.loads(...)["result"]) and use that in return
f"FINAL_ANSWER: {{parsed}}".
- End your function by returning a string that starts with 'FINAL_ANSWER: ' or
'FURTHER_PROCESSING_REQUIRED: '
- If the tool result is a document, webpage, or unstructured chunk, DO NOT return
it as the FINAL_ANSWER.
- Instead, return it with 'FURTHER_PROCESSING_REQUIRED:' so the agent can interpret
and summarize it next.

- No fallback, no multiple options.
- No explanation, no narration -- only valid Python code.
- If the user input already includes clean extracted webpage/document content, do
NOT call the tool again. Summarize or generate the final answer from it.
```

````
✅ Example 1: Output of last function parsed for next function
```python
import json
async def solve():
    # FUNCTION_CALL: 1
    """Convert characters to ASCII values. Usage: input={{"input": {{"string":
"BHARAT"}}}} result = await mcp.call_tool('strings_to_chars_to_int', input)"""
    input = {{"input": {{"string": "BHARAT"}}}}
    result = await mcp.call_tool('strings_to_chars_to_int', input)
    numbers = json.loads(result.content[0].text)["result"]

    # FUNCTION_CALL: 2
    """Sum exponentials of int list. Usage: input={{"input": {{"numbers": [65, 66,
67]}}}} result = await mcp.call_tool('int_list_to_exponential_sum', input)"""
    input = {{"input": {{"numbers": numbers}}}}
    result = await mcp.call_tool('int_list_to_exponential_sum', input)
    final_result = json.loads(result.content[0].text)["result"]

    # FINAL_RESULT
    return f"FINAL_ANSWER: {{final_result}}"

```

---

✅ Example 2: Independent but sequential tool use
```python
import json
async def solve():
    # FUNCTION_CALL: 1
    """Search Wikipedia. Usage: input={{"input": {{"query": "Artificial
Intelligence"}}}} result = await mcp.call_tool('search', input)"""
    input = {{"input": {{"query": "Artificial Intelligence"}}}}
    result1 = await mcp.call_tool('search', input)
    wiki_text = json.loads(result1.content[0].text)["result"]

    # FUNCTION_CALL: 2
    """Fetch News Articles. Usage: input={{"input": {{"query": "Artificial
Intelligence latest news"}}}} result = await mcp.call_tool('fetch_news', input)"""
    input = {{"input": {{"query": "Artificial Intelligence latest news"}}}}
    result2 = await mcp.call_tool('fetch_news', input)
    news_text = json.loads(result2.content[0].text)["result"]

    # FINAL_RESULT
    return f"FINAL_ANSWER: Wikipedia says {{wiki_text}}. News says {{news_text}}."
```
````

```
```
. Tips:

If the task can be solved by one tool, stop after that. You must return the result
immediately using 'FINAL_ANSWER:' if you got the result for the user's task, or
'FURTHER_PROCESSING_REQUIRED:'.
"""
```

Here is an example demonstrating function chaining, as generated by the Decision Layer, where the execution of function 2 is dependent on function 1 having completed.

*E.g.* ***"Find the ASCII values of characters in INDIA*** *and then* ***return sum of exponentials of those values"***

```
```python
import json
async def solve():
    # FUNCTION_CALL: 1
    """Convert characters to ASCII values. Usage: input={{"input": {{"string":
"INDIA"}}}} result = await mcp.call_tool('strings_to_chars_to_int', input)"""
    input = {{"input": {{"string": "INDIA"}}}}
    result = await mcp.call_tool('strings_to_chars_to_int', input)
    numbers = json.loads(result.content[0].text)["result"]

    # FUNCTION_CALL: 2
    """Sum exponentials of int list. Usage: input={{"input": {{"numbers": [65, 66,
67]}}}} result = await mcp.call_tool('int_list_to_exponential_sum', input)"""
    input = {{"input": {{"numbers": numbers}}}} ## numbers are coming from previous
function call
    result = await mcp.call_tool('int_list_to_exponential_sum', input)

    # FINAL_RESULT
    return f"{{result}}"

```
```

ASCII values of the characters in 'INDIA' have to be calculated first before performing the sum of the exponentials.

Contrast it with a user prompt that can compute either of the functions independently.

Who all own the DLF apartment Capbridge and also find the city in which Capbridge is located?
```

````
```python
async def solve():
    # FUNCTION_CALL: 1
    """Search documents to get relevant extracts. Usage: input={{"input":
{{"query": "Who is Modi?"}}}} result = await
mcp.call_tool('search_stored_documents', input)"""
    input = {{"input": {{"query": "DLF apartment Capbridge"}}}}
    result = await mcp.call_tool('search_stored_documents', input)

   # FUNCTION_CALL: 2
"""Find the location of a place Usage: input={{"input": {{"query": "India
Gate""}}}} result = await mcp.call_tool('search_places', input)"""
    input = {{"input": {{"query": "DLF apartment Capbridge"}}}}
    result = await mcp.call_tool('search_places', input)

    # FINAL_RESULT
    return f"{{result}}"
```
````

There is no dependence of the inputs on either of the function calls.

The Agentic Loop in PADM_FUNCT

The Agentic loop in this design closely mirrors the one in PADM, with one major difference: instead of calling individual functions in sequence, the **Decision module generates a single composite function—solve()**—that encapsulates the full execution plan.

This function is then executed inside a secure **Python sandbox**, and its results are stored in Memory.

> **Side Note**: A Python sandbox is an isolated execution environment that allows Python code to run safely under strict constraints on access, resources, and side effects. A sandbox is typically used when:
>
> - You need to run **untrusted or user-generated code**
> - You want to **experiment or prototype** without risk
> - You are building **agentic systems** that execute code dynamically
> - You want to **limit damage** from bugs, infinite loops, or malicious logic

Let's walk through how this loop operates step by step:

1. **Loop Control:**

   The loop continues running until either the **MAX_TRY** limit is reached or a **stop condition** is met.

2. **Perception:**

   The **Perception layer** identifies the user's intent, entities, and the tools that may be required to fulfill the query.

3. **Memory Retrieval:**

   The agent retrieves Memory to check whether similar function calls have been made previously, allowing it to reuse past context if available.

4. **Decision:**

   The **Decision module** generates the `solve()` function, which is a complete, structured plan containing all required tool calls in the correct order of execution.

5. **Action:**

   The **Action module** executes the `solve()` function within the sandbox environment and records the results in Memory.

6. **Iteration:**

   The loop repeats, comparing the current Memory state with the goal state.

   If the result matches the user's query, the loop exits. If not, the process restarts regenerating the entire plan.

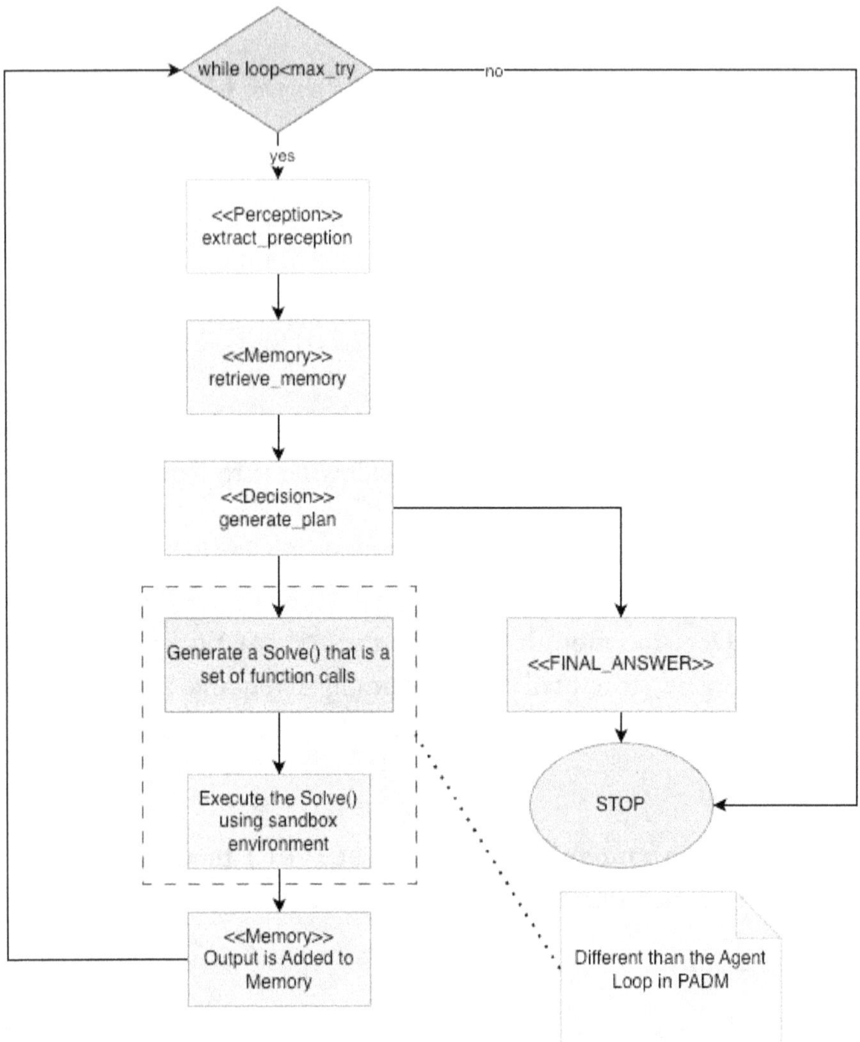

***Figure:** Agentic Loop for PADM_FUNCT*

In this setup, **Perception plays only a minimal role** and the recommendations from the Perception sometimes can often be bypassed entirely. This also largely depends on the strength of the LLM.The system lacks an internal reflection mechanism to evaluate *why* something failed. It only knows *that* it failed. The sole feedback signal comes from the Decision module comparing the Memory state before and after execution.

If the `solve()` function fails, produces invalid output, or runs into validation errors, the **entire plan is discarded** and the process begins again from the top. This can easily lead to **infinite or redundant loops**, especially if the LLM repeatedly misinterprets the goal or constructs an invalid function chain.

Drawbacks

In both **PADM** and **PADM_FUNCT**, the core weaknesses remain strikingly similar:

- **Limited Perception:**

  The Perception layer still lacks fine-grained understanding of progress. It operates only at the **macro level**, interpreting the user query as a single, global goal rather than evaluating intermediate steps.

- **Shallow Feedback:**

  Feedback is binary, either the goal was met or it wasn't. The system provides no guidance on *why* the result failed or *how* to correct the plan.

- **Fragile Recovery:**

  While **PADM_FUNCT** is far more efficient in terms of speed and LLM utilization, **any error**, however small, forces a **complete restart** from the first step, wasting computation and time.

Layers in Action

Let's look at an example to understand how PADM_FUNCT behaves when the Perception layer fails to correctly interpret the user's query.

In such cases, the agent tends to fall into a repetitive cycle of producing similar, redundant analyses in each iteration without making real progress toward the goal. This happens because the Perception layer keeps working with the same high-level understanding of the user's intent and doesn't adapt based on previous outcomes.

As a result, the Decision module keeps generating nearly identical execution plans, while the Memory dutifully logs each failed attempt creating the illusion of activity without meaningful advancement.

Let's walk through one such scenario to see how this repetition unfolds in practice.

☞ **Symbol denotes the Inline explaination of the code lines below it**

```
What do you want to solve today? → Find the sum of the log value of 5 and log value
of 8
Step 1/5 starting...

Note: here the perception is identifying the entities as log value of 5', 'log value
of 8

[perception] intent='Calculate the sum of logarithms.' entities=['log value of 5', 'log
value of 8'] tool_hint='python sandbox' tags=[] selected_servers=['math']
[plan] LLM output: ```python
import json
async def solve():
    # FUNCTION_CALL: 1
    """strings_to_chars_to_int: Convert characters to ASCII values. Usage:
input={"input": {"string": "INDIA"}} result = await
mcp.call_tool('strings_to_chars_to_int', input)"""
    input = {"input": {"string": "Find the sum of the log value of 5 and log value of
8"}}
    result = await mcp.call_tool('strings_to_chars_to_int', input)

    # FURTHER_PROCESSING_REQUIRED
    return f"FURTHER_PROCESSING_REQUIRED: {result}"
```
```
Note: The Decision layer identified the wrong function. It is trying to convert the
"log value of 5" from string to int

[loop] Detected solve() plan -- running sandboxed...
[action] Entered run_python_sandbox()
INFO     Processing request of type CallToolRequest
[loop] Forwarding intermediate result to next step:
Original user task: Find the sum of the log value of 5 and log value of 8

MEMORY output
Your last tool produced this result:

meta=None content=[TextContent(type='text', text='{\n  "result": [\n    70,\n    105,\n
110,\n    100,\n    32,\n    116,\n    104,\n    101,\n    32,\n    115,\n    117,\n
109,\n    32,\n    111,\n    102,\n    32,\n    116,\n    104,\n    101,\n    32,\n
108,\n    111,\n    103,\n    32,\n    118,\n    97,\n    108,\n    117,\n    101,\n
32,\n    111,\n    102,\n    32,\n    53,\n    32,\n    97,\n    110,\n    100,\n
32,\n    108,\n    111,\n    103,\n    32,\n    118,\n    97,\n    108,\n    117,\n
101,\n    32,\n    111,\n    102,\n    32,\n    56\n  ]\n}', annotations=None)]
isError=False

If this fully answers the task, return:
FINAL_ANSWER: your answer
```

```
Otherwise, return the next FUNCTION_CALL.


[loop] Continuing based on FURTHER_PROCESSING_REQUIRED -- Step 1 continues...
Step 2/5 starting...
Perception finds out the intent of the sub query, the entities which are the
parameters to work with and the MCP server and some tool hints. This time the output of
Perception is much better than the first time. Here the entities are changed.

[perception] intent='Calculate the sum of log(5) and log(8)' entities=['log(5)',
'log(8)', 'sum'] tool_hint='Math tools for logarithmic calculation' tags=[]
selected_servers=['math']

Decision has come up with its understanding of the suitable tool which is
"'strings_to_chars_to_int'. It is not giving attention to the tool suggestions by
Perception. Here the issue is that decision has totally missed the fact that the
'log(5)' is not some string but an actual mathematical expression that is required to be
run

[plan] import json
async def solve():
    # FUNCTION_CALL: 1
    """strings_to_chars_to_int: Convert characters to ASCII values. Usage:
input={"input": {"string": "INDIA"}} result = await
mcp.call_tool('strings_to_chars_to_int', input)"""
    input = {"input": {"string": "Find the sum of the log value of 5 and log value of
8"}}
    result = await mcp.call_tool('strings_to_chars_to_int', input)

    # FURTHER_PROCESSING_REQUIRED
    return f"FURTHER_PROCESSING_REQUIRED: {result}"
[loop] Detected solve() plan -- running sandboxed...
[action] Entered run_python_sandbox()
INFO     Processing request of type CallToolRequest
server.py:545
[loop] Forwarding intermediate result to next step:

MEMORY Output
Original user task: Find the sum of the log value of 5 and log value of 8
Your last tool produced this result:

meta=None content=[TextContent(type='text', text='{\n  "result": [\n    70,\n    105,\n
110,\n    100,\n    32,\n    116,\n    104,\n    101,\n    32,\n    115,\n    117,\n
109,\n    32,\n    111,\n    102,\n    32,\n    116,\n    104,\n    101,\n    32,\n
108,\n    111,\n    103,\n    32,\n    118,\n    97,\n    108,\n    117,\n    101,\n
32,\n    111,\n    102,\n    32,\n    53,\n    32,\n    97,\n    110,\n    100,\n
32,\n    108,\n    111,\n    103,\n    32,\n    118,\n    97,\n    108,\n    117,\n
```

```
101,\n    32,\n    111,\n    102,\n    32,\n    56\n  ]\n}', annotations=None)]
isError=False

If this fully answers the task, return:
FINAL_ANSWER: your answer

Otherwise, return the next FUNCTION_CALL.
```

Again continuing

```
[loop] Continuing based on FURTHER_PROCESSING_REQUIRED -- Step 2 continues...
Step 3/5 starting..
```

This time the perception is correct

```
[perception] intent='Calculate the sum of log values.' entities=['logarithm', '5', '8']
tool_hint='Use a calculator or math library to compute logarithms and sum them.' tags=[]
selected_servers=['math']
```

The plan is still wrong since this is a 2 step function where the first step is to perform the log function and the second step is to add the two logs. Decision is trying to pass the math.log(x) as a parameter assuming that the value of the log will be calculated automatically in the add function.

```
[plan] import json
import math
async def solve():
    # FUNCTION_CALL: 1
    """Add two numbers. Usage: input={"input": {"a": 1, "b": 2}} result = await
mcp.call_tool('add', input)"""
    input = {"input": {"a": math.log(5), "b": math.log(8)}}
    result = await mcp.call_tool('add', input)
    final_result = json.loads(result.content[0].text)["result"]

    # FINAL_RESULT
    return f"FINAL_ANSWER: {final_result}"
```

the sandbox is not able to run this as the add function expects int. There is a strict type validation through Pydantic

```
[loop] Detected solve() plan -- running sandboxed...
[action] Entered run_python_sandbox()
INFO     Processing request of type CallToolRequest
server.py:545
```

ERROR Thrown

```
[sandbox] ! Execution error: Expecting value: line 1 column 1 (char 0)
```

```
👉 since it was not captured why the things failed last time , perception will think its assessment was wrong and came up with some other analysis which is totally wrong.

[perception] intent='Calculate the sum of logarithms' entities=['logarithm of 5', 'logarithm of 8', 'sum'] tool_hint='Calculator or Math library' tags=[] selected_servers=['math']

👉 as perception is wrong the plan given out by Decision is also wrong

[plan] LLM output: ```python
import json
async def solve():
    # FUNCTION_CALL: 1
    """strings_to_chars_to_int: Convert characters to ASCII values. Usage: input={"input": {"string": "INDIA"}} result = await mcp.call_tool('strings_to_chars_to_int', input)"""
    input = {"input": {"string": "Find the sum of the log value of 5 and log value of 8"}}
    result = await mcp.call_tool('strings_to_chars_to_int', input)

    # FURTHER_PROCESSING_REQUIRED
    return f"FURTHER_PROCESSING_REQUIRED: {result}"
```

👉 Again the action is called

[loop] Detected solve() plan -- running sandboxed...
[action] 🔍 Entered run_python_sandbox()
INFO   Processing request of type CallToolRequest
server.py:545
[loop] ➡ Forwarding intermediate result to next step:
Original user task: Find the sum of the log value of 5 and log value of 8

Your last tool produced this result:
🧠 MEMORY Output
meta=None content=[TextContent(type='text', text='{\n "result": [\n   70,\n   105,\n   110,\n   100,\n   32,\n   116,\n   104,\n   101,\n   32,\n   115,\n   117,\n   109,\n   32,\n   111,\n   102,\n   32,\n   116,\n   104,\n   101,\n   32,\n   108,\n   111,\n   103,\n   32,\n   118,\n   97,\n   108,\n   117,\n   101,\n   32,\n   111,\n   102,\n   32,\n   53,\n   32,\n   97,\n   110,\n   100,\n   32,\n   108,\n   111,\n   103,\n   32,\n   118,\n   97,\n   108,\n   117,\n   101,\n   32,\n   111,\n   102,\n   32,\n   56\n]\n}', annotations=None)]
isError=False

If this fully answers the task, return:
FINAL_ANSWER: your answer
Otherwise, return the next FUNCTION_CALL.
```
```

```
[loop] Continuing based on FURTHER_PROCESSING_REQUIRED -- Step 3 continues...
Step 4/5 starting...
Again the perception has interpreted the user query in a wrong way

[perception] intent='Calculate the sum of logarithms.' entities=['log value of 5', 'log
value of 8'] tool_hint='math' tags=[] selected_servers=['math']

Decision made a blunder of considering the values of a and b as 5 and 8 without log.
Also the plan says that no further calculation is required which means whatever is the
result will the final result
[plan] import json
async def solve():
    # FUNCTION_CALL: 1
    """add: Add two numbers. Usage: input={"input": {"a": 1, "b": 2}} result = await
mcp.call_tool('add', input)"""
    input = {"input": {"a": 5, "b": 8}}
    result = await mcp.call_tool('add', input)
    final_result = json.loads(result.content[0].text)["result"]

    # FINAL_RESULT
    return f"FINAL_ANSWER: {final_result}"
[loop] Detected solve() plan -- running sandboxed...
[action] Entered run_python_sandbox()
[07/25/25 17:04:49] INFO     Processing request of type CallToolRequest
server.py:545
  the answer is totally wrong
  Final Answer: 13
```

The example above highlights a critical fragility in the **PADM_FUNCT** design: if either the **Perception** or **Decision** layer makes an incorrect assessment, the entire output can go wrong.

In this case, the **Perception module** provided only limited information both in terms of depth and diversity. Its output was narrow, focusing primarily on **entity extraction** and **tool hints**, without offering deeper reasoning, tool recommendations, or any measure of confidence.

This limitation stems largely from how the Perception stage is prompted. Because it isn't encouraged to think beyond surface-level parsing, it behaves more like a **syntactic interpreter** than a **cognitive analyst**.

To make matters worse, there is **no feedback mechanism** to validate whether the identified intent, entities, or tools were correct. The

Perception layer completes its task and moves on without knowing if it understood the query accurately. This lack of self-verification weakens its reliability and cascades into downstream errors.

The **Decision module**, meanwhile, struggles in the opposite direction. Even when Perception correctly identifies entities and tools, the Decision stage sometimes misuses that information, constructing faulty plans or calling incorrect functions. The result is a kind of **tug-of-war** between the two layers: when Perception is right, Decision falters; when Decision improves, Perception slips. Together, they can create a **never-ending loop** of minor misunderstandings and repetitive outputs.

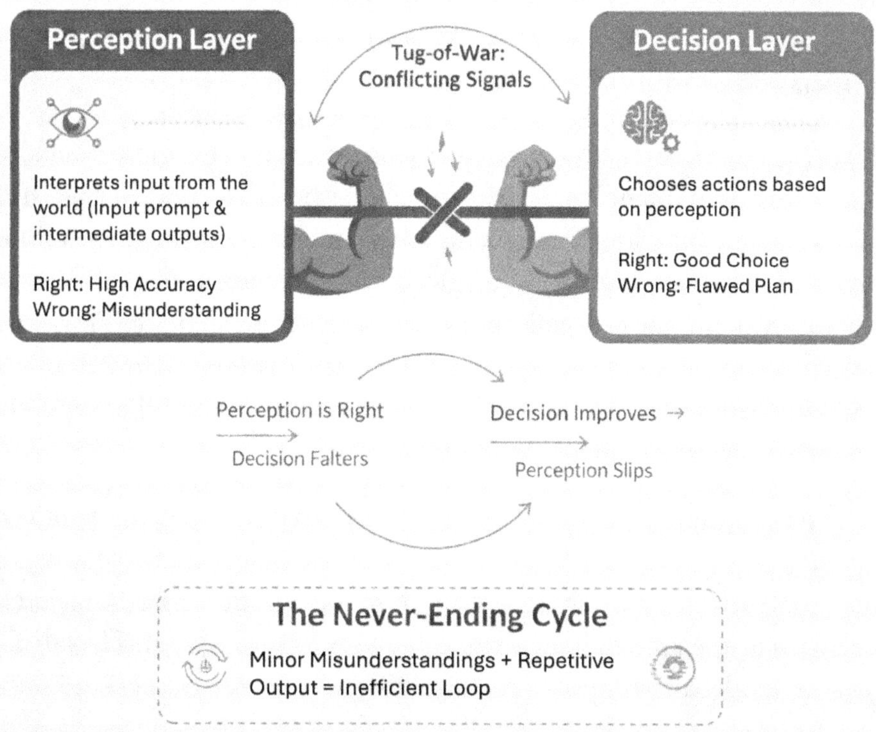

***Figure:** This diagram illustrates the inherent tension between Perception and Decision. Intelligence cannot be concentrated in just one. Errors in perception derail planning, and fragile decision logic nullifies accurate understanding*

In short, both layers operate intelligently on their own, but **without shared awareness or reflective feedback**, they fail to converge intelligently.

Evaluating PADM_FUNCT Through the Lens of the 4 R's

Every architecture we explore eventually comes back to the same four guiding principles—the 4 R's:

- **Reach**: How scalable and extensible the design is?
- **Reliability**: How consistently and accurately it performs?
- **Restraint:** How efficiently it uses resources?
- **Respect**: How responsibly it handles data and privacy?

Let's see how **PADM_FUNCT** stacks up.

1. Reach

PADM_FUNCT is designed with reach in mind by fundamentally rethinking how planning is performed. Rather than discovering and executing one function at a time, the Decision layer constructs the entire execution strategy upfront—a single, cohesive solve() plan that defines the full sequence of tool calls along with their dependencies. This shift significantly reduces back-and-forth between planning and execution and establishes a clear contract: the Action layer's responsibility is purely to execute what has already been planned.

In practice, this approach makes the system easier to scale across outlets, tenants, and workflows. Because the plan is explicit and self-contained, new tools can be introduced with minimal disruption, and the overall behavior of the system is easier to reason about and govern. The "*plan-as-code*" model also improves predictability, which is critical at scale.

The trade-off emerges when tasks become genuinely complex. Workflows that involve branching logic, conditional decisions, or data-dependent paths are harder to handle in a single-pass plan. Without a fine-grained feedback loop during execution, the system has limited ability to adapt mid-flight if assumptions made during planning turn out to be wrong.

Evaluation: *PADM_FUNCT excels at scalable, predictable execution, but it trades adaptability for* reach, making it best suited for well-structured workflows rather than highly dynamic ones.

2. Reliability

By front-loading reasoning into a single, coherent execution plan, PADM_FUNCT improves consistency in a meaningful way. Fewer handoffs between layers reduce prompt drift, and clearly defined inputs and outputs between tools make the system's behavior easier to reason about and reproduce. In this respect, reliability is stronger than in stepwise PADM, where each iteration introduces fresh variability.

That said, reliability remains highly sensitive to the quality of the initial perception. If intent or entities are misinterpreted at the outset, the error is effectively baked into the plan and propagated through every subsequent step. Additionally, when execution fails partway through—due to schema mismatches or sandbox errors—the system typically restarts rather than repairs. This conservative strategy favors safety and determinism but limits graceful recovery from partial failures.

Verdict: *PADM_FUNCT delivers more consistent behavior than iterative designs, but its reliability is front-loaded—strong when perception is correct initially, fragile when it is not.*

3. Restraint

Restraint is where PADM_FUNCT clearly excels. By requiring the model to reason once rather than repeatedly, it significantly reduces token consumption and overall latency for multi-step workflows. Execution is deterministic and inexpensive, and tool outputs can be cached or replayed without invoking the model again.

The trade-off emerges as complexity grows. Large tool catalogs or long execution chains can make the single planning call heavier, and a failed plan necessitates re-planning, which incurs additional cost. As with earlier PADM architectures, overall efficiency still depends on the capability and cost profile of the underlying LLM. Even so, for well-structured tasks, PADM_FUNCT offers a substantial improvement in cost control.

Verdict: *PADM_FUNCT is highly cost-efficient for structured workflows, trading adaptive reasoning for predictable and economical execution.*

4. Respect

Respect remains a strong pillar of architecture. The language model determines *what* to do but never directly accesses data; all data interaction occurs through controlled MCP tools. In PADM_FUNCT, the execution plan itself becomes an explicit, auditable artifact, clearly outlining tool usage, inputs, and expected outputs. When combined with sandboxed execution, this creates a clean and traceable boundary between reasoning and data access.

The primary risk lies in policy enforcement. A flawed plan could chain together sensitive operations if guardrails are too permissive. This makes strict MCP policies, pre-execution plan validation, and tightly scoped sandbox permissions essential. With these controls in place, PADM_FUNCT strengthens governance and auditability compared to more implicit, stepwise approaches.

Verdict: *With proper guardrails, PADM_FUNCT offers strong privacy guarantees and superior auditability, making Respect one of its most dependable strength*

Summary Table

Principle	Definition	Evaluation	Remarks
Reach	Ability to scale and extend efficiently across large deployments	🟡 **Moderate** — high scalability and improved throughput, depends entirely on LLM for complex workflow resolution	High throughput via single-pass planning; limited adaptability for complex or branching workflows
Reliability	Consistency and correctness of outcomes	🟡 **Moderate** — more deterministic, but fragile to early missteps	Early perception errors propagate; lacks in-loop correction.
Restraint	Efficiency and cost-effectiveness of LLM usage	🟢 **Better** — fewer calls, lower latency, better utilization	Fewer LLM calls reduce cost; full-plan retries remain expensive
Respect	Responsible handling of data, privacy, and governance	🟢 **High** — transparent and auditable design	Like PADM, all data still flows through MCP tools, maintaining strict isolation from the LLM. The generated plan acts as an auditable record. Every function call, parameter, and output can be traced.

Design Decisions and Infrastructure

Here are some of the key architectural choices that define the PADM_FUNCT design:

Design Area	Decision
Infrastructure	The framework remains model-agnostic, capable of running on any LLM from lightweight local models like *phi-4 on Ollama* to larger hosted ones such as *GPT-4* or *Gemini*. However, since PADM_FUNCT relies on generating structured code blocks (solve() functions), reasoning quality and syntax accuracy depend heavily on model capability. Production deployments generally prefer high-end models for consistent logic generation and fewer syntax errors.
Query Handling	All data access continues to flow through the **MCP server**. The LLM doesn't handle raw data or generate SQL, it plans which MCP tools to call and in what sequence. This enforces strict data boundaries while simplifying access management and ensuring auditability.
LLM Role	The language model has evolved from being a stepwise planner to a **reasoning-driven code generator**. Instead of deciding the next move at each step, it now produces a complete, executable plan upfront. The LLM effectively becomes a **compiler of reasoning**, turning user intent into runnable Python logic (solve()), which can then be validated, executed, and traced.
Action and Execution	The Action layer serves as a **sandboxed runtime** for executing the generated plan safely. It doesn't reason or modify the plan. It simply executes it line by line, logs results, and writes them back to memory. This separation ensures predictability and containment of errors.

Design Area	Decision
Memory and Feedback	Memory continues to record tool outputs and intermediate states, but feedback remains coarse—success or failure only. There's no reflective mechanism yet to refine partial results, which can lead to full-plan reruns. Future iterations could include light-weight validation and selective re-execution of failed steps.
Output Modalities	The output remains flexible: structured summaries, textual explanations, or JSON-formatted results depending on the query. Because plans are written as code, they can be **audited and replayed** easily, giving full transparency into how each result was produced.

```
```
import json
import math
async def solve():
    # FUNCTION_CALL: 1
    """Add two numbers. Usage: input={"input": {"a": 1, "b": 2}} result =
await mcp.call_tool('add', input)"""
    input = {"input": {"a": math.log(5), "b": math.log(8)}}
    result = await mcp.call_tool('add', input)
    final_result = json.loads(result.content[0].text)["result"]

    # FINAL_RESULT
    return f"FINAL_ANSWER: {final_result}"
```
```

Figure: Here is an example plan and we can find out what will be the output by just running this function and debugging it for any error

From POC to Production: Challenges of PADM_FUNCT

PADM_FUNCT performs impressively in controlled environments. In prototypes and research settings, where creativity and experimentation take precedence, the design's ability to generate complete execution plans (`solve()` functions) in one reasoning pass feels both elegant and efficient.

But production environments operate under a tougher rulebook often dominated by **predictability, cost, and scale**.

While PADM_FUNCT simplifies orchestration and improves determinism, several hurdles remain before it can operate seamlessly at production scale.

1. Model Dependency and Code Quality Variance

The first challenge stems from PADM_FUNCT's reliance on the LLM's ability to **generate valid, executable code**. At the prototype level, high-end models like GPT-4 or Gemini handle this task well, producing structured, syntactically correct `solve()` plans.

However, lower-tier or self-hosted models often struggle with **formatting, logic chaining, and dependency resolution**, leading to broken plans that require human intervention or retries. This creates a **practical model lock-in**, where the design is theoretically model-agnostic but practically tied to premium APIs increasing both operational cost and vendor dependency.

2. Limited Feedback and Adaptability

PADM_FUNCT trades iterative intelligence for speed. Once the plan is generated, it executes without ongoing reflection or contextual adjustment. If the perception or plan was slightly off, there's no mechanism to **course-correct midstream**. The system executes the wrong plan perfectly. At production scale, this can lead to consistent but systematically wrong outcomes. Building in lightweight feedback loops, for example, plan validation checkpoints or runtime confidence checks, will be essential for stable long-term deployment.

3. Governance and Plan Validation

Because PADM_FUNCT turns reasoning into executable code, governance becomes both easier and more important. Plans can be audited and versioned, providing transparency, but they also introduce the risk of chained sensitive actions if validation is weak. Each plan must pass through sandbox checks, policy filters, and tool-level permissioning before execution. This is a necessary safeguard that can add latency and operational overhead in production systems.

In Summary

PADM_FUNCT represents a major leap forward in efficiency and structure replacing iterative loops with single-pass reasoning and executable logic. However, that elegance introduces new practical challenges when moving from concept to scale: **model dependence, brittle recovery, limited feedback, and governance complexity.**

At POC scale, it's fast, explainable, and easy to experiment with. At production scale, it demands **stronger validation, smarter fallback strategies, and disciplined cost management.**

If your priority is **efficiency, transparency, and deterministic reasoning**, PADM_FUNCT delivers remarkable results. But if your environment values **adaptability, fault tolerance, and operational robustness**, this architecture still needs reinforcement before it can power large-scale, always-on deployments.

Agentic Test: Is This Architecture Agentic?

As we've discussed before, a truly agentic system rests on three foundational pillars—**Generation**, **Action**, and **Reflection**. These pillars define how independently a system can think, decide, and act, the true measure of machine agency.

Let's see how **PADM_FUNCT** performs when tested against each of these dimensions.

1. Generative Aspect

In PADM_FUNCT, the LLM moves from *reactive reasoning* to *proactive planning*.

Rather than generating one function at a time, it now produces a complete `solve()` function. It is a full execution plan that defines all steps needed to achieve the goal.

The generative capability here is not just about producing responses, but about **designing workflows**:

- **Intent Understanding:** Interpreting the goal behind the prompt, not just the literal request.
- **Tool Sequencing:** Deciding which tools to use and in what order.
- **Dependency Resolution:** Mapping how outputs from one step feed into the next.
- **Code Generation:** Converting reasoning directly into executable Python logic.

This makes the agent's thought process both **visible and verifiable**, a powerful trait in production-grade AI systems. The model no longer just "thinks in text"; it **thinks in code**.

Evaluation: *Strong, forward-looking generative intelligence; creates structured, executable reasoning.*

2. Action-Oriented Aspect

PADM_FUNCT enhances autonomy by **collapsing multiple decision loops into a single, self-contained plan**. Once the solve() function is generated, the system doesn't need further LLM guidance for each step. It simply executes the code in a sandboxed environment.

This design embodies true agentic behavior:

- The agent interprets, plans, and executes without human hand-holding.
- The execution layer performs tool calls automatically, ensuring consistency and speed.
- Each action produces a traceable log improving transparency while maintaining autonomy.

Evaluation: *Fully autonomous tool invocation*

3. Planning & Reasoning Aspect

Here lies the nuanced trade-off. PADM_FUNCT demonstrates **structured reasoning**, not **adaptive reasoning**. By front-loading all cognitive effort into a single reasoning step, the agent becomes faster and more predictable but less self-reflective.

It no longer pauses to re-evaluate after each action; instead, it assumes its initial plan is correct. This works beautifully for well-defined tasks but struggles when ambiguity or partial errors arise. Without a feedback loop or self-check mechanism, reasoning becomes **linear rather than cyclical**, more like a script than a conversation.

Evaluation: Strong structural reasoning, but limited adaptiveness or self-correction.

Assessment Against Agentic Principles

Pillar	Description	Evaluation
Generative Aspect	LLM designs complete workflows, chaining tools and logic into a single executable plan.	◯ Comprehensive reasoning-to-code generation.
Action-Oriented Aspect	Executes the full plan autonomously, with no stepwise human intervention.	◯ Full autonomy and traceable execution.
Planning & Reasoning Aspect	Reasoning is structured but lacks reflection or error adaptation.	◍ Strong reasoning but limited feedback awareness.

Conclusion

While the **PADM_FUNCT** architecture greatly improves efficiency by generating the entire execution plan upfront, it introduces a new set of limitations particularly around feedback, error correction, and adaptability.

One of the key drawbacks of this approach is the **lack of granular feedback** on the quality of the output.

In the earlier **PADM** approach, feedback was **stepwise** meaning that if only part of the output was incorrect, the agent could selectively re-evaluate that specific step. In contrast, **PADM_FUNCT** operates at an all-or-nothing level. If the final result is unsatisfactory, the **entire execution plan** is discarded, and a new one is generated from scratch.

The following radar chart illustrates the architecture's performance across the **4 R's** and core **Agentic Traits** for quick reference.

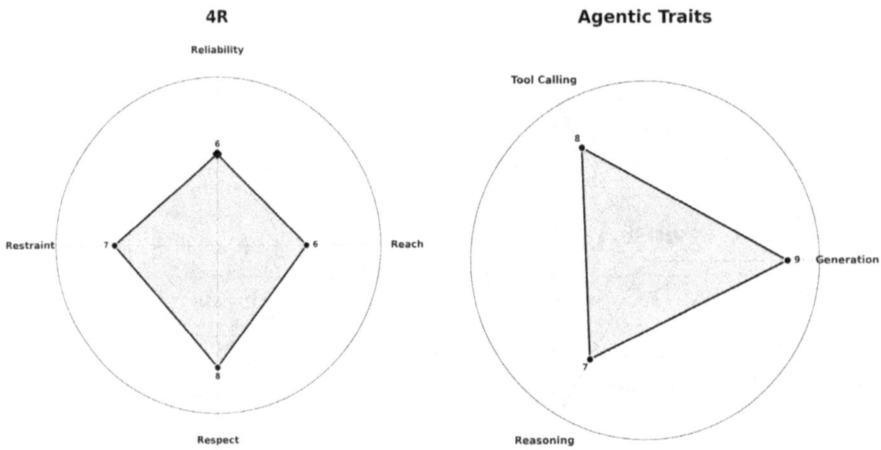

Figure: *The diamond bullet in 4R Radar highlights the fact that Reliability is still an issue in this architecture even though the Agentic traits have improved compared to PADM architecture*

In the next chapter, we'll explore a series of **techniques and design patterns** that address these issues enhancing the Perception and Decision layers with richer reasoning, structured validation, and feedback-driven refinement. These improvements transform the agent from a reactive executor into a truly **reflective cognitive system**.

CHAPTER 09

Towards True Agency: Reasoning, Reflection, and Refinement

"Where AI stops imitating and starts understanding"

By now, we've built and tested a few flavors of agentic systems.

We started with **PADM**, where the agent worked in loops—sensing, reasoning, remembering, and acting. Then we built on that to create **PADM_FUNCT**, which made things faster and leaner by having the Decision layer generate a complete execution plan in one go.

And while PADM_FUNCT felt like a huge leap forward, it also left us with a few headaches. It was quick, yes, but also a little *too confident*. Once it made up its mind about the plan, there was no turning back. If the plan went wrong, the agent simply started over, forgetting what it had just learned.

But as we began testing these architectures, we understood a few critical links were missing. The system could think, plan, and act, but it couldn't **learn from its own behavior**.

It's a bit like building a car with a powerful engine, a finely tuned transmission, and high-performance wheels but leaving out the differential. Without that one component, all the power in the world can't be delivered efficiently to the wheels. The car technically works, but it doesn't *move right.*

Our agentic systems faced a similar problem. We had all the major parts, but the **flow between them was broken**. Without proper feedback, reflection, and reasoning loops, each layer operated in isolation.

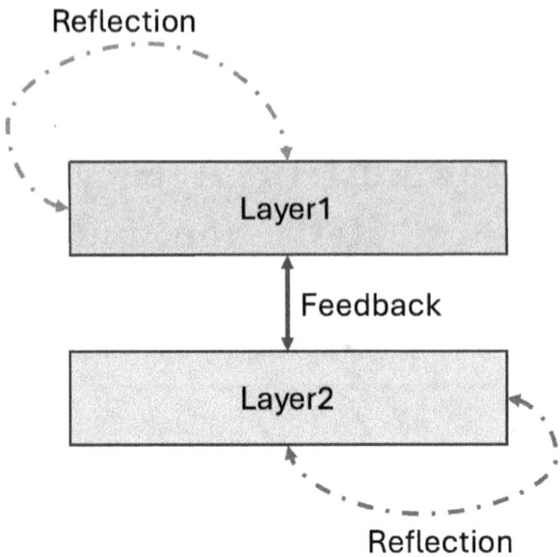

Perception interpreted the goal, Decision charted the next move, and Memory recorded the outcome. However, no one was verifying the synergy of these steps.

The result? *Agents that could execute but not improve; act but not adapt.*

The revised architecture fills in those missing links.

We call it **PADM_FEED**, short for *Perception–Action–Decision–Memory with Feedback.*

At its core, PADM_FEED introduces a **feedback-driven refinement mechanism**—a way for the agent to iteratively review its outputs, detect inconsistencies, and improve itself before proceeding further.

Here, the **Perception module** takes on a much more prominent role. It's no longer just parsing user intent or identifying entities; it's reasoning, analyzing, and validating the coherence of the results coming from other layers.

The **Decision module**, in contrast, becomes leaner, focused purely on planning and orchestration rather than deep reasoning.

This architecture shifts the balance of intelligence:

- **Perception** becomes the brain for reasoning, reflecting, and validating.
- **Decision** becomes the strategist to plan the sequence of the steps to reach the perceived goal.
- **Memory** becomes the conscience for remembering what worked and what didn't.
- **Feedback** becomes the connective tissue ensuring that every cycle improves upon the last.

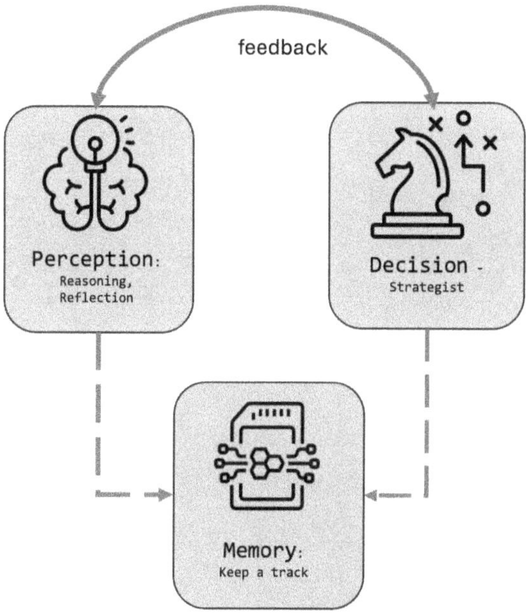

By introducing feedback into the cognitive loop, the agent gains the ability to *pause and reflect*, turning execution into an ongoing conversation between reasoning and action.

In the sections ahead, we'll explore how PADM_FEED works in practice, how feedback is captured, analyzed, and applied to refine each iteration. We'll see how this seemingly small change transforms the architecture from a reactive executor into a **self-correcting cognitive agent**.

The Perception Layer

In PADM_FEED, the **Perception layer** is no longer just an entry point. It's the *thinking eye* of the system. It not only interprets what the user is asking for but also continuously evaluates whether the system is moving in the right direction.

In many ways, it begins to emulate how a human approaches problem-solving: looking at the goal, checking progress, and adjusting course when things don't add up.

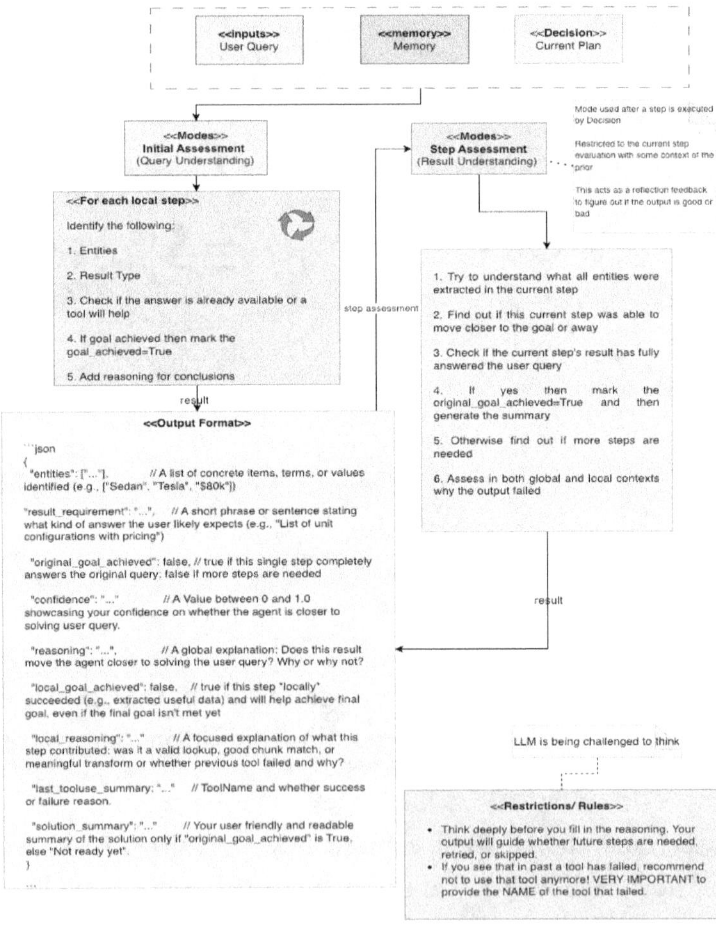

Figure: General Structure of the Perception Prompt in PADM_FEED.
Notice the stress on the format of the output and the additional fields in the output apart from just the entities and the intent.

Perception now operates in **two distinct modes:**

Mode 1. Initial Assessment (Query Understanding)

At the start, Perception performs an **initial assessment** of the user's query to identify the key entities, intent, and possible operations. Before any execution begins, it also checks **Memory** for past results or context that might already satisfy the goal. If relevant information is found, Perception records it and avoids redundant computation saving both time and cost.

Mode 2. Step Assessment (Result Understanding)

As the execution unfolds, Perception doesn't step aside; it stays engaged. After each intermediate step, it evaluates whether the results are aligned with the overall goal or if something has gone off course. This **ongoing self-check** acts as a feedback signal for the Decision module keeping the agent grounded, self-aware, and responsive to errors as they emerge.

Structured Output for Smarter Decisioning

Unlike earlier architectures, the output from Perception in PADM_FEED is far more structured and explicit. It produces a **JSON object** that serves as a detailed status report. It is a snapshot of progress so far and a guide for what comes next.

Here are some of the key fields included in the Perception output:

- **Entities:** Lists all the identified entities, parameters, and operations relevant to the task. This is the foundation for planning and execution.
- **Original_goal_achieved:** A critical field that forces Perception to reason about whether the *overall goal* has been met. If this flag is true, the agent loop can stop and no further iterations would be done.
- **Reasoning:** A textual explanation of *why* Perception reached its conclusions. This transforms Perception into a genuine reasoning engine that doesn't just report findings but explains them.

- **Local_goal_achieved:** Evaluates whether the *current step's* objective has been fulfilled. If there's any deviation or partial failure, Perception flags it, creating an intelligent feedback loop that is much richer than the simple vector comparison used in earlier versions.
- **Last_tooluse_summary:** Captures which tool was used most recently and what outcome it produced. This prevents redundant tool invocations and helps the Decision layer understand what's already been tried.
- **Confidence:** Expresses how certain Perception is about its analysis and conclusions.
- This gives the Decision layer a sense of reliability for each input, allowing it to weigh results intelligently.

Perception is now called **after every plan step** is executed. Each call updates the fields above, ensuring that the system remains context-aware and grounded in its progress.

This design transforms Perception from a one-time interpreter into a **continuous reasoning and reflection engine** that observes, questions, and guides the agent through each stage of its cognitive journey.

The Decision Layer

Let's now look at the **Decision module.** In this architecture, the Decision layer is deliberately **restricted to a single, disciplined purpose,** creating a structured plan based on the insights coming from the **Perception module.**

It no longer tries to reason or interpret; instead, it focuses on **planning and adaptation,** ensuring that each step of the execution aligns with the agent's evolving understanding of the goal. The focus is more on how to implement the analysis of the Perception Module, the reason why the layer was created in the first place but was not working in that mode in the previous two architectures. This architecture strictly adheres to the Separation of Concerns principle, preventing, for instance, the Decision component from attempting the work of Perception.

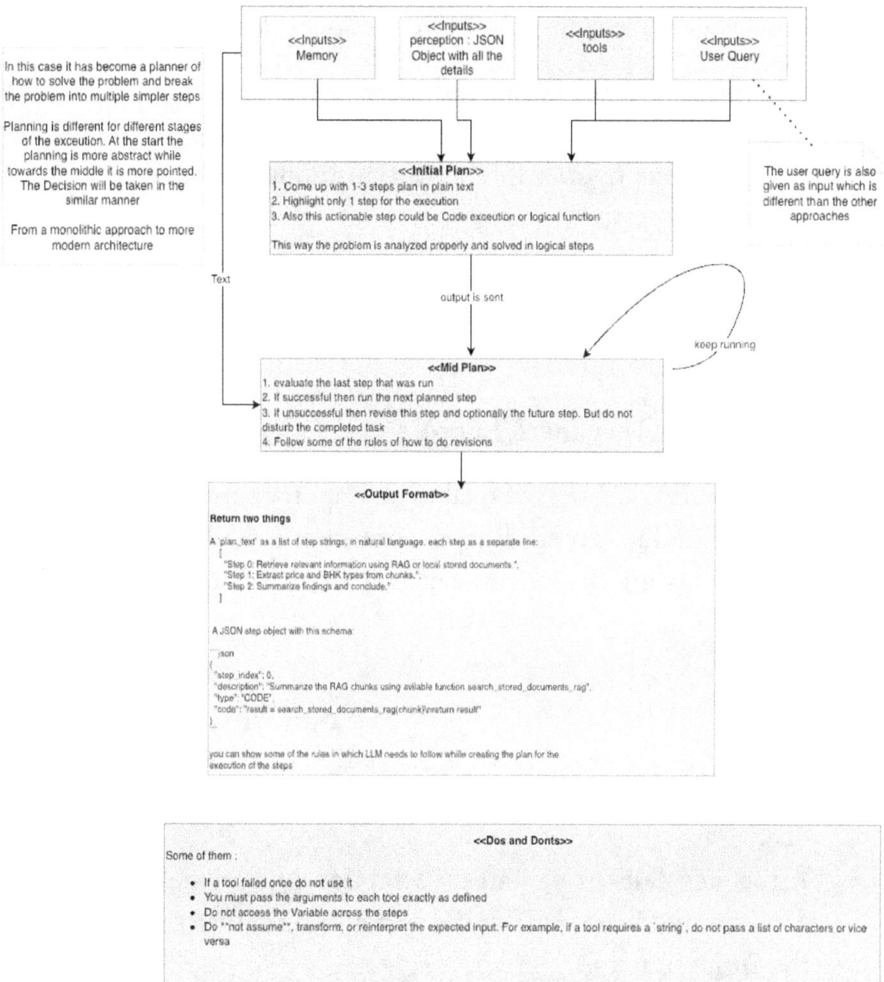

Figure: General Structure of the Decision Prompt in PADM_FEED. *Notice the emphasis of reasoning at each steps and presence of two modes*

Just like Perception, the Decision module in **PADM_FEED** operates in **two distinct modes:**

Mode 1. Initial Plan

At the beginning, based on the **initial assessment** provided by Perception, the Decision module constructs a **structured execution plan** containing a sequence of actionable steps to achieve the user's goal.

Each step in this plan represents a specific tool or function call, defined with clear inputs, dependencies, and expected outputs.These steps are then passed **one by one** to the **Action module** (the executor) for implementation.

This modular approach allows the system to maintain visibility into progress, execution flow, and dependencies making the process transparent and traceable.

Mode 2. Mid Plan (Feedback Loop)

This is where **PADM_FEED** takes a leap forward. In this mode, the Decision module enters into a **continuous feedback loop** with Perception, evaluating the outcome of each executed step.

After every action:

- **Perception** assesses whether the result aligns with the intended goal.
- If the step is **successful**, Decision simply moves on to the next one.
- If the step **fails or deviates,** Perception immediately signals the Decision module to adjust the current step rather than restarting the entire process.

Decision then revises that specific part of the plan, generating an alternative step or reconfiguring parameters as needed, while **preserving previous progress**.

This tight collaboration between Perception and Decision creates a genuinely **adaptive loop**, where the agent corrects itself dynamically instead of starting over.

This design marks a **significant improvement** over earlier architectures like **PADM** and **PADM_FUNCT**, where even a minor failure would trigger a full restart of the execution. In contrast, **PADM_FEED** enables **localized correction** fixing only what's broken while keeping everything else intact.

Unlike PADM_FUNCT, this approach does not generate a single solve() function upfront. Instead, it produces an incremental plan that operates on the information provided by the Perception layer. Each step is executed sequentially, with the agent evaluating success or failure before deciding how to proceed next.

It's a subtle change in logic but a profound leap in capability: the agent now learns *within* the loop, not *after* it.

The Agentic Loop

Let us now look at the **Agentic Loop**, the heart of the PADM_FEED architecture.

Compared to earlier loops in PADM or PADM_FUNCT, this version behaves very differently. It doesn't just move in a fixed sequence of steps. Instead, it acts as a **true orchestrator**, intelligently managing the flow between modules based on real-time feedback. The sequence of events can change dynamically as new information emerges, much like how a human might pause, reassess, and change direction while solving a problem.

Because this loop has multiple moving parts, it's worth walking through it step by step.

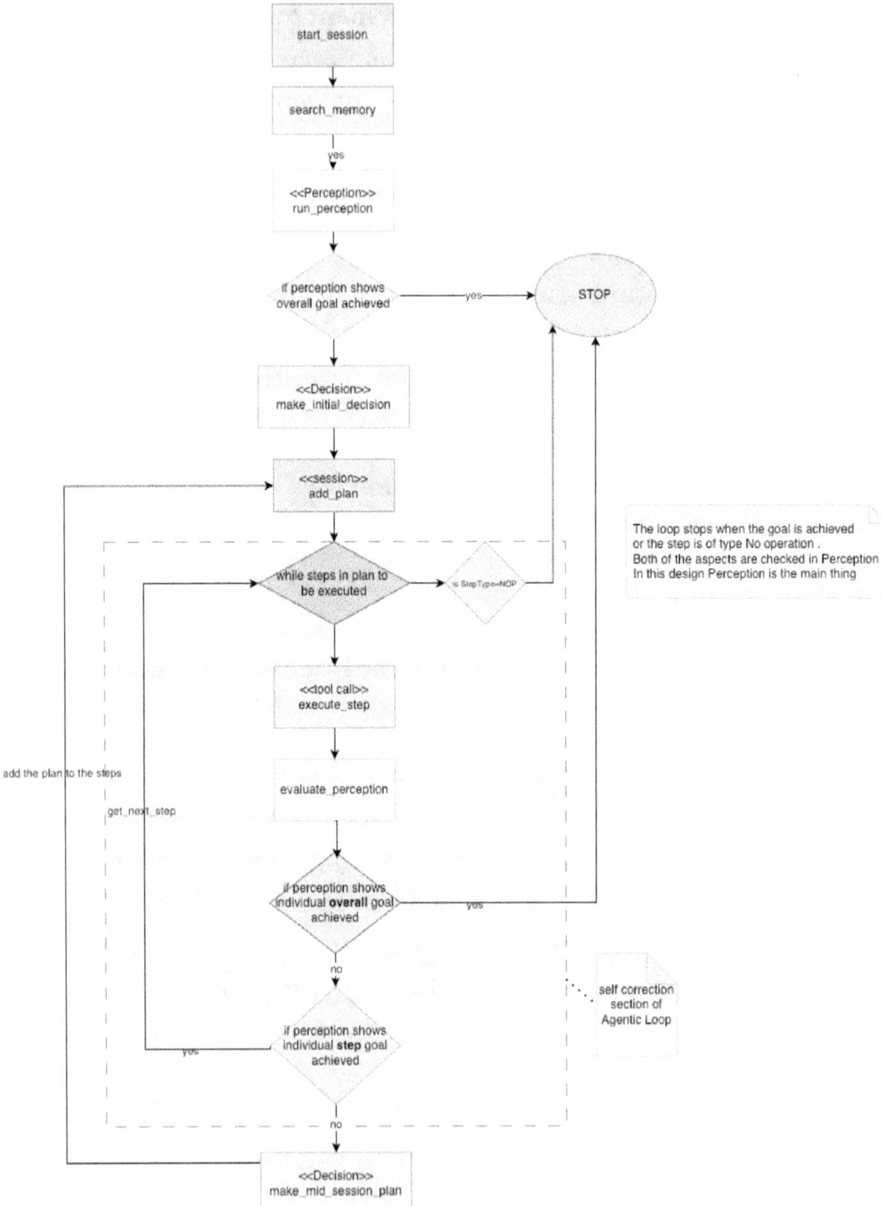

Figure: The Agentic Loop In PADM_FEED. Notice in the diagram how the loop between Perception and Decision forms a small circular pathway, a self-correcting cycle that refines each step in real time.

Step-by-Step Flow of the PADM_FEED Agentic Loop

1. Session and Memory Initialization

The process begins with two key components of state management:

- **Session Object (Short-Term Memory):**

  This acts as the shared workspace storing intermediate messages, temporary results, and context passed between **Perception** and **Decision** during a single run.

- **Long-Term Memory (Vector DB):**

  Once a run is complete, important insights are stored in a vector database for future reference. This ensures the agent doesn't start from scratch each time but learns from prior experiences.

2. Initial Perception

The loop begins by invoking **Perception** in its *Initial Mode*. Using the **user query** and available data from **Memory**, it performs an initial assessment to identify key entities, intent, and context.

- If Perception determines that the user's goal has *already been met*, meaning it successfully retrieved the result directly from memory, it immediately signals to **halt execution**.
- If not, the system proceeds to planning.

3. Initial Decision and Plan Creation

The **Decision module** is called next. Based on Perception's analysis, it generates an **initial structured plan**—a sequence of logical steps that together will accomplish the user's goal.

Each step may correspond to a function call, data retrieval, or reasoning operation. This plan is then stored in the **session object**, which keeps track of progress and results.

4. Execution Loop Begins

The **Agentic Loop** now enters its main execution cycle. Each step in the plan is processed one by one, and the loop continues until all steps are completed or the goal is achieved.

For each iteration:

- The system checks whether the step is a **no-op** (no operation) or an **actionable step**.
    - If it's a **no-op**, the system can safely skip execution and move ahead.
    - If it's **actionable**, the step is handed over to the **Action module**, which executes the function call or code block.

5. Post-Execution Reflection (Perception Feedback)

Once the Action module completes a step, **Perception** is called again to **evaluate the outcome**.

It checks:

- Whether the output contributes meaningfully toward the overall goal.
- Whether the output deviates from the expected result.
- And whether the *goal has now been achieved.*

Depending on this evaluation:

- If the **goal is achieved**, the loop exits successfully.
- If the **step output is valid but incomplete**, the loop proceeds to the next step.
- If the **output deviates or fails**, Perception signals **Decision** to intervene.

6. Dynamic Replanning (Feedback Mode)

When a step fails or drifts off course, the **Decision module** is reactivated but only to fix the specific issue.

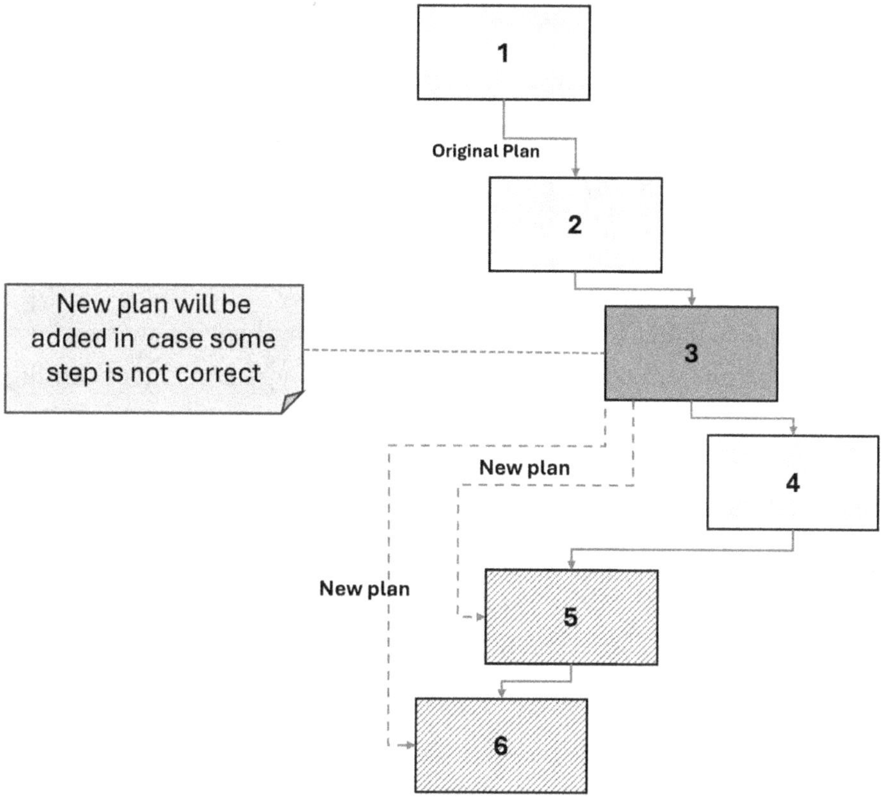

Figure: *The cross in the 4R radar indicates that the framework has limited reliability in its outputs. Similarly, the Agentic Traits radar shows that the system struggles to demonstrate strong, consistent cognitive reasoning.*

It generates **alternative steps** or modified function calls to correct the error, without discarding prior progress. These new steps are added to the existing plan in **LIFO (Last-In, First-Out)** order, allowing the system to immediately address the most recent issue before resuming the broader sequence.

This localized correction mechanism is what gives PADM_FEED its flexibility and resilience.

7. Loop Exit and Safeguards

The loop continues until:

- All steps are completed successfully,
- The **goal is confirmed as achieved**, or
- The **MAX_TRY** limit is reached (a safeguard to control excessive LLM calls).

At the end of execution, the **Memory** is updated with new learnings, outcomes, and context enriching the agent's long-term understanding for future runs.

Illustration

Lets see how Perception, Decision, Memory will play their role in this approach. I have taken the example similar to PADM_FUNCT to be able to understand the difference in the two approaches better:

User Prompt: *Find the ASCII values of characters in BHARAT and then return sum of exponentials of those values*

```
⭐ All of the following happens in a Agent Loop
checking memory : Searching Recent Conversation History. This is the vectorDb
search

🔍 Found 10 JSON file(s) in 'memory/session_logs'
✅ d20ed0a3-f506-4734-ba47-23fc06851e6a.json: 1 matching entries
✅ Extracted: what is the exponential of the character → The exponential sum of
the ASCII values
✅ 673b5bea-bd8f-4aa3-a0f6-43cdc99533bb.json: 1 matching entries
✅ Extracted: what is the sum of the number 3 and 4 → The sum of 3 and 4 is 7.
✅ 1bd5fc5f-1001-4b26-a7ab-787381b9ae48.json: 1 matching entries
✅ Extracted: Find the ASCII values of characters in I → The final result of the
calculation is 7
✅ fd14f7cd-81fb-4691-a430-89d59751e6d0.json: 1 matching entries
📦 Total usable memory entries collected: 6

⭐ results after accessing the stored memory from previous runs. It seems there was
a similar query but it was for "INDIA". This time the word is "BHARAT"
🎯 Top Matches:

[1] File: fd14f7cd-81fb-4691-a430-89d59751e6d0.json
Query: Find the ASCII values of characters in INDIA and then return sum of
exponentials of those values
Result Requirement: Final numerical result of the calculation.
Summary: The final result of the calculation is 7.599822246093079e+33.

[2] File: 673b5bea-bd8f-4aa3-a0f6-43cdc99533bb.json
Query: what is the exponential of the characters in INDIA
Result Requirement: The exponential sum of the ASCII values of the letters in
'INDIA'.
Summary: The exponential sum of the ASCII values for the string 'INDIA' is
7.599822246093079e+33.

[3] File: 1bd5fc5f-1001-4b26-a7ab-787381b9ae48.json
Query: what is the sum of the number 3 and 4
Result Requirement: The sum of 3 and 4
Summary: The sum of 3 and 4 is 7.
```

```
calling the initial perception layer with memory and the user query. Notice the
reasoning section where the Perception output clearly says what has happened till
now and how to proceed further

[Perception Result]:
{
  "entities": [
    "BHARAT",
    "ASCII values",
    "sum of exponentials"
  ],
  "result_requirement": "Final numerical result of the calculation.",
  "original_goal_achieved": false,
  "confidence": "0.9",
  "reasoning": "The user is asking for a calculation that can be done by extracting
the ASCII values and calculating the sum of their exponentials. This is similar to
previous queries in memory, so I will proceed with the calculation directly.",
  "local_goal_achieved": true,
  "local_reasoning": "The request is clear, and the necessary steps are understood.
The problem is well-defined.",
  "last_tooluse_summary": "Not applicable",
  "solution_summary": "Not ready yet"
}

session is created. This act like a short term memory only restricted to this
particular run

✅ Session stored:
memory/session_logs/2025/07/21/3db5805d-90f8-4efb-8df3-7f2de26e6497.json
✍ Session live-updated.

Decision Step: this is where the initial planning will happen. It will create a
3 step plan as per the prompt

[Decision Plan Text: V1]:
the name of the function has been identified correctly with the help of the tool
list
  Step 0: Convert the string 'BHARAT' to a list of ASCII values using
strings_to_chars_to_int tool.
  Step 1: Calculate the exponential sum of the ASCII values using
int_list_to_exponential_sum tool.
  Step 2: Return the final result.

Agent will start the execution of the step 0

[Step 0] Convert the string 'BHARAT' to a list of ASCII values using
strings_to_chars_to_int tool.
```

```
-------------------------------------------------
[EXECUTING CODE]
👉 This is the mcp call for the function strings_to_chars_to_int
 result = strings_to_chars_to_int('BHARAT')
return result

👉Now calling the Perception to verify the results. In this particular design
Perception has a major role to play. It is performing the self reflection and
understanding if the result so far is as per the user prompt or it has deviated
away

[Perception Result]:
{
  "entities": [
    "[66, 72, 65, 82, 65, 84]",
    "ASCII values"
  ],
  "result_requirement": "Exponential sum of the ASCII values",
  "original_goal_achieved": false,
  "confidence": "0.9",
  "reasoning": "The step successfully converted the input string to a list of ASCII
values. This is a necessary step towards calculating the exponential sum. The
original goal is not yet achieved, as the exponential sum still needs to be
calculated.",
  "local_goal_achieved": true, 👉 Reasoning part tells that the step goal was met
  "local_reasoning": "The string 'BHARAT' was correctly converted to its ASCII
representation [66, 72, 65, 82, 65, 84]. This result is now ready for the next
step, which will calculate the exponential sum.",
  "last_tooluse_summary": "strings_to_chars_to_int tool success", 👉 this is
important to make sure that the decision don't keep planning for the same step
again and again
  "solution_summary": "Not ready yet" 👉 summary will be ready only when the
complete solution has been achieved
}

👉 update the session.. Store in the memory. This help in tracking what has been
done till now

✅ Session stored:
memory/session_logs/2025/07/21/3db5805d-90f8-4efb-8df3-7f2de26e6497.json
📝 Session live-updated.

👉 Now back to the decision step and now execute the step1
[Decision Plan Text: V2]:
  Step 0: Convert the string 'BHARAT' to a list of ASCII values using
strings_to_chars_to_int tool.
  Step 1: Calculate the exponential sum of the ASCII values using
```

```
int_list_to_exponential_sum tool.
  Step 2: Return the final result.

👉 Agent will start the execution of the step1
[Step 1] Calculate the exponential sum of the ASCII values [66, 72, 65, 82, 65, 84]
using int_list_to_exponential_sum tool.
--------------------------------------------------
[EXECUTING CODE]
👉 calling mcp function call int_list_to_exponential_sum
result = int_list_to_exponential_sum([66, 72, 65, 82, 65, 84])
return result

👉 again recheck the obtained result at this step using perception
[Perception Result]:
{
  "entities": [
    "3.4344956851009924e+36"
  ],
  "result_requirement": "Final result of exponential sum calculation",
  "original_goal_achieved": true,
  "confidence": "1.0",
  "reasoning": "The final step is completed, providing the exponential sum, which
is the final answer to the user's implicit query. Since the current plan consists
of all steps, this step achieved the original goal.", 👉 reasoning states that the
overall goal has been achieved
  "local_goal_achieved": true,
  "local_reasoning": "The int_list_to_exponential_sum tool successfully computed
the exponential sum, which is the intended result of the step.",
  "last_tooluse_summary": "int_list_to_exponential_sum: success",
  "solution_summary": "The exponential sum of the ASCII values of the characters in
'BHARAT' is 3.4344956851009924e+36." 👉 since the overall goal has been met the
summary has been produced
}

👉 session updated
✅ Goal achieved.
✅ Session stored:
memory/session_logs/2025/07/21/3db5805d-90f8-4efb-8df3-7f2de26e6497.json
🖊 Session live-updated.
● Agent: The exponential sum of the ASCII values of the characters in 'BHARAT' is
3.4344956851009924e+36.
```

We can observe that the agent validates its progress at every step, continuously checking whether it is moving in the right direction. While this approach requires more iterations than the PADM_FUNCT method, it results in greater confidence and clarity in the agent's reasoning and evaluation. This step-by-step verification allows the agent to correct the course early rather than committing to a flawed plan. With that in mind, let us now revisit the earlier example where PADM_FUNCT took an incorrect path and was unable to recover, highlighting the trade-off between efficiency and adaptability.

Comparing PADM_FEED and PADM_FUNCT

Lets now see how PADM_FEED will keep track of the progress while solving the same problem which PADM_FUNCT struggled to solve.

"Find the sum of the log value of 5 and the log value of 8."

Perception and **Decision** layers in PADM_FEED work more intelligently through feedback driven reasoning.

In **PADM_FEED**, the process is much more thoughtful. The **Perception module** first analyzes the query deeply identifying not just entities but also relationships, dependencies, and reasoning steps.

Let's break it down:

1. Perception identifies key entities and operations:
    - Entities: log value of 5, log value of 8
    - Operations: log, sum
    - Relationships: "Take log of 5 and 8, then add the results."
2. Checks goal completion:
    - Perception determines whether the goal ("sum of the logs") has already been achieved in previous runs.
    - If yes, it halts execution immediately.
    - If not, it sets the stage for Decision to create a plan.
3. Provides reasoning context:
    - Perception outputs a reasoning field describing *why* it interpreted the problem this way.
    - Example: *"To find the sum of log values, first compute log(5), then log(8), and finally add the two results."*
4. Assesses confidence:
    - It assigns a confidence score (e.g., 0.92) to indicate how certain it is about this interpretation. This helps the Decision layer gauge how aggressively it can proceed.

Cleaner, More Informed Decisioning

Now, when **Decision** receives this structured Perception output, it no longer starts from a blank slate.

It has a clear understanding of:

- **What needs to be done** (the identified entities and operations),
- **Why it needs to be done** (the reasoning behind the query),
- **Whether it's already achieved** (goal flags), and
- **How confident the Perception is** in its assessment.

```
[Perception Result]:
{
  "entities": [
    "log value of 5",
    "log value of 8"
  ],
  "result_requirement": "The sum of the log value of 5 and the log value of 8.",
  "original_goal_achieved": false,
  "confidence": "0.9",
  "reasoning": "The user wants to calculate the sum of two logarithmic values. This
requires calculating the individual log values first and then summing them. This
can be achieved using a calculator tool or a Python execution tool.",
  "local_goal_achieved": false,
  "local_reasoning": "The initial query needs to be processed to calculate the
final result.",
  "last_tooluse_summary": "Not ready yet",
  "solution_summary": "Not ready yet"
}
  session which acts as the short term memory

  Session stored:
memory/session_logs/2025/07/25/a7fe9035-5b2f-42a2-933e-e42848d35729.json
  Session live-updated.

 Decision comes up with the 3 step plan which is basically the logical steps of
solving the problem even by a human. Since Decision is encouraged to think clearly
the approach identified is correct even in the first go
[Decision Plan Text: V1]:
  Step 0: Calculate the natural logarithm of 5 and 8 using the available
mathematical functions.
  Step 1: Sum the calculated logarithms from the previous step.
  Step 2: Present the final sum as the answer.

 First Step is being executed which will find the log values of 5 and 8
[Step 0] Calculate the natural logarithm of 5 and 8 and store them for the next
step.
```

```
----------------------------------------------------
[EXECUTING CODE]
 import math
log_5 = math.log(5)
log_8 = math.log(8)
return log_5, log_8

 Perception is called to evaluate the result . This is where it will now check if
the answer to the last step is leading towards the overall goal or going in a
different direction. It will also register the last tool run status as success just
to indicate that this tool was the correct choice.
[Perception Result]:
{
  "entities": [
    "1.6094379124341003",
    "2.0794415416798357"
  ],
  "result_requirement": "The sum of the natural logarithm of 5 and 8.",
  "original_goal_achieved": false,
  "confidence": "1.0",
  "reasoning": "This step provides the natural logarithms of 5 and 8, which are
necessary to calculate their sum, as requested in the original query. The agent is
closer to solving the query.",
  "local_goal_achieved": true,
  "local_reasoning": "The mathematical functions were successfully used to compute
the natural logarithms of 5 and 8.",
  "last_tooluse_summary": "Successful calculation of logarithms",
  "solution_summary": "Not ready yet"
}

 session will register this evaluation as the ongoing execution log
 Session stored:
memory/session_logs/2025/07/25/a7fe9035-5b2f-42a2-933e-e42848d35729.json
 Session live-updated.

 no change in the Decision plan and the next step is picked up
[Decision Plan Text: V2]:
  Step 0: Calculate the natural logarithm of 5 and 8 using the available
mathematical functions.
  Step 1: Sum the calculated logarithms from the previous step.
  Step 2: Present the final sum as the answer.

[Step 1] Sum the logarithms obtained in the previous step.
----------------------------------------------------
[EXECUTING CODE]
 import math
log_5 = 1.6094379124341003
```

```
log_8 = 2.0794415416798357
result = log_5 + log_8
return result
👉 The result is evaluated by the Perception and it concludes that the goal has
been reached by the previous step
[Perception Result]:
{
  "entities": [
    "3.688879454113936"
  ],
  "result_requirement": "The sum of the natural logarithms of 5 and 8.",
  "original_goal_achieved": true,
  "confidence": "1.0",
  "reasoning": "The result represents the sum of the natural logarithms of 5 and 8,
thus achieving the original goal.",
  "local_goal_achieved": true,
  "local_reasoning": "The step successfully computed and presented the final sum.",
  "last_tooluse_summary": "Calculator tool - success",
  "solution_summary": "The sum of the natural logarithms of 5 and 8 is
3.688879454113936."
}
👉 Session is updated
✅ Session stored:
memory/session_logs/2025/07/25/a7fe9035-5b2f-42a2-933e-e42848d35729.json
📝 Session live-updated.

✅ Goal achieved.
✅ Session stored:
memory/session_logs/2025/07/25/a7fe9035-5b2f-42a2-933e-e42848d35729.json
📝 Session live-updated.
👉 execution is stopped
🔵 Agent: The sum of the natural logarithms of 5 and 8 is 3.688879454113936.
```

This execution is noticeably cleaner and follows a well-defined reasoning and feedback loop. Compared to the earlier approach, which failed to converge within the allowed number of attempts, this method demonstrates greater clarity, control, and robustness in reaching the final answer.

Pros and Cons of the PADM_FEED Approach

Like all architectures, **PADM_FEED** comes with its own trade-offs. It solves many of the reliability and reasoning issues found in earlier designs like **PADM** and **PADM_FUNCT**, but it also introduces new challenges particularly around cost and speed.

The main difference now is that the agent doesn't just *plan*, it also *reflects*. That reflection adds intelligence, but it also adds overhead. Each course correction requires another LLM call, and because LLMs are computationally expensive and relatively slow, the architecture inherits those limitations.

That said, the **checks and balances** built into PADM_FEED greatly reduce the chances of the agent wandering endlessly in the wrong direction. If a wrong tool is chosen or a step fails, the system now corrects itself mid-loop rather than starting over. The risk of infinite execution remains, as with any self-correcting system, but it can be controlled through **forced termination** after a set number of retries.

Pros of PADM_FEED

- **Increased Accuracy Through Feedback Loops**

  The introduction of self-evaluation dramatically improves the reliability of outcomes. If a suboptimal tool or function is chosen, the feedback mechanism detects the issue and prompts a correction leading to higher accuracy and consistency in results.

- **Lower Risk of Resource Wastage**

  Because each action is verified before proceeding, the agent is less likely to pursue a faulty path for too long. Even though LLM calls are expensive, the overall cost of *wrong* executions is reduced.

- **Fail-Safe Mechanism**

  The architecture includes configurable safeguards, such as a **MAX_TRY** limit, to prevent infinite loops. This ensures that even if reasoning diverges, the system can gracefully exit rather than consuming unbounded resources.

- **Self-Corrective Behavior**

  The biggest conceptual win is that PADM_FEED introduces a kind of "situational awareness." The agent can now *notice when it's wrong* and attempt to fix itself, rather than blindly continuing. This makes it far more aligned with human-style reasoning and decision-making.

Cons of PADM_FEED

- **High Computational Cost**

  PADM_FEED uses LLMs not just for planning but also for verification and feedback. This multiplies the number of calls required per task. In large-scale systems, this can become prohibitively expensive.

- **Slow Execution**

  Because each iteration involves multiple LLM evaluations, the architecture is slower by design. The benefit of self-correction comes at the expense of responsiveness.

- **LLM Dependency**

  The overall performance still depends heavily on the quality of the underlying language model.A weaker model may produce poor feedback loops, leading to degraded accuracy or unstable behavior.

- **Potential Infinite Execution**

  Despite safeguards, there's always a risk of the agent falling into an endless loop of self-correction particularly when the reasoning or feedback logic is ambiguous.

While this can be mitigated through iteration limits, it remains a structural limitation of feedback-driven systems.

Evaluating PADM_FEED Through the Lens of the 4R's

As we've seen throughout this book, every agentic design can be measured not only by how well it performs technically but also by how it balances the broader trade-offs that define practical, responsible AI systems.

To assess **PADM_FEED**, we'll look at it through the lens of the **4R's—Reach, Reliability, Restraint, and Respect**—each corresponding to a critical dimension of scalability, consistency, cost efficiency, and privacy.

1. Reach

PADM_FEED introduces a more intelligent and adaptive feedback loop, allowing agents to correct themselves mid-execution rather than restarting from scratch. From a scalability standpoint, this makes the architecture **more resilient but less lightweight**.

While the system scales well in reasoning quality (handling complex, multi-step tasks with higher success rates), it comes at the cost of **computational scalability** (lots of steps are needed to run to compute).

Because the architecture depends on multiple LLM calls for reasoning and verification, horizontal scaling becomes expensive, both in terms of compute and time. In production environments, this may require hybrid approaches of using lighter models for step verification and stronger models only for reasoning-heavy steps to balance Reach and cost.

Verdict: PADM_FEED improves *cognitive reach* (the ability to handle complex queries) but compromises on *operational reach* (the number of queries it can handle efficiently at scale).

2. Reliability

This is where **PADM_FEED** truly shines. By introducing structured reflection and feedback at every stage, the design significantly improves the **consistency** and **accuracy** of outcomes.

Earlier systems like **PADM** or **PADM_FUNCT** could easily drift off course, executing wrong tool calls or looping indefinitely without correction.

PADM_FEED's feedback-driven refinement ensures that each step is evaluated for logical consistency and goal alignment before moving forward. This drastically reduces the chances of hallucination, incorrect tool usage, and silent failures.

Verdict: *High reliability through structured reflection. The system is slower, but far more dependable and auditable in its decision-making.*

3. Restraint

Restraint refers to the **discipline of resource usage** that optimizes for efficiency, not just accuracy.

Here, **PADM_FEED** inherits one of the biggest challenges of feedback-heavy architectures: **cost inefficiency**.

Because LLMs are used not just to reason and plan but also to validate each step, the number of calls, and therefore, the cost multiplies quickly. While the system wastes fewer tokens on wrong paths, it still pays a premium for intelligence.

The design also runs slower due to sequential feedback cycles, which can be problematic for real-time or latency-sensitive use cases.

Verdict: *High reasoning efficiency, low computational efficiency. PADM_FEED demonstrates restraint in logic, but not yet in cost.*

4. Respect

Respect, in this context, speaks to **data governance**, **transparency**, and **trust**.

PADM_FEED maintains strong control boundaries by ensuring that **all data access happens through defined MCP tools** rather than direct queries. This architectural discipline ensures better auditability, reduced data leakage risk, and clear accountability for every action taken by the agent.

However, because the design depends heavily on LLMs for reasoning and validation, **data exposure risk** remains tied to model deployment choices. A self-hosted or hybrid model setup would mitigate this risk and strengthen the Respect dimension further.

Verdict: *High privacy assurance through MCP-based data access and traceable reasoning; dependent on deployment choices for full compliance.*

Summary

4R Principle	Focus Area	PADM_FEED Performance	Remarks
Reach	Scalability & Adaptability	◍ Moderate	Excellent at reasoning-rich scaling; costly for large-scale deployments
Reliability	Consistency & Accuracy	○ High	Feedback loops and reasoning validation greatly improve correctness
Restraint	Cost & Efficiency	● Low	Frequent LLM calls slow execution and raise costs
Respect	Privacy & Control	○ High	MCP tool boundary preserves security and traceability

Design Evolution Summary: Comparing PADM, PADM_FUNCT, and PADM_FEED

Over the last few chapters, we've seen the agent evolve from a simple, linear executor (PADM) to a more intelligent planner (PADM_FUNCT) and finally into a self-reflective, feedback-driven system (PADM_FEED). Each stage represents a distinct trade-off between scalability, reliability, efficiency, and control—the four pillars of our 4R framework.

The table below summarizes this journey:

Dimension (4R)	PADM	PADM_FUNCT	PADM_FEED
Reach	● **Basic scalability** Each loop runs step by step, leading to slow performance. Handles simple queries effectively but struggles with complex reasoning	◍ **Improved scalability** Due to one-shot plan generation; handles moderately complex tasks faster but lacks adaptability	◍ **Adaptive scalability** Through feedback loops; handles complex, multi-step reasoning well, though at higher computational cost
Reliability	● ***Low*** Non-deterministic outcomes, prone to tool misfires and hallucinations. No error correction mechanism.	◍ **Moderate** Executes structured plans reliably, but errors in planning cause total restarts	○ **High** Feedback loops validate and correct results step-by-step, reducing hallucinations and improving convergence
Restraint	● **Inefficient**; multiple sequential LLM calls without validation lead to wasted compute	◍ **More efficient than PADM** due to reduced LLM calls, but still costly for complex queries	● **Costly;** multiple feedback and validation steps increase LLM usage. However, it reduces long-term waste through fewer failed runs.

Dimension (4R)	PADM	PADM_FUNCT	PADM_FEED
Respect	◯ **High;** uses MCP-based tool calling for structured data access.	◯ **High;** uses MCP-based tool calling for structured data access.	◯ **High;** strict tool boundaries, transparent reasoning, and strong traceability make it enterprise-friendly and compliant

Following Radar diagram pictographically depicts the above discussion

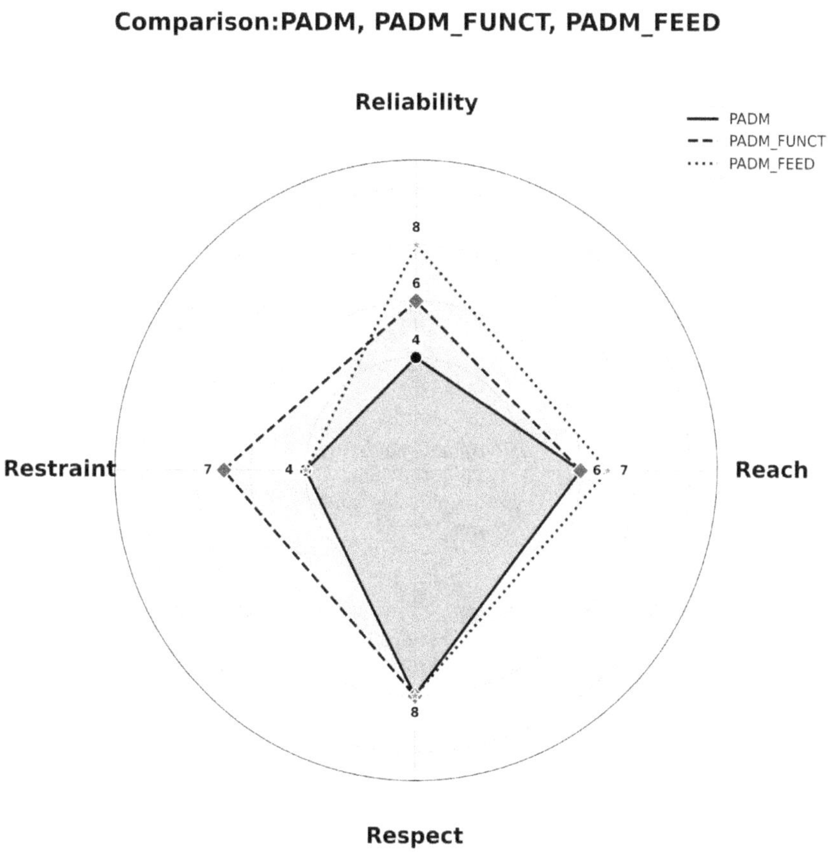

Figure: PADM_FEED clearly lags in the Restraint while Scores most in the Reliability

At a Glance: The Evolution of Intelligence

This table summarizes some of the key features of the three PADM architectures we have seen so far.

Architecture	Key Innovation	Core Weakness	Ideal Use Case
PADM	Introduced the 4-layer agent loop (Perception–Decision–Memory–Action)	Lacks reasoning and feedback; high error rate	Simple workflows and proof-of-concept demos
PADM_ FUNCT	Combined multi-step reasoning into one executable plan; faster and cleaner.	No reflection; any error requires a full restart.	Medium-complexity tasks where speed matters more than precision
PADM_ FEED	Added self-correction through feedback-driven Perception and Decision loops.	Expensive and slower; depends heavily on LLM strength.	High-stakes, reasoning-intensive tasks demanding accuracy and adaptability

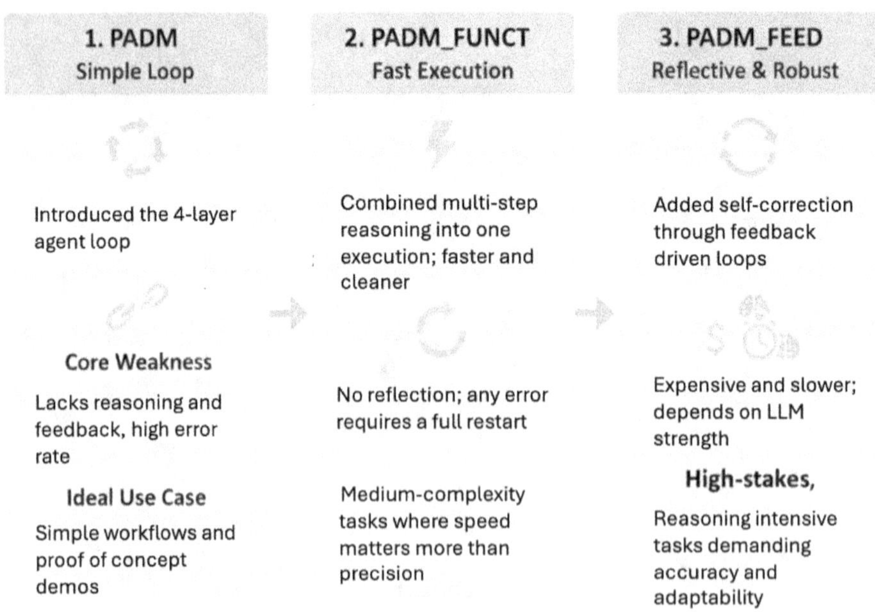

Figure: Evolving Architectures: From Simple Loops to Reflective Systems. Comparing PADM, PADM_FUNCT, PADM_FEED

Design Decisions and Infrastructure

The PADM_FEED architecture builds upon the foundation laid by earlier designs like PADM_FUNCT, but it transforms the agent from a task executor into a *self-correcting cognitive system*. While many infrastructural components remain consistent, the interaction patterns between them evolve significantly due to the introduction of feedback-driven reasoning.

Below are the key architectural choices embedded in this design:

Infrastructure

The framework remains model-agnostic, capable of operating across a wide range of language models from open-source, self-hosted options like *phi-4 on Ollama* to enterprise-grade APIs such as *Gemini*, *Claude*, or *GPT-5*.

However, because PADM_FEED depends heavily on nuanced reasoning and self-reflection, the quality of the LLM directly determines the system's stability and convergence. Lighter models may struggle with consistency in feedback interpretation, often requiring multiple correction cycles. Hence, for production-grade deployments, higher-end reasoning models are typically preferred.

Query Handling

All data access continues to be routed through the MCP server, maintaining a strict separation between reasoning and data retrieval.

The LLM's job is not to generate raw SQL but to select the appropriate MCP tools that can fetch the required data safely and efficiently.

This ensures:

- Clean modularity between logic and execution
- Strong governance of data access
- Reduced risk of query-based hallucinations

What's new in PADM_FEED is that the Perception layer now validates whether the data retrieved actually aligns with the user's goal, adding a layer of reflection between data access and reasoning.

LLM Role

This is where PADM_FEED diverges most meaningfully from its predecessors.

The LLM is no longer a single-shot planner, it's now a multi-role cognitive engine that:

- Perceives the user's intent and the evolving task context.
- Plans a structured execution sequence via the Decision module.
- Reflects on each step's outcome to determine alignment with the overall goal.
- Refines subsequent steps based on internal reasoning and feedback from previous outputs.

In essence, the LLM acts not just as the *planner and narrator*, but also as the *critic and teacher* of its own work. This reflexive loop transforms it from a static reasoning tool into an adaptive problem solver capable of improving within a session.

Output Modalities

The system continues to support diverse output formats like structured tables, analytical summaries, and expressive natural-language explanations.

However, PADM_FEED adds one subtle but important layer: **self-explanatory outputs**.

Every final output is accompanied by a reasoning trace, which is a short narrative of *why* the agent took certain steps and *how* it validated the results.

```
[Perception Result]:
{
  "entities": [
    "3.688879454113936"
  ],
  "result_requirement": "The sum of the natural logarithms of 5 and 8.",
  "original_goal_achieved": true,
  "confidence": "1.0",
  "reasoning": "The result represents the sum of the natural logarithms of
5 and 8, thus achieving the original goal.",
  "local_goal_achieved": true,
  "local_reasoning": "The step successfully computed and presented the
final sum.",
  "last_tooluse_summary": "Calculator tool - success",
  "solution_summary": "The sum of the natural logarithms of 5 and 8 is
3.688879454113936."
}
```

This enhances interpretability and trust, particularly in enterprise contexts where understanding *why* an answer was produced is as critical as the answer itself.

From POC to Production: Shortcomings of PADM_FEED

The true value of any architecture isn't proven in the lab, it's tested in the real world. A proof of concept (POC) can be impressive on paper, but for an AI system to deliver sustainable business value, it must scale efficiently, predictably, and cost-effectively.

While PADM_FEED represents a major evolution in reasoning quality and reliability, several challenges emerge as soon as we begin thinking about production-scale deployment.

1. High Cost

Despite its self-corrective strengths, PADM_FEED becomes prohibitively expensive when deployed at scale. Each feedback cycle between the Perception and Decision modules triggers additional LLM calls for reasoning, verification, and reflection.

In practice, a single user query can result in three to four LLM calls and sometimes more if a step fails and must be revised. While this structure ensures accuracy and robustness, it also introduces a high per-query cost, which quickly multiplies across millions of transactions.

In a production setup, say, spanning millions of outlets, product SKUs, or dashboards, the economics simply don't hold up without major optimization.

2. Cost Unpredictability Due to Dynamic Planning

One of PADM_FEED's greatest strengths is its ability to re-plan dynamically based on feedback. However, it also becomes one of its biggest challenges in production.

Because the Decision module can generate new steps *on the fly*, it's impossible to predict in advance how many LLM calls a single query will require. Some tasks may finish in two calls, while others might loop through five or six iterations before converging.

This variability in cost and latency makes it difficult to estimate, budget, or cap resource consumption, posing a major hurdle for enterprise environments that demand predictable performance.

3. Scalability Bottleneck for Large Deployments

As the number of users or data entities grows, the combined latency of repeated LLM reflection loops becomes a severe bottleneck.

For instance, consider deploying this architecture across 10 million retail outlets, each generating data for hundreds of SKUs. Even with aggressive caching, batching, or parallelization, the cumulative runtime and compute cost would make real-time responsiveness impractical.

This isn't a failure of the design. It's a limitation of the current generation of LLM-based feedback systems, which prioritize accuracy and autonomy over speed.

4. Inherent Limitations in Agentic Architectures

These challenges are not unique to PADM_FEED. They reflect a broader reality of agentic AI systems that depend heavily on language models for reasoning and reflection.

Every feedback-driven architecture faces the same trade-off: *you gain intelligence, but you pay for it in cost and latency.*

Until LLMs become significantly faster and cheaper or until reasoning can be partially offloaded to lighter models or cached frameworks, agentic systems like PADM_FEED will remain better suited for high-value, low-frequency workflows rather than continuous, large-scale automation.

5. Practical Strength: Structured Feedback and Reliable Convergence

Despite these limitations, PADM_FEED excels where it matters most for experimentation and prototyping.

Its structured approach and feedback-driven reasoning ensure that results are found quickly and effectively, often with fewer failed runs compared to previous architectures.

In smaller-scale implementations, such as decision-support dashboards, planning assistants, or internal analytics agents, PADM_FEED provides excellent reliability and explainability, even if it sacrifices raw speed.

In Summary

PADM_FEED represents a milestone in cognitive agent design: a system that thinks before it acts and reflects before it decides again. However, this intelligence comes with a cost. At scale, the feedback-heavy architecture introduces economic and operational constraints that make it challenging to adopt widely in production today. As models continue to evolve and optimization techniques mature, the goal will be to retain PADM_FEED's reasoning depth while bringing its efficiency closer to production-grade expectations.

That journey—from reflection to real-world resilience—is where the next generation of agentic systems will be born.

Agentic Test: Is This Architecture Truly Agentic?

Let's now examine **PADM_FEED** through the lens of the three defining pillars of agentic intelligence—**Generation, Action, and Reflection**—to see how closely this design aligns with true agentic behavior.

1. Generative Aspect

PADM_FEED is deeply LLM-centric. Every aspect of the user's request from interpreting intent to generating the final execution plan is guided by the language model's reasoning ability.

Here, **Perception** and **Decision** work hand-in-hand:

- *Perception* decodes the user's goal, identifies entities, and reasons about the relationships between them.
- *Decision* translates that understanding into a structured plan of action consisting of a sequence of tool calls or code steps designed to achieve the goal.

Both modules are driven by carefully designed system prompts that shape their behavior and enforce discipline in reasoning. Unlike earlier designs, **PADM_FEED's self-corrective feedback loop** gives the LLM space to reflect and detect hallucinations, verify assumptions, and converge on more consistent solutions.

2. Action-Oriented Aspect

A true agent doesn't just plan; it acts. In **PADM_FEED**, the LLM autonomously invokes tools, makes data-driven decisions, and executes actions without human intervention or manual triggers.

The **Action** module becomes the executor of the LLM's intent, running the steps that the Decision module generates and feeding outcomes back to Perception for evaluation. This creates a complete **perception–action loop**, where the agent can:

- Identify what needs to be done.
- Execute the right tool at the right time.
- Evaluate the success or failure of that action and adapt accordingly.

This end-to-end autonomy marks the design as distinctly **agentic**, where the LLM doesn't just assist the process, it *owns* it

3. Planning & Reasoning Aspect

The third pillar—**Reasoning**—is where **PADM_FEED** truly advances beyond its predecessors. Here, the agent isn't limited to static decision-making; it reasons dynamically.

At each stage, it determines:

- **When** a tool should be executed.
- **Which** tool or method is most appropriate.
- **How** to validate the outcome before moving forward.

This reasoning process is anchored in the collaboration between **Perception** (which reflects and critiques) and **Decision** (which plans and adapts). Together, they form a feedback-driven reasoning engine capable of self-correction and incremental improvement.

In essence, the system doesn't just *run tasks,* it *thinks about how it's running them.*

Assessment Against Agentic Principles

Pillar	Description	Evaluation
Generative Aspect	The LLM understands user intent, decomposes complex queries, selects relevant tools, and constructs structured, well-formed function calls	◯ Strong orchestration from intent to execution

Action-Oriented Aspect	The LLM autonomously calls and manages tools, executing steps without external triggers or supervision	◯ Truly autonomous tool invocation and control
Planning & Reasoning Aspect	The system dynamically decides when and how to act, evaluates intermediate results, and refines execution paths using feedback	◯ Built-in reasoning, reflection, and adaptive control flow

Agentic Traits Comparison: PADM, PADM_FUNCT, PADM_FEED

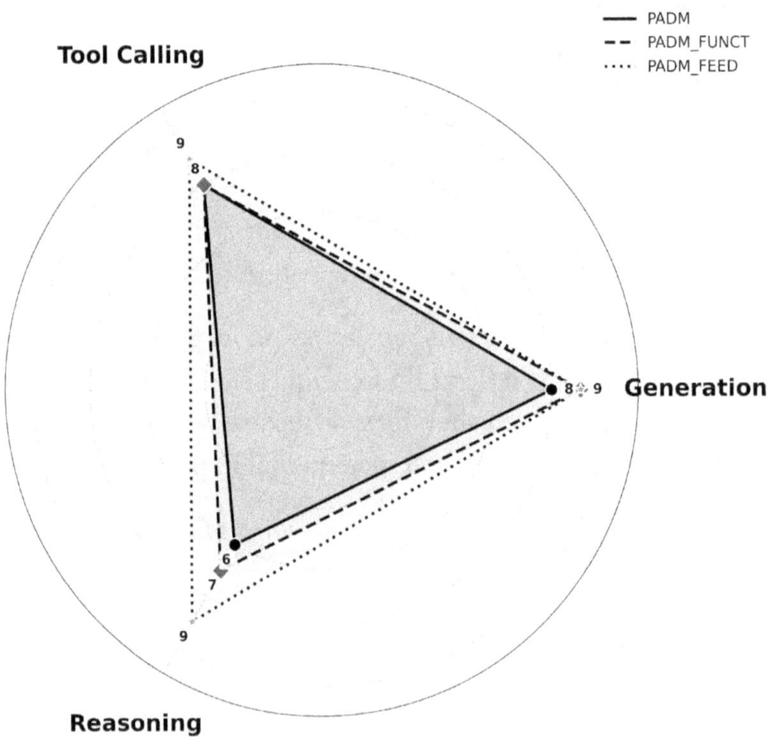

Figure: The radar chart compares the Agentic Traits across the three PADM architectures. The key differentiating trait is Reasoning, which reflects the system's ability to adapt when errors occur and to steer itself toward the correct output.

Conclusion

The **PADM_FEED** architecture marks a significant leap in the evolution of agentic systems, transforming them from simple executors of logic into reflective, self-correcting cognitive frameworks.

By tightly integrating **Perception**, **Decision**, and **Memory** within a feedback-driven control loop, PADM_FEED introduces a more *human-like* way of solving problems.

Each step is now reasoned through, validated, and refined before proceeding ensuring that the agent doesn't just act, but *thinks about its actions* in real time.

Unlike its predecessors, **PADM** and **PADM_FUNCT**, which operated linearly and lacked introspection, PADM_FEED creates a continuous dialogue between its components.

Perception reasons and assesses, **Decision** plans and adapts, and **Memory** preserves both context and learning across iterations. The result is an agent that can interpret intent, invoke tools autonomously, and dynamically adjust its course—all while maintaining awareness of the larger goal.

This feedback-rich design offers several tangible advantages:

- It enhances **accuracy** by catching and correcting reasoning errors mid-execution.
- It **reduces resource waste**, avoiding redundant computations and failed runs.
- And it **minimizes hallucinations**, grounding the agent's decisions in validated data and structured reasoning.

However, this sophistication comes with a cost. PADM_FEED's intelligence depends heavily on frequent **LLM calls** for perception, planning, reflection, and validation. These multiple reasoning cycles add **latency** and drive up **operational costs**, which limits the architecture's scalability in high-volume production environments. The dynamic, adaptive nature of planning also makes **cost prediction** difficult, challenging organizations that demand tight efficiency controls.

From an engineering standpoint, PADM_FEED proves that it is possible to build **agents that can think, act, and self-correct**, basically, the systems capable of autonomous reasoning loops that approach human cognitive patterns. But it also exposes the reality that such intelligence must be tempered with pragmatism.

To make architectures like this production-grade, the next evolution must focus on **optimization.** This involves reducing reasoning overhead, improving inference speed, and adopting **hybrid designs** that selectively apply LLM intelligence where it adds the most value.

In essence, **PADM_FEED** stands as both a breakthrough and a bridge and a powerful demonstration of what reflective cognition in AI can achieve today. It is also a reminder of the challenges that must be solved to make such intelligence scalable tomorrow.

CHAPTER 10

The GAP Advantage: Deterministic Agentic Systems at Scale

"Graphs don't just map data, they map the path to intelligence."

In the earlier chapters, we introduced the PADM family of architectures—systems designed to let an agent determine which function or tool to use in order to solve a task.

The goal was straightforward: build an agentic workflow where natural-language prompts could be interpreted, analyzed, and executed with minimal manual intervention. And in many cases, these systems performed well. The ability of an LLM to select tools, organize steps, and generate structured plans was encouraging and often effective.

However, as we expanded the scope and scale of these systems, certain limitations became more visible. We observed variability in outputs, higher operational costs due to repeated LLM calls, and occasional execution loops that affected reliability.

These issues do not undermine the potential of the architecture, but they do highlight the gap between promising prototypes and production-level dependability. When considering deployment at large scale, for instance, across millions of retail outlets producing high-volume daily transactions, consistency and cost-efficiency become essential requirements rather than optional refinements.

Rethinking the Agentic Ideal

So, how do we preserve the magic of autonomy while solving the problems of chaos and cost?

To address these limitations, we need to design a more **deterministic and structured approach** that keeps the intelligence of PADM but trades a bit of autonomy for stability, predictability, and efficiency.

This approach doesn't try to make the agent "more human." Instead, it makes the system *more practical*.

It's what we call a **pseudo-agentic architecture**. It is intelligent enough to reason through operations and dependencies, but grounded enough to remain fully predictable.

It may not talk back, improvise, or self-reflect like PADM_FEED, but it *delivers results consistently*, and at scale.

What Do We Want From a Pseudo-Agentic System?

To build this more deterministic design, we identified two critical capabilities, the non-negotiables for any realistic, scalable architecture:

1. **Ability to Execute Tools:**

   The system must be able to call the right function or tool autonomously (without human intermediary) and pass it the correct parameters in the right format.

2. **Ability to Know the Order of Operations (Dependencies):**

   It must understand *when* and *how* to run those tools. If one function's output (say, Func1) feeds into another (Func2), the agent should automatically detect and manage that dependency.

These two abilities form the backbone of the pseudo-agentic design. For the agent to execute any tool, MCP is the way to do so.

Function Landscape (Mapping the Tools to the Data)

In our dataset, every query ultimately revolves around two core entities: **SKUs** and **Outlets**. Together, they form the backbone of the entire analytical universe we've been exploring.

For each of these domains, the system leverages a set of **MCP-based functions (tools)** to extract, compute, and interpret different insights.

These functions act as the agent's hands and eyes within the structured world of data helping it answer questions like *"Which SKUs are selling fastest?"* or *"Which outlets are underperforming this month?"*

Below is a summary of the key functions used across both **SKU-level** and **Outlet-level** analyses.

Domain Entity	**Function/Tool**	**Purpose**
SKU	`get_most_selling_SKUs(input Data:OutletSpecificInput)->SkuListOutput`	This function will give out a list of SKUs that are most selling in a particular outlet
SKU	`get_slow_moving_SKUs(input Data:OutletSpecificInput)-> SkuListOutput`	This function will give out a list of SKUs that are not selling much in a particular outlet
Outlet	`get_struggling_outlets(input Data:UserSpecificInput)-> OutletListOutput`	Find out the list of outlets that are struggling for the given salesman

Domain Entity	Function/Tool	Purpose
Outlet	`get_improved_outlets(inputData:UserSpecificInput)->OutletListOutput`	Find out the list of outlets that have showed improvement

These tools return **filtered lists of SKUs or Outlets** based on specific conditions. For example, top-selling products, underperforming outlets, or items nearing expiry.

Once these filtered lists are retrieved, we can apply a set of **operations or transformations** on top of them. These operations typically relate to **sales performance metrics**, such as total sales amount or total quantity sold, allowing the system to move from simple filtering to deeper, more actionable analysis.

In essence, the tools help the agent *find what to look at*, while the operations help it *understand what's happening*

Operations	Purpose
`get_total_sales_for_SKUs(inputData:OutletSKUListInput) -> floatOutput`	Calculate the total sales for a given outlet across a specified list of SKUs
`get_total_qty_for_SKUs(inputData:OutletSKUListInput) -> intOutput`	Calculate the total qty for a given outlet across a specified list of SKUs
`get_total_sales_for_outlets(inputData:CombinedOutletInput) -> floatOutput`	Calculate the total sales of all the outlets that are visited by a specific user
`get_average_sales_for_outlets(inputData:CombinedOutletInput) -> floatOutput`	Calculate the average sales of all the outlets that are visited by a specific user

Most real-world queries aren't solved by a single function call. In practice, it's usually a **combination of domain-specific functions** and **operations** that need to work together to produce the final answer.

Take this example:

> *"Calculate the total sales and quantity for the most selling SKUs for outlet 75757."*

At first glance, it sounds like one simple request. But under the hood, this query can be decomposed into multiple steps, each handled by a different function:

```
get_most_selling_SKUs(inputData: OutletSpecificInput) → SkuListOutput
get_total_sales_for_SKUs()
get_total_qty_for_SKUs()
```

Here, the **domain function** viz. get_most_selling_SKUs, first identifies the key SKUs for a specific outlet.

Then the **operations** viz. get_total_sales_for_SKUs, get_total_qty_for_SKUs perform calculations on that filtered list.

Finally, the results from these operations are **merged into a single structured output**, summarizing both total sales and quantities.

This relationship between domain functions and operations can be visualized more clearly as a **function graph** where data flows from one function to the next, forming a chain of dependent computations that lead to the final result.

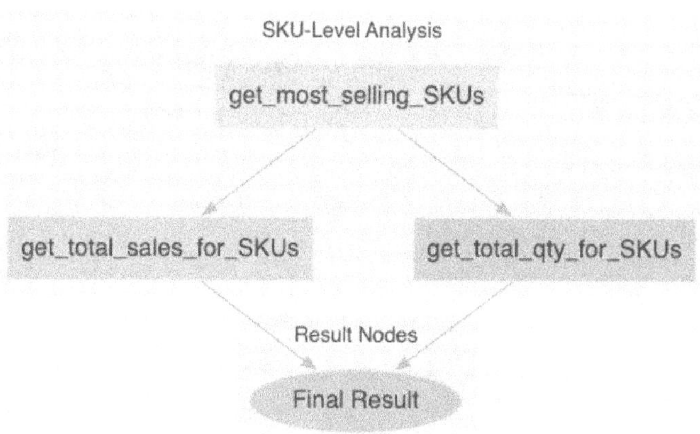

This graphical representation is not only intuitive for human readers, but also makes the system's logic explicitly visible. It shows how each function contributes to the overall outcome, which functions depend on upstream results, and how data is passed and transformed at every step. By structuring execution logic as a function graph, dependencies become transparent, data flow is easy to trace, and the path from input to final result can be understood at a glance.

These **graphs make complex calculations easier to visualize**, transforming what might otherwise look like a black box of function calls into a transparent, traceable sequence of steps.

They act as both a **blueprint for execution** and a **diagnostic tool**, helping developers and systems alike understand how the agent arrives at its answers.

Here is a much more complex graph:

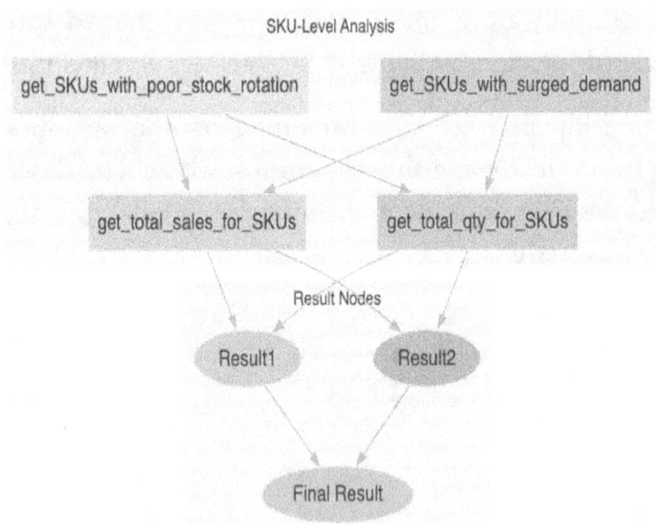

This is basically saying that we need to do the following:

```
1. Get_skus_with_poor_stock_roation
     a. get_total_sales_for_SKUs()
     b. get_total_qty_for_SKUs()
2. Get_SKUs_with_surged_demand
     a. get_total_sales_for_SKUs()
     b. get_total_qty_for_SKUs()
3. Finally combine the Results of each of the step 1 and step2
```

Now, imagine if we tried to express all of these steps directly in a single natural-language prompt.

It might look something like this:

```
"Calculate the total sales and quantity for the SKUs that showed poor stock rotation for outlet 75757. Then calculate the total sales and quantity for the SKUs that have shown a surge in demand for the same outlet. After that, find the most valuable outlets for the user 6382, and finally calculate the total sales for these outlets."
```

Even in this one example, you can see how quickly things become complicated. To a human reader, the sequence of actions is fairly clear. Each step depends on the previous one, and the order matters.

But for an LLM, this single paragraph contains multiple entities, operations, and dependencies that must be correctly interpreted, sequenced, and executed.

Without a structured way to represent this flow, the system can easily lose track of what depends on what leading to incorrect results or repeated calculations.

That's exactly why **function graphs** are so powerful: they turn a tangled prompt like this into a **clear, visual execution plan**, where every operation, dependency, and data hand-off is explicit.

GraphViz

The graphs in this chapter were created using Graphviz (https://dreampuf.github.io/GraphvizOnline/), a widely used tool for generating diverse graph structures. While Graphviz satisfies the visualization needs, our requirements go beyond drawing diagrams. We need graphs that encode semantic meaning and domain-specific constraints.

In our system, different entities support different operations. For example, calculating the total quantity sold using `get_total_qty_for_SKUs` is valid for SKUs but makes no sense for outlets. Each entity type, such as SKUs or outlets, has its own set of permissible functions:

Entity	Operations
SKU	`get_total_qty_for_SKUs`
SKU	`get_total_sales_for_SKUs`
Outlet	`get_total_sales_for_Outlets`
Outlet	`get_average_sales_for_Outlets`

To ensure users do not accidentally create invalid graphs or apply the wrong operations to an entity, we built a custom tool called **Parseboard**. Parseboard serves as an interactive environment for constructing, validating, executing, and storing semantic graphs aligned with our agentic framework.

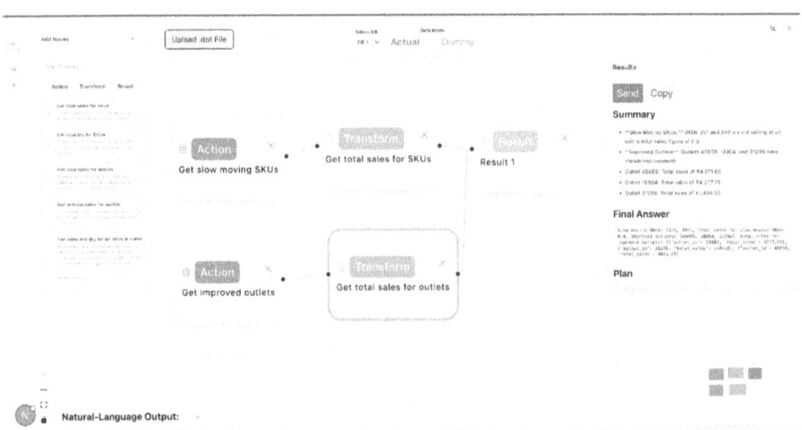

Figure: Screenshot of the Parseboard tool which is used to quickly and correctly build the graph based prompts for GAP

Further technical details about Parseboard, including its design philosophy and integration with the agentic framework, are provided in Appendix D.

LLM Call Footprint in PADM Architectures

In a typical PADM architecture, lets calculate the number of LLM calls that will be made to resolve this prompt assuming that Perception and Decision are working perfectly together

```
"Calculate the total sales and quantity for the SKUs
that showed poor stock rotation for outlet 75757. Then
calculate the total sales and quantity for the SKUs that
have shown a surge in demand for the same outlet. After
that, find the most valuable outlets for the user 6382,
and finally calculate the total sales for these outlets."
```

In the example prompt there are 3 different subqueries that need to be executed to get the final answer:

Subquery1: Calculate the total sales & quantity for the skus that showed poor stock rotations for outlet 75757

SubQuery2: Calculate the total sales & qty for the Skus that have shown surge in the demand for the outlet 75757

SubQuery3: find the most valuable outlets for the user 6382 and also find the total sales for these outlets

SubPrompt	PADM Module	What will it do	# of LLM Calls
Calculate the total sales & quantity for the skus that showed poor stock rotations for outlet 75757	Perception	Identify `Get_skus_with_poor_stock_roation`	1
Calculate the total sales & quantity for the skus that showed poor stock rotations for outlet 75757	Decision	Create Function Call	1

SubPrompt	PADM Module	What will it do	# of LLM Calls
Calculate the total sales & quantity for the skus that showed poor stock rotations for outlet 75757	Perception	Identify the tool `get_total_sales_for_SKUs`	1
Calculate the total sales & quantity for the skus that showed poor stock rotations for outlet 75757	Decision	Create Function call	1
Calculate the total sales & quantity for the skus that showed poor stock rotations for outlet 75757	Perception	Identify the tool `get_total_qty_for_SKUs`	1
Calculate the total sales & quantity for the skus that showed poor stock rotations for outlet 75757	Decision	Create Function call	1
Calculate the total sales & quantity for the skus that showed poor stock rotations for outlet 75757	Perception	This Subquery is done	1
Calculate the total sales & quantity for the skus that showed poor stock rotations for outlet 75757	Decision	Final Call	1
Calculate the total sales & qty for the Skus that have shown surge in the demand for the outlet 75757	Perception	Identify `get_SKUs_with_surged_demand`	1
Calculate the total sales & qty for the Skus that have shown surge in the demand for the outlet 75757	Decision	Create Function Call	1
Calculate the total sales & qty for the Skus that have shown surge in the demand for the outlet 75757	Perception	Identify the tool `get_total_sales_for_SKUs`	1

SubPrompt	PADM Module	What will it do	# of LLM Calls
Calculate the total sales & qty for the Skus that have shown surge in the demand for the outlet 75757	Decision	Create Function call	1
Calculate the total sales & qty for the Skus that have shown surge in the demand for the outlet 75757	Perception	Identify the tool `get_total_qty_for_SKUs`	1
Calculate the total sales & qty for the Skus that have shown surge in the demand for the outlet 75757	Decision	Create Function call	1
Calculate the total sales & qty for the Skus that have shown surge in the demand for the outlet 75757	Perception	This Subquery is done	1
Calculate the total sales & qty for the Skus that have shown surge in the demand for the outlet 75757	Decision	Final Call	1
find the most valuable outlets for the user 6382 and also find the total sales for these outlets	Perception	Identify the tool `get_mostValuable_outlets`	1
find the most valuable outlets for the user 6382 and also find the total sales for these outlets	Decision	Create a Function Call	1
find the most valuable outlets for the user 6382 and also find the total sales for these outlets	Perception	Identify the tool `get_total_sales_for_outlets`	1
find the most valuable outlets for the user 6382 and also find the total sales for these outlets	Decision	Create a Function Call	1
find the most valuable outlets for the user 6382 and also find the total sales for these outlets	Perception	This subquery is done	1

SubPrompt	PADM Module	What will it do	# of LLM Calls
find the most valuable outlets for the user 6382 and also find the total sales for these outlets	Decision	Final Call	1
find the most valuable outlets for the user 6382 and also find the total sales for these outlets	Perception	Collate all the subquery data together to make the final output	1
		Total Calls	**23**

The query makes approximately 20 LLM calls, with the first subquery *(calculating total sales and quantity for SKUs with poor stock rotation in outlet 75757*) making 8 calls, the second subquery (*calculating total sales and quantity for SKUs with surging demand in outlet 75757*) making 8 calls, and the final subquery *(identifying most valuable outlets for user 6382 and their total sales*) making 6 calls. This number of calls is excessive. Considering a Pan-India scale, with a conservative estimate of 10 million outlets served daily, the number of queries would escalate into the millions.

The above example illustrates the practical issue with overreliance on LLMs to resolve the NLP based user prompts. ***As user prompts become more complex, NLP-based prompting will lead to an exponential increase in LLM consumption.***

Introducing the Graph as a Prompt (GAP)

Let's try to understand the issues that will come with PADM architectures when the prompts become more and more complex to handle real-world query. Consider the following prompt, a monster of a request that blends multiple objectives, dependencies, and intermediate results:

```
{
  "prompt":"For the company {companyId}, identify the most selling SKUs and near expiry SKUs for the outlet {outletId}. For both types of SKUs, calculate the total sales and total quantity. Use these metrics to generate two intermediate results: Result1 derived from most selling SKUs and Result2 derived from near expiry SKUs. Then, combine these results into a unified Result. Next, evaluate struggling outlets for the user {userId}. For each, compute their total sales and average sales, and use these to generate Result3, which also contributes to the final Result. Additionally, analyze surge demand SKUs for the outlet {outletId}. Compute relevant metrics to generate Result4 and incorporate this into the overall Result. The final Result should reflect a comprehensive view derived from SKU sales performance, expiry risks, outlet-level performance, and sudden demand surges."
}
```

Even for a human analyst, that's a dense task. It involves multiple domains (SKUs, outlets, users), several levels of dependency (outputs from one step feeding into another), and four separate result sets that must be merged into one coherent answer.

Now, let's see how our previous PADM architectures would handle this.

PADM Struggles

In the **naïve PADM** setup, the agent tries to resolve each part of the query sequentially, identifying tools, calling them, and looping through perception–decision–action cycles until all goals are met.

The problem? It often gets lost in its own reasoning. Complex dependencies confuse the Perception layer, and without a clear sense of completion, the agent may enter an **infinite resolution loop**, calling tools repeatedly without ever assembling the final result.

In simpler terms, the agent keeps *thinking*, but never *finishes thinking.*

PADM_FUNCT: Faster, But Not Predictable

The PADM_FUNCT approach introduces a clear improvement by allowing the agent to generate an entire execution plan in a single step. For example, producing the full solve() function upfront. This makes the workflow more efficient because the LLM does not need to re-plan after each action. The process becomes faster, cleaner, and structurally closer to how real systems operate.

```
async def solve():
    # FUNCTION_CALL: 1
    """get_near_expiry_SKUs: Identifies SKUs which are near expiry."""
    input = {"inputData": {"company_id": 800, "outlet_id": 75757, "query_date":
"2025-06-18"}}
    result1 = await mcp.call_tool('get_near_expiry_SKUs', input)
    poor_stock_rotation_skus = json.loads(result1.content[0].text)["result"]

    # FUNCTION_CALL: 2
    """get_total_sales_for_SKUs: Calculates total sales for SKUs which are near
expiry"""
    input = {"inputData": {"company_id": 800, "outlet_id": 75757, "lstSKUs":
poor_stock_rotation_skus, "query_date": "2025-06-18"}}
    result2 = await mcp.call_tool('get_total_sales_for_SKUs', input)
    total_sales_poor_stock_rotation =
json.loads(result2.content[0].text)["result"]

    # FUNCTION_CALL: 3
    """get_total_qty_for_SKUs: Calculates total quantity sold for the same
SKUs."""
    input = {"inputData": {"company_id": 800, "outlet_id": 75757, "lstSKUs":
poor_stock_rotation_skus, "query_date": "2025-06-18"}}
    result3 = await mcp.call_tool('get_total_qty_for_SKUs', input)
    total_qty_poor_stock_rotation =
json.loads(result3.content[0].text)["result"]

    ...
    # (Subsequent function calls continue similarly)
```

However, a key limitation remains: **non-determinism**. Re-running the same prompt can produce variations in the generated function including differences in ordering, tool selection, or parameter naming.

Each time the LLM is asked to generate the same solve() function, the output could vary, sometimes in ordering, sometimes in function selection, sometimes even in parameter names.

This inconsistency makes it impossible to guarantee reproducibility, which is again a deal-breaker for production-grade systems.

As the number of sub-queries increases, these variations accumulate, making the system harder to control and scale.

Note: *We are not showing PADM_FEED as it would be a long list of Perception - Decision handshaking to execute the entire prompt*

Lets see how Graphs Can Help

In software engineering, **graphs** have long been used to represent dependencies whether between microservices, APIs, or even logical processes. They bring one critical property that the PADM family lacked: **determinism**.

When represented as a graph, each node corresponds to a function, and each edge captures the flow of data or dependency between them. You can visualize it, trace execution paths, and validate dependencies before anything actually runs removing ambiguity from the execution process.

Languages such as DOT, commonly used with Graphviz, have become standard tools for defining and persisting these graphs. They provide a formal, machine-readable representation that preserves both execution **order** and **intent**, making complex workflows auditable, reproducible, and predictable.

This led us to a simple but provocative question: ***What if we could apply the same graph-based thinking to natural language intent?***

What if a user's prompt could be translated into a structured graph that explicitly captures intent, dependencies, and data flow?

That question became the foundation for our next architectural leap: **Graph as a Prompt (GAP)**, a framework designed to bridge the gap between raw data and intelligent action by grounding language-driven intent in deterministic, graph-based structure.

The Core Idea of GAP

Instead of relying on the LLM—through the Decision layer in PADM—to dynamically reason through each step at runtime, **GAP leverages the user's prompt as a directed graph.**

Note: *The graph has to be created by the user. Instead of giving a NLP input, the user will submit a graph in the DOT form to the GAP.*

This graph explicitly encodes what needs to be done, the order in which actions should occur, and the dependencies between them. By doing so, GAP ensures that the agent understands not just *what* to execute, but *how* the overall task is structured before execution begins, reducing ambiguity and eliminating the need for sequential trial-and-error reasoning.

Each node in the graph represents a function call (like `get_most_selling_SKUs or get_total_sales_for_SKUs`), and the edges define how their outputs feed into the next operation.

Once the graph is built, the execution becomes predictable, traceable, and most importantly, **reproducible**.

- No more guessing.
- No more infinite loops.
- Just structured reasoning, visual clarity, and deterministic outcomes.

Lets try to create a graph for the user query:

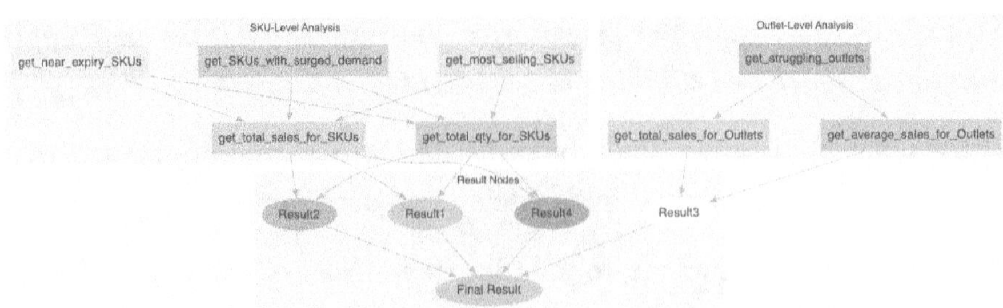

The graph can be conveniently converted to a DOT file which is how the graphs can be saved in a database or a file. In this representation, each **node** is a function, and each **edge** defines the flow of data or dependency between them. Here is the DOT version of the same graph.

```
digraph G {

  get_most_selling_SKUs->get_total_sales_for_SKUs->Result1;
  get_most_selling_SKUs->get_total_qty_for_SKUs->Result1;


  get_near_expiry_SKUs->get_total_sales_for_SKUs->Result2;
  get_near_expiry_SKUs->get_total_qty_for_SKUs->Result2;

  get_struggling_outlets->get_total_sales_for_outlets->Result3
  get_struggling_outlets->get_average_sales_for_outlets->Result3

  get_SKUs_with_surged_demand->get_total_sales_for_SKUs->Result4
  get_SKUs_with_surged_demand->get_total_qty_for_SKUs->Result4

  Result1 -> Result
  Result2 -> Result
  Result3 -> Result
  Result4 -> Result
}
```

Once the graph has been constructed, it can be **sent directly as a prompt** to the LLM because it's written in **natural language (NL)**, which every language model can understand.

The prompt is exactly the same as the DOT language just encapsulated with a keyword **prompt.**

```
{
    "prompt": digraph G {

      get_most_selling_SKUs->get_total_sales_for_SKUs->Result1;
      get_most_selling_SKUs->get_total_qty_for_SKUs->Result1;


      get_near_expiry_SKUs->get_total_sales_for_SKUs->Result2;
      get_near_expiry_SKUs->get_total_qty_for_SKUs->Result2;

      get_struggling_outlets->get_total_sales_for_outlets->Result3
      get_struggling_outlets->get_average_sales_for_outlets->Result3

      get_SKUs_with_surged_demand->get_total_sales_for_SKUs->Result4
      get_SKUs_with_surged_demand->get_total_qty_for_SKUs->Result4

      Result1 -> Result
      Result2 -> Result
      Result3 -> Result
      Result4 -> Result

    }
}
```

In fact, you could even represent the same graph visually (as a PNG or SVG) and send it to a **multimodal LLM** for interpretation.

However, multimodal models tend to be more expensive and resource-intensive, so for most use cases, the **natural language version of the graph** works perfectly well and keeps things simple.

In this representation, each node is a function, and each edge defines the flow of data or dependency between them. The LLM's job is straightforward: it simply reads the graph and converts it into a list of function calls just like in the PADM_FUNCT approach, but this time with a built-in guarantee of order and structure. Because the graph explicitly defines the dependencies and execution sequence, the LLM no longer needs to infer or guess them. That makes the entire process deterministic. Every time you send the same graph, you'll get the same ordered list of function calls. *The execution flow now becomes clean, predictable, and scalable.*

The Flow in Action

1. **Graph Creation**: The system (or a user) constructs a dependency graph describing how different functions connect.
2. **Prompt Conversion:** The graph, written in natural language, is sent as a prompt to the LLM.
3. **Function Extraction**: The LLM parses the graph and generates the corresponding function call sequence and puts them under solve().
4. **Execution**: These functions are executed deterministically via MCP tools, ensuring consistency and repeatability.
5. **Aggregation**: The outputs from all branches of the graph are combined to form the final result, the "Result" node in the graph.

In short, instead of asking the LLM to *plan the logic* dynamically, we now ask it to simply *read and translate* an already structured plan. This subtle shift from "**reasoning over instructions**" to "**executing a predefined map**" dramatically reduces variability while keeping the system intelligent and flexible.

Benefits of the Graph-Based Approach

The **Graph-based approach** introduces a refreshing simplicity and determinism to agentic design. By representing tasks and dependencies explicitly as a graph, this method eliminates much of the ambiguity and complexity that plagued earlier PADM-style architectures.

One of its key advantages is a **simplified architecture**. It removes the heavy dependence on the Perception and Decision modules, reducing both cognitive and computational overhead. Instead, the **graph itself becomes the source of truth**, defining all function calls, their dependencies, and even the stopping conditions directly within its structure.

This design also enables **graph-driven execution**, where every operation is mapped and sequenced ahead of time. The LLM's role is limited to interpreting and executing what's already defined which dramatically improves consistency and repeatability.

Through **guided prompting (in the form of graph/DOT file)**, the system provides the LLM with a concise, unambiguous instruction set, ensuring that it executes the right functions in the correct order. The result is a clean, predictable workflow that's easy to debug, monitor, and scale.

Finally, because there is **no agentic loop**, the architecture avoids the endless back-and-forth of perception–decision–action cycles. This not only cuts down on latency and cost but also removes the risk of infinite reasoning loops that previously made fully agentic systems unstable.

In essence, the Graph-based approach transforms complex, open-ended reasoning into **structured, deterministic execution,** offering the reliability of traditional software engineering with the flexibility of modern AI.

Inside the Engine: How the Graph-Based Execution Works

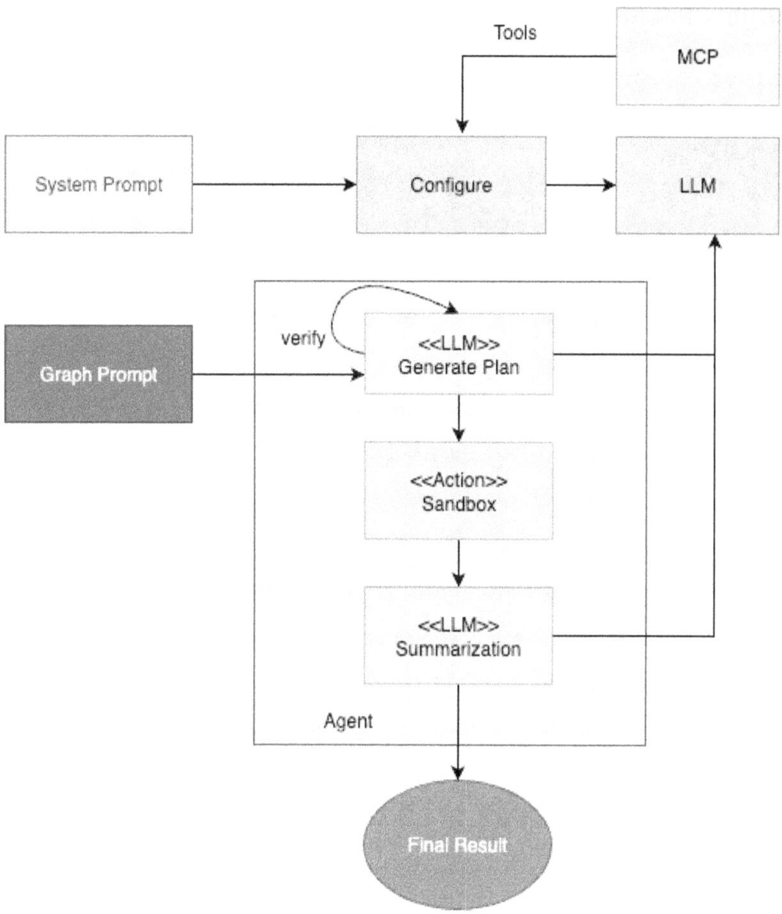

Let's now go step by step to understand the internal workflow of this solution and how the system transforms a structured graph into real, executable results.

1. System Prompt Configuration

The process begins with the **Agent configuring the LLM** using a carefully designed **system prompt**. This prompt is similar to the one used in the **PADM_FUNCT** approach, as the goal here is also to generate an asynchronous solve() function.

The prompt sets clear expectations for the LLM specifying that it must follow the graph structure, respect dependencies, and output a complete execution plan in code form.

Here is an example of such prompt.

```
prompt = f"""
You are a reasoning-driven AI agent responsible for generating a simple, structured
execution plan using ONLY the tools currently available to you.

 Define what is available
 Tool Catalog:
{tool_descriptions}

 User Query:
"{user_input}"

 Goal:
Write a valid async Python function named `solve()` that solves the user query using exactly
ONE FUNCTION_CALL.

 Do's and Don'ts
 STRICT RULES:

- You must always define a function `async def solve():`
- Each tool call must follow the Usage docstring format exactly.
- You MUST call only those tools that are available in Tool Catalog.
- Call a tool using its tool name string, not function variable.
  E.g., await mcp.call_tool('add', input)
  (NOT await mcp.call_tool(add, input))
- Call the tool exactly as per its function signature: tool(input)
- If one FUNCTION_CALL depends on another, parse the previous result using
json.loads(result.content[0].text)["result"] to extract the value from the tool's JSON
output.
- ! Important: Never inline json.loads(...) inside f"" strings. Always assign it to a
variable first (e.g., parsed = json.loads(...)["result"]) and use that in return
f"FINAL_ANSWER: {{parsed}}".
- End your function by returning a string that starts with 'FINAL_ANSWER: ' or
'FURTHER_PROCESSING_REQUIRED: '
- If the tool result is a document, webpage, or unstructured chunk, DO NOT return it as the
FINAL_ANSWER. Instead, return it with 'FURTHER_PROCESSING_REQUIRED:' so the agent can
interpret and summarize it next.
- Assume that the call_tool() is already defined and so no need to generate the mock code it
- Do not add import json or import re
- Do not add 'Result' as a function call
- No fallback, no multiple options.
- No explanation, no narration -- only valid Python code.
- If the user input already includes clean extracted webpage/document content, do NOT call
the tool again. Summarize or generate the final answer from it.
- Indent the code correctly as per python rules
- Most of the user input will have companyId and outletId which needs to be passed as a
argument to the function call .
e.g. For the companyId 123 Calculate the most selling SKUs for the outlet 1234
in this case the function will be like

 Give Some examples of how to resolve the dependencies among the function calls

```python
```
```

````
async def solve():
    # FUNCTION_CALL: 1
    """get_most_selling_SKUs:
    returns the top skus that are mostly sold in this outlet"""
    input = {{"inputData": {{"company_id":123,"outlet_id": 1234}}}}
    result1 = await mcp.call_tool('get_most_selling_SKUs', input)
    most_selling_skus = json.loads(result1.content[0].text)["result"]

    return f"FINAL_ANSWER: Most selling SKUs: {{most_selling_skus}}"
```

- Some times there might be multiple function calls required like
For the companyId 123 Calculate the slow moving SKUs for the outlet 1234 and also the most
selling SKUs for the outlet 1234
In this case the function call will be
```python
async def solve():
    # FUNCTION_CALL: 1
    """get_slow_moving_SKUs:  Returns a list of SKUs which are not getting sold"""
    input = {{"inputData": {{"company_id":123,"outlet_id": 1234}}}}
    result1 = await mcp.call_tool('get_slow_moving_SKUs', input)
    slow_moving_skus = json.loads(result1.content[0].text)["result"]

    # FUNCTION_CALL: 2
    """get_most_selling_SKUs:
    returns the top skus that are mostly sold in this outlet"""
    input = {{"inputData": {{"company_id":123,"outlet_id": 1234}}}}
    result2 = await mcp.call_tool('get_most_selling_SKUs', input)
    most_selling_skus = json.loads(result2.content[0].text)["result"]

    return f"FINAL_ANSWER: Slow moving SKUs: {{slow_moving_skus}}, Most selling SKUs:
{{most_selling_skus}}"
```

- Some times there might be a dependence between the next function call where the result of
first function call will be the input for the next function call
For the companyId 123 Calculate the most selling SKUs for the outlet 1234 and then find out
the total sales of those SKUs and the total quantity sold for those SKUs
In this case the function call will be
```python
async def solve():
    # FUNCTION_CALL: 1
    """get_most_selling_SKUs:
    returns the top skus that are mostly sold in this outlet"""
    input = {{"inputData": {{"company_id":123,"outlet_id": 1234}}}}
    result1 = await mcp.call_tool('get_most_selling_SKUs', input)
    most_selling_skus = json.loads(result1.content[0].text)["result"]

    # FUNCTION_CALL: 2
    """Get the total sales of the SKUs"""
    input = {{"inputData": {{"company_id":123,"outlet_id": 1234,"lstSKUs":most_selling_skus
}}}}
````

```
    result2 = await mcp.call_tool('get_total_sales_for_most_selling_SKUs', input)
    total_sales = json.loads(result2.content[0].text)["result"]


    # FUNCTION_CALL: 3
    """Get the total sales of the SKUs"""
    input = {{"inputData": {{"company_id":123,"outlet_id": 1234,"lstSKUs":most_selling_skus
}}}}
    result3 = await mcp.call_tool('get_total_qty_for_most_selling_SKUs', input)
    total_qty = json.loads(result3.content[0].text)["result"]


    return f"FINAL_ANSWER: Most selling SKUs: {{most_selling_skus}} and the total sales of
the SKUs is {{total_sales}} and the total qty sold is {{total_qty}}"
```
"""
```

## 2. Plan Generation from Graph

Once the prompt is initialized, the **LLM reads the provided graph** and translates it into an **execution plan**, essentially the `async solve()` function.

This function includes all the required **function calls arranged in the precise order** dictated by the graph's dependencies.

Unlike earlier architectures, there's no ambiguity or reasoning required; the flow is deterministic because the graph already defines what needs to happen and when.

The planning module will use a prompt similar to the PADM_FUNCT as the main purpose is to generate the `async solve()`.

The major difference between PADM_FUNCT approach and Graph approach is that NLP resolution of the functions is already available through the DOT file so translation of the NLP text to the function name using Perception is not required. The Planning stage can directly be called which will generate the `solve()`.

## 3. Verification Loop

Since this architecture no longer relies on the **Perception** and **Decision** modules for validation, a lightweight **verification loop** is introduced.
```

This step ensures that the generated plan fully covers all nodes and edges of the graph confirming that no function has been skipped or duplicated.

While optional for simple graphs, verification is strongly recommended for complex workflows. Interestingly, when the LLM is explicitly asked to **validate its own plan**, it tends to enter a "**reflective mode**," checking each function call carefully and improving overall reliability.

4. Sandbox Execution

After the verification step, the finalized `solve()` function is executed inside a **secure Python sandbox**. This sandbox handles all MCP tool invocations sequentially, ensuring proper isolation and logging. The execution engine follows the exact sequence defined in the graph, producing consistent and repeatable outputs every time.

5. Result Summarization

Once all functions have been executed, the system moves to the **summarization phase**. Here, the final results are aggregated and presented either by the same LLM or by a **secondary summarization model** for better clarity and presentation.

The process then concludes, returning a comprehensive, structured output derived from the entire execution graph.

At this point, the agent has successfully **read, validated, executed, and summarized** a graph-based workflow—all without relying on complex perception–decision loops.

This combination of structure and simplicity makes the Graph-based approach both **deterministic and scalable**, while maintaining the expressiveness of natural language.

Graph in Action

Lets see the graph being executed in Action:

Suppose we want to execute the following NLP prompt:

> "*Calculate the total sales and quantity for the SKUs with the poor stock rotation*"

This can be represented as:

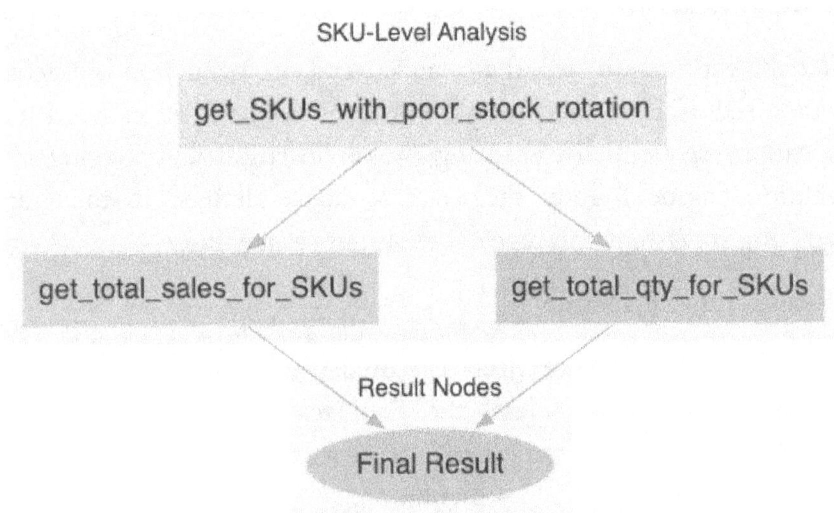

This will be converted to a dot file and then sent as a prompt to the agent.

```
{
  "prompt": "digraph G {{ subgraph cluster_0{{
get_SKUs_with_poor_stock_rotation->get_total_sales_for_SKUs->Result;
get_SKUs_with_poor_stock_rotation->get_total_qty_for_SKUs->Result; }} }}"
}
```

Here is the log trace of agentic execution.

```
configuration step: The tools list is being read. At the start of the execution the agent
will get a list of all the tools that are needed.

INFO     Processing request of type ListToolsRequest
→ Tools received: ['get_SKUs_with_poor_stock_rotation', 'get_SKUs_with_surged_demand',
'get_SKUs_with_dip_demand', 'get_slow_moving_SKUs', 'get_near_expiry_SKUs',
'get_most_selling_SKUs', 'get_total_sales_for_SKUs', 'get_total_qty_for_SKUs',
'get_total_sales_for_outlets', 'get_average_sales_for_outlets', 'get_improved_outlets',
'get_struggling_outlets', 'get_mostValuable_outlets', 'get_most_visited_outlets',
'get_sales_for_particular_outlet', 'get_sales_and_qty_for_all_SKUs_in_outlet']

 The following is the request obtained by the agent
follow the following order of operations as in the graph. Replace the values of the
paramters with the ones given in the payload e.g. companyId with
    {companyId}, queryDate with {queryDate} and userId with {userId} , outletId with
{outletId}.
    Make sure all the nodes in the graph are covered in the final output : digraph G {{
subgraph cluster_0{{ get_SKUs_with_poor_stock_rotation->get_total_sales_for_SKUs->Result;
get_SKUs_with_poor_stock_rotation->get_total_qty_for_SKUs->Result; }} }}
user_input follow the following order of operations as in the graph. Replace the values of
the parameters with the ones given in the payload e.g. companyId with
    800, queryDate with 2025-06-18 and userId with 186 , outletId with 69124.
    Make sure all the nodes in the graph are covered in the final output : digraph G {
subgraph cluster_0{ get_SKUs_with_poor_stock_rotation->get_total_sales_for_SKUs->Result;
get_SKUs_with_poor_stock_rotation->get_total_qty_for_SKUs->Result; } }

 The planning stage is called to generate the solve() from the given prompt

[loop] Detected solve() plan — running sandboxed...
async def solve():
    # FUNCTION_CALL: 1
    """get_SKUs_with_poor_stock_rotation: Identifies SKUs with poor stock rotation in a
specific outlet."""
    input = {"inputData": {"company_id": 800, "outlet_id": 69124, "query_date":
"2025-06-18"}}
    result1 = await mcp.call_tool('get_SKUs_with_poor_stock_rotation', input)
    poor_stock_rotation_skus = json.loads(result1.content[0].text)["result"]

    # FUNCTION_CALL: 2
    """get_total_sales_for_SKUs: Calculates the total sales amount for a list of SKUs at a
specific outlet."""
    input = {"inputData": {"company_id": 800, "outlet_id": 69124, "lstSKUs":
poor_stock_rotation_skus, "query_date": "2025-06-18"}}
    result2 = await mcp.call_tool('get_total_sales_for_SKUs', input)
    total_sales_poor_stock_rotation = json.loads(result2.content[0].text)["result"]

    # FUNCTION_CALL: 3
    """get_total_qty_for_SKUs: Calculates the cumulative quantity sold for a list of SKUs at
a specific outlet."""
    input = {"inputData": {"company_id": 800, "outlet_id": 69124, "lstSKUs":
poor_stock_rotation_skus, "query_date": "2025-06-18"}}
    result3 = await mcp.call_tool('get_total_qty_for_SKUs', input)
```

```
    total_qty_poor_stock_rotation = json.loads(result3.content[0].text)["result"]

    return f"FINAL_ANSWER: SKUs with poor stock rotation: {poor_stock_rotation_skus}, Total
sales: {total_sales_poor_stock_rotation}, Total quantity: {total_qty_poor_stock_rotation}"

  The Python Sand Box Environment is called to run each of the function calls one by one
[action] 🔍 Entered run_python_sandbox()

[INSIDE] get_SKUs_with_poor_stock_rotation
[data] {'inputData': {'company_id': 800, 'outlet_id': 69124, 'query_date': '2025-06-18'}}
INFO     Processing request of type CallToolRequest
server.py:551
[INSIDE] get_total_sales_for_SKUs
[data] {'inputData': {'company_id': 800, 'outlet_id': 69124, 'lstSKUs': [421, 420, 383],
'query_date': '2025-06-18'}}
INFO     Processing request of type CallToolRequest
server.py:551
[INSIDE] get_total_qty_for_SKUs
[data] {'inputData': {'company_id': 800, 'outlet_id': 69124, 'lstSKUs': [421, 420, 383],
'query_date': '2025-06-18'}}
INFO     Processing request of type CallToolRequest
server.py:551
RAW Results=> FINAL_ANSWER: SKUs with poor stock rotation: [421, 420, 383], Total sales:
58688.62, Total quantity: 1087

  Once the raw output is obtained then the formatting happens. For this we are calling
another LLM call to just do the proper output creation

FORMATTED=> - **Key Issues Identified:**
  - SKUs 421, 420, and 383 have poor stock rotation, indicating potential inventory issues.
  - Despite a total sales amount of ₹58,688.62, the total quantity sold is only 1,087 units,
suggesting a need to analyze sales efficiency.

- **Actionable Insights:**
  - Investigate the reasons behind the poor stock rotation of SKUs 421, 420, and 383.
  - Review sales strategies to improve sales efficiency given the current sales figures.
```

Pros and Cons of GAP Approach

Like every architectural evolution, the **Graph as a Prompt (GAP)** approach introduces both powerful advantages and a few important trade-offs. By replacing the dynamic reasoning of PADM architectures with a graph-driven, deterministic workflow, GAP achieves remarkable gains in **efficiency**, **predictability**, and **clarity**, but it also changes how we think about prompting and automation.

Let's look at the strengths and challenges of this design in more detail.

Pros

1. **Low LLM Usage and Predictable Costs**

   One of the standout benefits of GAP is its extremely low dependency on LLM calls. A typical workflow requires only **three LLM invocations**: two before the sandbox execution stage (for graph interpretation and validation) and one at the end of the sandbox for formatting result. This predictable and minimal usage allows organizations to estimate both **system load** and **budget requirements** with confidence. Since LLM calls are the most expensive part of any agentic pipeline, **cost predictability** is a key enabler for large-scale adoption.

2. **Deterministic and Accurate Results:** Unlike traditional agentic systems where outputs may fluctuate across runs, the GAP approach delivers **deterministic results**. For any given prompt graph, the underlying numerical outputs remain consistent, ensuring both **reliability and reproducibility**. While natural language formatting may vary slightly depending on the LLM's phrasing, the **core data never changes**. This consistency makes GAP especially well-suited for business-critical use cases where accuracy and auditability are non-negotiable.
3. **Fast and Efficient Execution:** Although LLMs are inherently slower than traditional compute processes, limiting their use to just three calls ensures quick execution. This balance between efficiency and precision makes GAP both practical and scalable
4. **No Infinite Loops or Dead Ends:** A major issue in PADM architectures was the risk of infinite reasoning loops, where the agent kept iterating without ever reaching completion. GAP avoids this entirely. It follows a single-entry, single-exit execution model, which is a linear path defined by the graph. Once all functions have been executed, the process ends cleanly, making the system far more robust and reliable.

5. **Simplicity in Expressing Complex Prompts:** Perhaps the most user-friendly advantage of GAP lies in how it handles complexity. Instead of writing long, carefully worded natural-language prompts, users can now draw them.

Graphs provide an intuitive, visual way to represent intricate dependencies between functions, making it easier to both design and validate what the agent needs to do.

As the saying goes, *"A picture is worth a thousand words."*

To make this even easier, a dedicated UI for graph creation has been built (see **Appendix D** for details), allowing users to visually construct and deploy their prompts with no coding required.

The following Infographics summarizes the key benefits of the approach

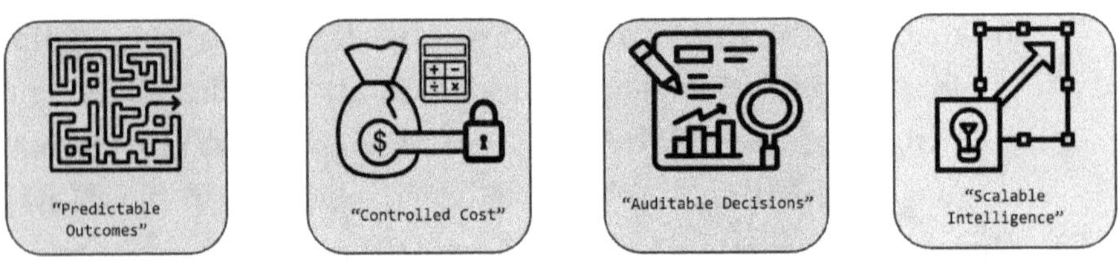

Cons

1. **Challenging Perception of "Prompting":** One of the biggest hurdles is not technical. It's **perceptual**. Many people associate GenAI systems with conversational, natural-language prompts. Convincing teams that a graph is simply another form of prompting—more structured, visual, and reliable—can take some effort. In essence, GAP reframes how we think about interaction with AI. It's still prompting, just in a language of **connections instead of sentences**.
2. **Heavy Dependence on MCP:** The GAP architecture is tightly coupled with the **Model Context Protocol (MCP)** ecosystem. It relies on MCP tools for data retrieval, transformation, and computation which works beautifully for structured, API-driven tasks.

However, this dependence comes with a limitation. If an intermediate step requires **generative reasoning** (for instance, summarization or text generation), GAP alone cannot handle it elegantly. In such cases, a **hybrid setup** of combining GAP for deterministic workflows with LLM reasoning layers for creative tasks may be necessary.

Design Decisions and Infrastructure

The **Graph as a Prompt (GAP)** architecture represents a mature stage in the evolution of agentic systems that replaces free-flowing LLM reasoning with structured, deterministic orchestration. Its design decisions reflect a deliberate balance between **intelligence and engineering discipline**, ensuring that the system remains intelligent enough to reason but predictable enough to deploy at scale.

Here are some of the key architectural choices that define GAP.

Infrastructure

The framework is **LLM-agnostic** by design, capable of operating with any large language model, including compact, self-hosted variants such as *phi-4 on Ollama* or enterprise-hosted models like *Claude Enterprise* or *GPT-4 Turbo.*

However, in production, **model quality directly influences consistency** in graph interpretation and `solve()` generation.

To ensure determinism and precision, organizations often choose **premium models** with stable token embeddings and consistent parsing behavior. Because the LLM is used sparingly (typically three calls per workflow), **even high-end models remain economically feasible** in large-scale deployments.

The architecture treats the LLM as an enabler, not the engine, minimizing dependency while maximizing precision.

Query Handling

All data retrieval and computation are routed through the **Model Context Protocol (MCP)** layer. In this setup, the LLM's role is limited to **reading the graph and constructing the corresponding execution plan (`solve()`)**, rather than generating SQL or free-form logic. This makes GAP inherently **secure, auditable, and schema-aware**, as all data access is governed by pre-defined MCP tools.

Each node in the graph represents an MCP function, and edges define the **execution order and data dependencies.**Once the graph is parsed, the sandbox environment executes it deterministically without any reasoning loops or hidden side effects.

LLM interprets intent; MCP ensures integrity.

LLM Role

In GAP, the language model plays a **surgical role** invoked only where human-like intelligence is needed.

Specifically:

- To interpret the graph and generate the executable plan (solve() function).
- To optionally verify that all graph nodes and dependencies are covered correctly.
- To format and summarize final outputs for user-friendly presentation.

By limiting the LLM's role to **interpretation, validation, and presentation,** GAP achieves both **cost efficiency** and **high predictability**. Earlier architectures struggled to maintain this equilibrium.

Execution Environment

Execution occurs within a **controlled Python sandbox,** where each MCP call is made sequentially as per the generated solve() plan.

This sandboxed runtime ensures:

- Isolation from the main system (for security and debugging).
- Full traceability of execution steps.
- Immediate error handling and logging.

Unlike the PADM family, which relied on iterative reasoning to reach convergence, GAP's sandbox runs in **single-entry, single-exit mode** ensuring **deterministic execution** and **guaranteed termination**.

Output Modalities

The architecture supports a wide variety of output formats like **structured tables**, **narrative summaries**, **visual graphs**, and even **meme-style explanations** for creative dashboards. Because outputs are built on MCP data, they are inherently **consistent, complete, and query-driven**. The final formatting, powered by the LLM, adds a natural-language or visual interpretation layer for end users.

In Summary

GAP reimagines how intelligence is embedded into enterprise systems. It's not about more reasoning, it's about **better reasoning, with control**. By grounding execution in graphs and MCP-based data access, while reserving LLMs for selective high-value reasoning tasks, GAP achieves **repeatable intelligence at production scale,** which earlier agentic architectures could not. In this sense, GAP is not the next evolution of PADM. It is the *industrialization* of agentic design.

Evaluating GAP Through the Lens of the 4Rs

Every architectural evolution we've discussed so far, from PADM to PADM_FUNCT to PADM_FEED, has been an attempt to bring AI agents closer to production-grade reliability. The **Graph as a Prompt (GAP)** approach takes that evolution one step further, focusing on **determinism, scalability, and cost-efficiency**.

Let's now assess how it performs across our four guiding design principles: **Reach, Reliability, Restraint, and Respect.**

1. Reach

GAP shines when it comes to **scalability**. By shifting from dynamic reasoning to structured execution, it dramatically reduces computational load and makes the architecture **horizontally scalable**. Since each prompt graph leads to a fixed number of LLM calls (usually three), system architects can **accurately predict throughput and cost** across millions of parallel queries.

Unlike agentic loops that require continuous orchestration, GAP workflows are **stateless and modular,** meaning they can easily be distributed across multiple compute nodes or microservices. In a Pan-India deployment scenario, this predictability translates directly into **operational feasibility**.

Verdict: *Exceptionally strong on Reach. Scalable, predictable, and cloud-friendly.*

2. Reliability

Reliability has long been the Achilles' heel of agentic systems. GAP tackles this head-on.

Because all dependencies and function sequences are **explicitly encoded in the graph**, there's **no ambiguity** in execution. Each run produces the same results for the same input, eliminating the nondeterminism typical of LLM-driven loops.

The optional **verification step** before sandbox execution adds another layer of assurance, allowing the model to re-check its own plan for completeness. This self-validation, combined with deterministic sequencing, gives GAP **machine-like consistency with AI-level flexibility**.

Verdict: *Highly reliable and repeatable. A major improvement over PADM Architectures*

3. Restraint

In terms of **cost efficiency**, GAP is arguably the most restrained architecture so far. It calls the LLM **only three times** per query: for graph interpretation, verification, and summarization.

This means that even complex multi-stage queries can be handled with **minimal API usage**, making large-scale operations economically viable.

Moreover, because the system is not looping or reasoning in real time, compute overhead is drastically lower. This is restraint by design. The architecture does less, but with greater precision and control.

Verdict: *Strong on Restraint. Predictable, efficient, and economically scalable.*

4. Respect

Respect, in our framework, relates to **data privacy, governance, and user control** to ensure that AI operates within clear, auditable boundaries. GAP naturally enforces this principle. All data access happens exclusively through **MCP tools**, which are authenticated and pre-approved interfaces.

Because the graph explicitly defines which tools will be called and in what sequence, there's complete **transparency and traceability** in how data is processed.

This clarity makes GAP well-aligned with enterprise compliance requirements and minimizes the risks of unintended data exposure that can occur in free-form agentic loops.

Verdict: *Excellent on Respect. Secure, transparent, and governance-friendly.*

Summary Table

4R Principle	Focus Area	GAP Performance	Remarks
Reach	Scalability & Adaptability	○ High	Fixed LLM calls enable predictable scaling across millions of queries.
Reliability	Consistency & Accuracy	○ High	Graph-based execution guarantees reproducible outputs
Restraint	Cost & Efficiency	○ High	Minimal LLM dependency; no looping; cost predictable and controlled
Respect	Privacy & Control	○ High	All data flows are explicit, tool-bound, and auditable via MCP

From POC to Production: Is GAP the real deal?

The **Graph as a Prompt (GAP)** approach isn't just a research prototype like PADM, it's a **production-ready** framework that was *designed specifically* to overcome the scalability, cost, and unpredictability issues of earlier agentic architectures.

This architecture has been designed to remove the shortcomings of all the previous architectures. As a refresher we are listing down the major flaws in the previous architectures

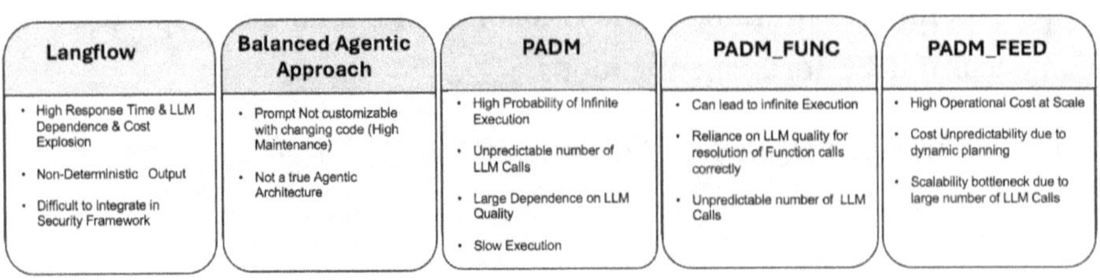

Let's explore what makes GAP ready for production, and where careful design still matters.

1. Ready for Scale

In a production environment, the most valuable property of any AI system is **predictability**. That is, knowing exactly what it will do, how long it will take, and how much it will cost.

GAP delivers all three. Because each graph represents a fully deterministic workflow with a fixed sequence of MCP function calls, every execution behaves exactly the same way, every time. This not only ensures **accuracy and repeatability**, but also makes it possible to **precisely forecast compute load and API costs** before deployment.

In short, GAP doesn't just scale well. It scales *responsibly*, with total visibility into performance and economics.

2. Graphs as a System of Record

One of the biggest challenges in production AI systems is **traceability**. It refers to understanding how a decision was made or a result was derived. GAP solves this elegantly.

Each prompt graph acts as a **system of record**, defining exactly which tools were used, in what order, and with what dependencies. That means every execution can be **audited, replayed, or versioned** making the system transparent by design.

3. Maintainability and Extensibility

Unlike agentic loops that can degrade unpredictably as they scale, GAP is **modular by construction**. Each node in the graph corresponds to an independent MCP function that can be **reused, updated, or replaced** without affecting the overall system. This modularity allows for rapid adaptation as business requirements evolve. For example, swapping a sales model or integrating a new API.

In essence, GAP turns the chaos of agentic reasoning into a **governed, graph-based execution framework** that enterprises can actually trust to run at scale.

It offers:

- **Predictable cost and performance** (no runaway LLM calls)
- **Guaranteed reproducibility** (no nondeterministic reasoning)
- **Native auditability and compliance** (clear data lineage via MCP)
- **Ease of monitoring and control** (explicit function graphs)

Agentic Test: Is This Architecture Truly Agentic?

After exploring GAP's internals and production readiness, it's time to ask the big question,

Is this architecture truly agentic?

We'll assess it through the same three lenses we've applied throughout this book: **Generation**, **Action**, and **Reflection**.

And as we'll see, GAP doesn't aim to be fully autonomous, it aims to be *reliably intelligent*.

Generative Aspect

The GAP architecture strikes a deliberate balance between **automation and control**.

It uses LLM generation only where it genuinely adds value. For example, when creating the `solve()` function from the graph or formatting the final results for user consumption.

Unlike earlier architectures:

- **PADM_FEED**, which relied heavily on generation at every stage,
- or the **Balance Approach**, which minimized it almost entirely,

GAP walks the middle path. It leverages the creative strengths of LLMs for orchestration and summarization, but keeps execution deterministic and rule-bound. This ensures that **outputs are reliable, consistent, and scalable**, without losing the adaptive flexibility that makes agentic systems powerful.

Verdict: *Generation used purposefully. Precise, efficient, and enterprise-ready.*

Action-Oriented Aspect

In GAP, the agent demonstrates true action-oriented behavior by **executing all functions in the correct sequence** based on the predefined graph. Each node in the graph represents a callable function, and the system executes them autonomously through the sandbox environment.

However, the system's autonomy is bounded by design. If a particular tool fails during execution, the framework does not yet have the capacity to adapt dynamically or select an alternative function since tool resolution follows the **graph definition** strictly. This limitation, while intentional, prioritizes **predictability over improvisation**, making the architecture more production-friendly but less exploratory.

Verdict: *Strong structured execution, limited adaptability.*

Planning & Reasoning Aspect

Planning in GAP doesn't emerge from LLM reasoning, it's encoded in the **graph itself**. The sequence of tools, their dependencies, and the flow of data are all explicitly defined upfront, ensuring that the agent's "plan" is transparent and auditable.

The Decision-like behavior comes into play when the LLM translates the graph into the executable `solve()` function. This translation is followed by a **light validation pass**, where the model checks whether all nodes and edges have been properly represented.

However, GAP does not yet include a full-fledged feedback mechanism to verify whether every step executed successfully in real time, a feature that, if added, would further strengthen its reasoning loop.

Verdict: *Structured reasoning with strong determinism, but minimal in-execution reflection.*

Assessment Against Agentic Principles

Here is the summary of how the architecture fairs against the Agentic Principles:

Pillar	Description	Evaluation
Generative Aspect	Uses generation selectively for `solve()` creation and output formatting. Balances reliability and adaptability better than minimal (Balance) or heavy (PADM_FEED) generation approaches	◯ Balanced, reliable, and scalable
Action-Oriented Aspect	Executes all functions in `solve()` sequentially. Cannot adapt if a tool fails, as it relies strictly on the predefined graph without Perception or Decision layers	◍ Strong execution, limited adaptability
Planning & Reasoning Aspect	Relies on Graph input for tool selection and dependencies. Validates translation to `solve()`, but lacks robust feedback to ensure all steps succeed	◍ Structured but limited feedback and reasoning

This table highlights a stark gap between the current reality and the ideal of a fully autonomous agentic system. While a fully autonomous system remains highly desirable, it is not yet sustainable at scale. The proposed solution, though not entirely autonomous, offers a scalable approach that still retains a meaningful degree of intelligence

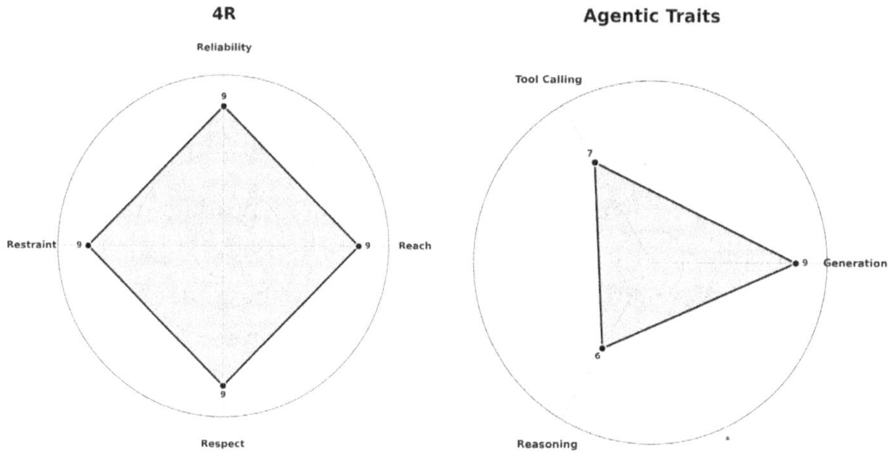

Figure: The radar chart above highlights our discussion on the 4R Framework and the Agentic Traits. The framework scores perfectly across the Reliability, Reach, Respect, and Restraint dimensions, while its performance on the Agentic Traits shows a more mixed profile.

Conclusion

Our journey through PADM, PADM_FUNCT, PADM_FEED, and finally GAP reflects the broader evolution of agentic design—from experimentation to engineering, from autonomy to assurance. Early PADM architectures demonstrated the raw cognitive potential of large language models: flexible reasoning, adaptive behavior, and human-like problem solving. But that freedom came at a cost of unpredictability, high operational expense, and fragile execution that struggled to scale beyond controlled environments.

Each iteration addressed a different dimension of this challenge. PADM_FUNCT improved efficiency through plan-first execution, PADM_FEED strengthened reliability through feedback and reflection, and GAP ultimately brought these lessons together. By translating intent into a structured, graph-driven execution model, GAP replaces free-form reasoning with determinism, making behavior predictable, costs measurable, and outcomes auditable.

Viewed through the lens of the 4 R's—Reach, Reliability, Restraint, and Respect—GAP emerges as the most balanced architecture. It does not abandon intelligence; it refines it. GAP embraces bounded intelligence, where reasoning is encoded in structure and governed by design.

In closing, the path from proof of concept to production is not a test of intelligence, but of discipline. GAP closes the gap between aspiration and execution, delivering agentic systems that are not just intelligent but trustworthy, scalable, and ready for the real world.

Final Thoughts

This book has been a chronicle of both simple and deeply sophisticated experiments designed to uncover what truly works when building agentic systems that can scale, remain cost-effective, and operate securely in the real world. Along the way, we explored a spectrum of architectures, from naive and exploratory designs to highly structured, enterprise-ready systems. Each experiment revealed not just new capabilities but also new constraints.

While a PADM_FEED–style architecture may appear to be the most compelling choice in many scenarios, the reality is more nuanced. Such designs are not always practical at today's scale or cost. Even so, I would strongly encourage readers to experiment with them at least once. They offer a rare glimpse into the true potential of large language models. They also hint at a future where computations become affordable enough to host powerful models in-house, making deeper cognitive autonomy more viable.

The deeper purpose of this book, however, has not been to advocate for a single "best" architecture. It has been to surface the trade-offs that accompany every design decision and trade-offs that are too often obscured or ignored in vendor narratives. The market today is crowded with solutions promising "fully autonomous agentic intelligence," yet few are transparent about the operational costs, reliability challenges, or governance risks beneath the surface. Without a clear mental model of how these systems actually work, teams are easily drawn into choices that lead to fragile, expensive, or unmanageable deployments.

My hope is that this book equips you with that missing mental model. By understanding the architectural patterns, their strengths and limitations, and the dimensions along which they should be evaluated, you are better positioned to assess what is truly agentic, what is merely reactive, and what aligns with your real objectives.

To reinforce these insights, the final section of the book presents a set of summary tables or concise reference maps that distill the journey we have taken. They capture the evolution from PADM to GAP, the evaluation through the lens of the 4 R's, the Agentic Maturity Ladder, and the progression from prototype to production. Together, they represent the accumulated learnings of every experiment explored in these pages.

In the end, building agentic systems is not about chasing autonomy for its own sake. It is about designing intelligence with intent, balancing ambition with discipline, creativity with control, and possibility with responsibility. If this book helps you ask better questions, see beyond the hype, and design systems that are both intelligent and trustworthy, then it has served its purpose.

Snapshots

Here are few tables to capture the comparisons of the different architectures as a quick snapshot

1. The Evolution Map

Stage	Essence	Personality	Strength	Limitation
PADM	The origin story is modeled on human cognition (Perception → Action). A curious thinker that explores everything, even at the cost of control.	*The Thinker*	Exploration, Creativity	Unstable loops, high cost

Stage	Essence	Personality	Strength	Limitation
PADM_ FUNCT	Streamlined logic in a single flow that is faster, more focused, but fragile under failure.	*The Planner*	Efficiency, Speed	Brittle when errors occur
PADM_ FEED	Introduces reflection and feedback. Smarter, self-correcting, yet burdened by its own introspection.	*The Reflector*	Reliability, Reasoning	Slower, expensive
GAP	Graph-based determinism where structure replaces uncertainty. Reliable, auditable, and enterprise-ready.	*The Executor*	Balance, Scalability, Governance	Limited improvisation

2. The 4R Balance Sheet

Principle	PADM	PADM_ FUNCT	PADM_ FEED	GAP
Reach (Scalability)	◍ Exploratory but chaotic	◍ Faster but nondeterministic	◍ Reflective but slower	○ Predictable and scalable
Reliability (Consistency)	● Unstable	◍ Moderate	○ High	○○ Very High
Restraint (Cost Efficiency)	● Costly	○ Controlled	◍ Heavy feedback load	○○ Optimized and predictable
Respect (Governance)	● Weak controls	◍ Some governance	○ Secure via MCP	○○ Fully auditable and compliant

3. The Agentic Maturity Ladder

Trait	PADM	PADM_FUNCT	PADM_FEED	GAP
Generative Power	Creative	Focused	Reflective	Purposeful
Action Autonomy	Full but unstable	Structured	Controlled	Deterministic
Reasoning Depth	Emergent	Linear	Multi-step	Structured logic
Operational Simplicity	High orchestration	Moderate	Complex	Streamlined

4. From POC to Production

Stage	Readiness	Ideal Context
PADM	Prototype	Cognitive experiments and innovation labs
PADM_FUNCT	Controlled pilot	Fast analytical agents
PADM_FEED	Research-grade	Precision reasoning prototypes
GAP	Production-ready	Enterprise automation at scale

4. The Final Verdict

Architecture	Tagline	Essence in One Line
PADM	*The Thinker*	Creative but chaotic
PADM_FUNCT	*The Planner*	Fast but fragile
PADM_FEED	*The Reflector*	Wise but costly
GAP	*The Executor*	Structured, scalable, and enterprise-ready

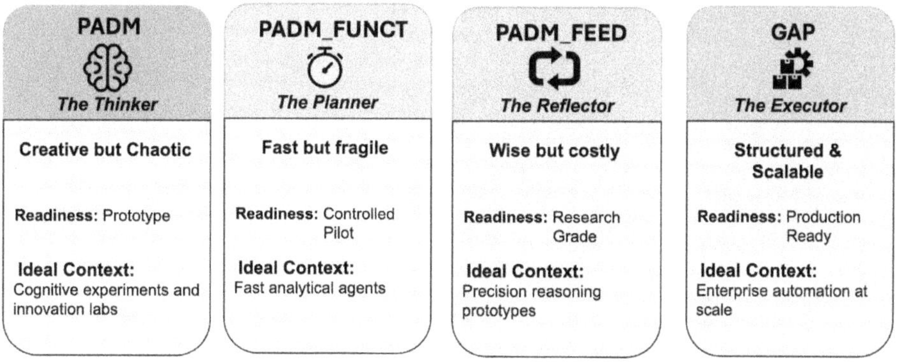

Figure: Summarizes the four approaches

If there is one takeaway from this journey, it is this:

Agentic AI is not defined by how intelligent a system appears, but by how intelligently it is designed.

The difference between a dazzling prototype and a dependable platform lies not in the model, but in the architecture around it and how we manage cost, enforce boundaries, design feedback loops, and balance autonomy with control. The era of experimentation proved what is possible. The next era will determine what is sustainable. The experimentation phase is over. The engineering phase has begun. And the future of Agentic AI will belong to those who design it with discipline, not just ambition.

Appendix A
Extending the SQL Agent with Langflow

As we saw earlier, the SQL Agent architecture demonstrated how natural language queries can be translated into structured SQL operations. While powerful, such architectures still require significant implementation effort—wiring components together, writing glue code, and handling edge cases in a traditional programming language. For anyone learning, prototyping, or experimenting, this quickly becomes a distraction. The focus shifts from understanding concepts to wrestling with setup, configuration, and inevitable bugs often draining momentum at the very stage when curiosity and exploration should be highest.

This creates a familiar dilemma: should we spend our energy mastering the ideas, or debugging the plumbing required to make them work?

Low-code development frameworks offer a way out of this trap. With the rapid rise of LLM-first frameworks, much of the underlying complexity in tool orchestration, prompt handling, memory management, and execution flow can now be abstracted away. These platforms allow practitioners to experiment, iterate, and learn at a higher level of abstraction, focusing on agent behavior and system design rather than infrastructure details.

Langflow is a prominent visual, low-code platform for Low Code Development. It enables users to design, configure, and deploy agentic workflows efficiently, minimizing the need for extensive code writing.

Langflow provides drag-and-drop components for **LLMs, prompts, tools, memory, and control flow**, letting you assemble full-fledged agentic systems that previously required hundreds of lines of Python and multiple orchestration layers. It's the perfect environment to experiment, iterate, and visualize your logic making it ideal for proof-of-concepts, internal demos, or rapid prototyping of Agentic AI applications.

Note: The discussion of Langflow in this Appendix is based on hands-on experimentation conducted during an earlier phase of our work. The observations and conclusions reflect practical experience with the platform at that point in time and are intended to illustrate architectural trade-offs, not to serve as an exhaustive or current assessment. Langflow continues to evolve through active development and community contributions, and it is likely that some of the constraints or behaviors described here have since changed. Readers interested in the latest capabilities, updates, or recommended usage patterns should refer to the official Langflow documentation (https://docs.langflow.org/) for up-to-date information.

Illustration

To see how Langflow can simplify things, let's take a familiar example we've used repeatedly throughout this book:

> "Show the top 5 selling SKUs in this outlet, and then retrieve the sales and quantities for these 5 SKUs."

This problem is small but meaningful.

It has two distinct steps, ranking SKUs by sales, then drilling into detailed metrics, making it a great test case for any agentic framework.

It also checks three important boxes:

1. **Data access:** pulling structured data from a sales database.
2. **Sequential logic:** chaining one result (top SKUs) into another query (sales and quantity).
3. **Context retention:** maintaining awareness of intermediate results.

In short, it's simple enough to build, yet complex enough to expose design strengths and weaknesses.

Why Langflow Works Well Here

Langflow makes this kind of use case easy to design through its **node-based architecture**. Each component—an LLM, tool, prompt, or memory—is represented as a node, and you can visually define how data flows between them using the connectors.

Langflow also allows you to implement a conversational agent in a very easy manner.

For our example, the workflow might look like this:

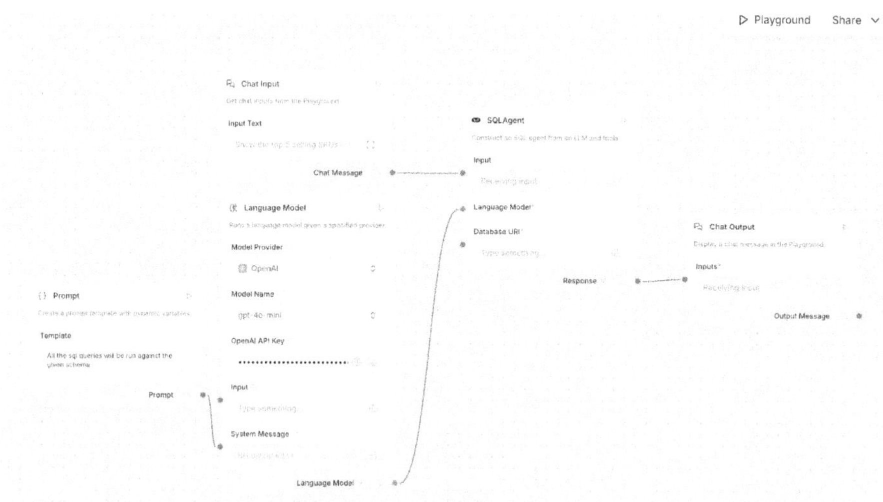

1. **Prompt Node:** This allows the user to add some user level prompt optionally. E.g. "All the sql queries need to be run on the given schema"
2. **Chat Input Node:** Accepts the user input (e.g., "*Show the top 5 selling SKUs for outlet 75757*").
3. **SQLAgent Tool Node:** Connects to the database and executes a parameterized SQL query.
4. **OpenAI Node:** This is the LLM that we are providing for the NLP2SQL and formatting of the results
5. **Chat Output Node:** Shows the output for the query.

Langflow takes care of **data passing, context management, and orchestration**, allowing you to focus on the business logic rather than the plumbing.

Why does Langflow Make Sense?

The biggest advantage of Langflow is that it **replaces code with clarity**.

Instead of scripting the orchestration logic, you can see the workflow unfold visually:

- Data flows from one node to another.
- You can trace where the query starts, how it's processed, and where results end up.
- Non-technical users can design, understand, and even modify the logic without deep coding knowledge.

It also makes experimentation effortless. You can swap models, tweak prompts, or plug in new tools instantly, all without redeploying code.

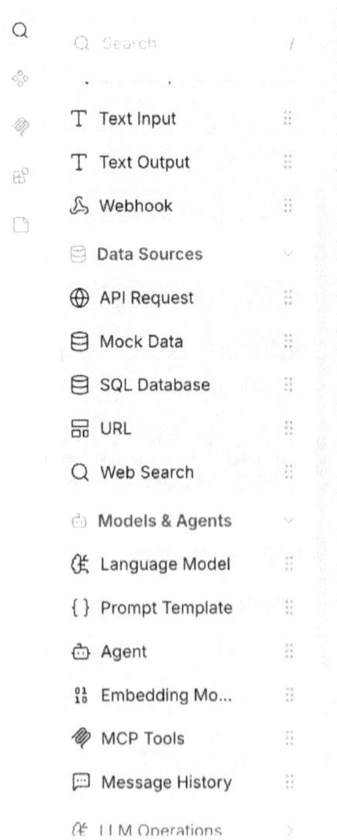

For internal data teams, this means faster prototyping; for enterprises, it means more interpretable and maintainable AI systems.

Langflow transforms the original SQL Agent from a coded experiment into a **production-ready, low-code workflow**. It simplifies design, reduces setup time, and gives teams the freedom to build, test, and iterate agentic data experiences quickly with full visibility and control.

If the SQL Agent was our first working prototype, Langflow is its polished successor,

a way to build intelligent, data-aware workflows that are both **powerful and approachable**.

Pros and Cons of the Langflow Approach

Like every architectural choice we've explored so far, Langflow brings its own set of strengths and trade-offs. It stands out for its simplicity and transparency, but certain practical limitations make it better suited for rapid prototyping than large-scale enterprise deployment.

Let's break it down.

Pros

1. Ease of Setup and a True No-Code Experience

One of Langflow's biggest strengths lies in its simplicity. Setting up a new project is refreshingly easy. You don't need a software engineering background or a deep understanding of orchestration frameworks.

Langflow truly delivers on the "no-code" promise: users can build sophisticated agentic flows simply by linking pre-built components through an intuitive drag-and-drop interface.

Each block represents a logical function, such as a prompt, LLM, or database connection, and connecting them is as straightforward as drawing a line between nodes.

There's no need to manage complex dependencies or write glue code; just connect the pieces, add your API keys, and hit run.

This makes Langflow ideal for experimentation, prototyping, and educational use cases where speed matters more than raw flexibility.

2. Transparent Workflow and Debugging

Langflow's **playground view** offers an unmatched level of transparency. It visually traces how data moves through the system from user prompt to LLM reasoning to final output. This real-time feedback helps users understand *exactly* what's happening under the hood, making it easier to debug, optimize, and validate each stage of execution.

You can inspect intermediate outputs at every node, tweak parameters, and instantly see how your changes affect the result. This kind of clarity is invaluable in LLM-based systems, where understanding *why* a response was generated is often just as important as the response itself.

3. Extensive Integration Capabilities

Langflow shines when it comes to **flexibility**. It supports a wide range of integrations across major **LLMs (OpenAI, Anthropic, Gemini, Mistral, etc.)**, **vector databases**, and **third-party APIs**.

This broad compatibility allows teams to easily switch between models, tools, and configurations and is perfect for **A/B testing** or performance benchmarking. Want to compare GPT-4's results against Claude or Llama-3? Just drop in two LLM nodes, feed them the same input, and observe the outputs side by side. This plug-and-play approach encourages rapid iteration and fosters a deeper understanding of how different components perform under the same workflow.

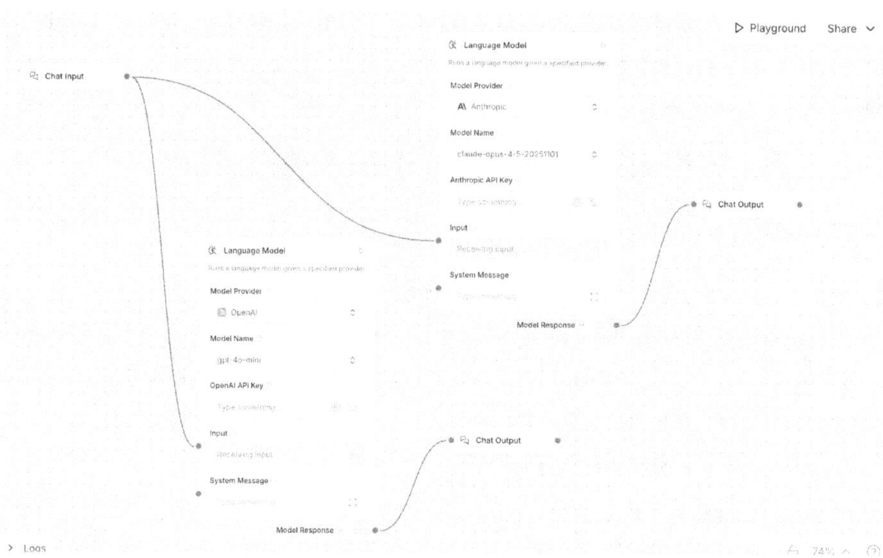

Figure: Shows the concept where the same input is being fed to two different LLMs and the output can be seen in the different "chat output" nodes.

Cons

1. Hosting and Deployment Challenges

Langflow currently lacks **native integration** with major cloud platforms like AWS, Azure, or GCP. As a result, organizations must either **self-host** Langflow (adding DevOps overhead) or rely on Langflow's proprietary cloud, which might not align with corporate **security, compliance, or cost** policies. This limitation makes scaling or production deployment less straightforward, particularly for large enterprises with strict governance standards.

2. Limited "Low-Code" Practicality

While Langflow's interface feels wonderfully simple at the prototype stage, true **enterprise integration** often breaks the illusion of "no-code."

Connecting Langflow agents with production systems like ERP, CRM, or platforms like Bizom, typically requires **custom scripting**, API wrappers, or authentication logic.

This means that while Langflow drastically lowers the barrier to entry, it doesn't completely remove the need for coding once you move beyond sandbox experiments.

In short, it's low-code for experiments but not for deployment.

3. Difficulty with Complex Logic

Langflow's architecture is **prompt-centric**, which can make implementing **complex logic** (loops, conditionals, state management) cumbersome. If an action depends on specific runtime conditions, say, *"fetch sales only if stock rotation is below threshold,"* expressing that logic purely through prompts can be error-prone.

Additionally, integrating secure authentication tokens or multi-step verification workflows often requires manual handling, which introduces potential **security and maintainability concerns.** This limits Langflow's suitability for deeply conditional or logic-heavy business workflows.

4. Other Limitations

Beyond the major constraints, a few additional considerations exist:

- **Version Control and Collaboration:** Limited built-in support for multi-user environments or Git-based versioning.
- **Performance Constraints:** Execution can be slower than code-based implementations, especially for large data pipelines.
- **Specialized Connectors:** Enterprise-grade connectors (for proprietary APIs or internal systems) are not always available out-of-the-box.

While these are not deal-breakers, they do affect scalability and long-term maintainability in production environments.

From POC to Production: Shortcomings of the LLM-Driven Langflow Architecture

Langflow offers an appealing vision: a low-code interface where LLMs, databases, and external tools work together seamlessly to create intelligent, conversational agents. It's fast to prototype, visually intuitive, and remarkably easy to use.

However, as we transitioned from early experimentation to production-grade deployments, particularly for SQL-based querying and natural language data access, several critical challenges surfaced.

What worked well in the lab began to strain under the demands of scale, security, and cost.

This section highlights the core limitations we observed when evaluating Langflow for enterprise-ready environments.

1. Response Time and Execution Architecture

The first and most noticeable bottleneck is **latency**. Langflow doesn't run natively on cloud ecosystems like **AWS, Azure, or GCP**. Instead, it operates as a standalone service typically deployed on a VM or container. This setup introduces **network and orchestration overhead** with every request, particularly when agents need to make multiple LLM or database calls in sequence.

By default, Langflow executes workflows **synchronously and sequentially**, meaning each step must complete before the next begins. In real-world systems, however, agents often need to perform **parallel tasks** such as fetching multiple KPIs from different databases simultaneously.

Achieving this requires manually rewriting nodes for **asynchronous execution**, which quickly undermines the "low-code" advantage that Langflow promotes.

Once asynchronous orchestration is custom-built, Langflow effectively becomes a **wrapper** around direct API calls (to OpenAI, Postgres, etc.). At that point, one has to ask the uncomfortable question:

"If we're coding asynchronous pipelines anyway, why not just call the APIs directly?"

2. Database Compatibility and Infrastructure Coupling

Langflow's current SQL agent implementation is **tightly coupled with PostgreSQL**.

While this works well for basic use cases, it becomes restrictive in heterogeneous enterprise environments where systems may rely on **MySQL, BigQuery, Snowflake, Redshift, or proprietary data warehouses**.

Re-architecting or replicating databases solely to accommodate Langflow is not only inefficient but also introduces compliance risks and additional maintenance overhead.

Security adds another layer of complexity. Langflow requires **open network access** between its agent runtime and the target database. In enterprises enforcing **VPC isolation, zero-trust policies, or private data enclaves**, this is often a non-starter.

As a result, Langflow struggles to integrate cleanly within modern, locked-down infrastructure environments.

3. LLM Dependence and Cost Escalation

Langflow's greatest strength lies in its deep integration with LLMs, but it also becomes its biggest weakness at scale.

The architecture relies heavily on LLMs for reasoning, planning, and **NLP-to-SQL translation**, which introduces several cost and performance issues:

- **Accuracy risks:** LLMs struggle with complex SQL involving **joins, subqueries, and dynamic filters**. Even when the schema is provided as context, the generated queries can be syntactically valid but semantically wrong.
- **Retry loops:** When the SQL fails to execute correctly, Langflow often re-invokes the LLM with corrective prompts, multiplying both cost and latency.

- **Premium model dependency:** Reasoning-focused models like GPT-4-Turbo or Claude 3 Opus perform better but are **far more expensive** than smaller open models.

In large deployments, where agents may run **hundreds of thousands of queries daily**, these costs add up quickly. A single complex query that triggers multiple LLM calls for metadata, query validation, and summarization can cost several cents. At enterprise scale, this can easily translate to **thousands of dollars per day** in operational expenditure.

4. Platform and Security Constraints

Langflow's simplicity, while ideal for prototyping, becomes a liability when scaling to production.

There is **no built-in mechanism** for implementing enterprise-grade security measures such as **user authentication, authorization policies, or API usage quotas**.

Session management, audit trails, and usage throttling must all be implemented manually, increasing development complexity and the potential for error.

Even more concerning is the **data exposure risk**. To generate SQL queries, Langflow must provide the LLM with **database schema details**, and in some cases, real data samples, as context. This introduces multiple security and compliance challenges:

- Potential for **data leakage** through model logging or API misuse
- Difficulty ensuring compliance with **GDPR, HIPAA, and SOC2**
- Inability to tightly control data visibility for specific users or roles

In short, what feels safe in a sandbox becomes a red flag under an enterprise audit.

5. Determinism and Repeatability Challenges

Finally, Langflow inherits one of the fundamental challenges of all LLM-based systems: **non-determinism**. Even when given the same schema and prompt, the generated SQL query can differ slightly between runs, especially for complex logic.

This inconsistency breaks **repeatability**, a core principle for enterprise analytics, where reproducibility and auditability are non-negotiable. Without deterministic outputs, debugging and regression testing become tedious. Teams cannot easily verify whether discrepancies in reports stem from data changes or model variability.

In regulated domains like finance, healthcare, and manufacturing, this alone can make LLM-driven agents unsuitable for production deployment.

Conclusion

Langflow remains one of the most approachable tools for **rapid agentic experimentation**, but as of today, it falls short of being production-ready for **enterprise-grade, SQL-driven use cases**.

Its low-code visual interface simplifies early development but introduces significant limitations in **scalability, security, latency, determinism, and cost control** once deployed at scale.

To move beyond POC, organizations would need to supplement Langflow with:

- **Asynchronous orchestration** for speed
- **Custom middleware** for authentication and governance
- **Specialized LLM fine-tuning** for deterministic SQL generation

Until such capabilities are natively supported, Langflow is best positioned as a **prototyping platform**—a place to experiment, learn, and iterate quickly before transitioning to a custom-built, production-grade agentic stack

Reference:

For more details on Langflow please refer to the langflow page: https://docs.langflow.org/

Appendix B
Amazon Bedrock: Scaling Generative AI for Real-World Enterprise Systems

Generative AI has rapidly evolved from a niche research topic into a mainstream capability embedded across business applications. But as enterprises shift from demos to production, one truth becomes painfully clear: **scaling large language models (LLMs) is difficult.** The challenges involving cost, infrastructure complexity, privacy, unpredictable load patterns, and model drift can easily overwhelm teams who try to self-host or directly call public APIs.

Amazon Bedrock emerges as a platform designed explicitly to solve these problems. It is not just an interface to LLMs, it is a complete ecosystem for building, scaling, customizing, and governing generative AI applications reliably. *Bedrock abstracts away the engineering burdens that usually block real-world adoption, offering a "just works" experience without compromising flexibility or control.*

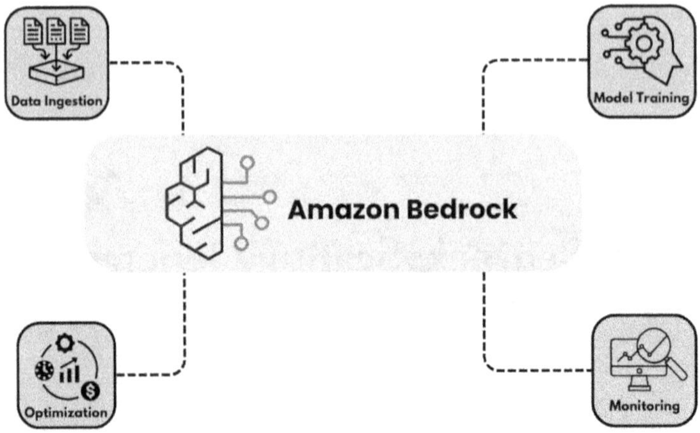

Figure: Core components of the Amazon Bedrock platform, highlighting data ingestion and management, scalable model training infrastructure, flexible deployment options, and built-in monitoring and optimization capabilities that together support end-to-end AI operations.

Note: This appendix provides a high-level set of bullet points on Amazon Bedrock to help readers assess whether it is a suitable choice for production deployments. The intent is not to offer a comprehensive evaluation, but to highlight practical considerations based on our experience. For a detailed and up-to-date understanding of Bedrock's full capabilities, readers should refer to the official Amazon Bedrock documentation.

What is Amazon Bedrock? A Unified Foundation for Modern AI

Amazon Bedrock is a **fully managed, serverless service from AWS** designed to make large-scale generative AI practical, secure, and production-ready. It provides access to a broad range of **best-in-class foundation models** including Anthropic Claude, Meta Llama, Cohere Command, Mistral, Stability AI, and Amazon's own Titan models through a **single, unified API**. Developers can invoke these models without provisioning servers, managing GPUs, or handling the operational complexity traditionally associated with running large language models.

One of Bedrock's defining characteristics is that it is **model-agnostic by design**. Applications are not tightly coupled to a single provider or model family. Instead, teams can experiment with, evaluate, and benchmark different models using the same interface, and switch between them as requirements evolve whether the priority is reasoning quality, latency, throughput, or cost.

Bedrock also integrates deeply with the broader **AWS ecosystem**, allowing seamless connections to data stores, security services, networking controls, and monitoring tools. Organizations can **fine-tune models securely using private datasets**, with workflows that preserve data isolation and regulatory compliance. Fine-tuned models remain private to the customer and do not affect shared base models.

Most importantly, Bedrock enables organizations to **deploy generative AI at scale** without worrying about GPU capacity planning, inference bottlenecks, or infrastructure failures. By abstracting away model hosting and operations, Bedrock shifts the focus from managing technology to solving business problems, making advanced generative AI accessible to teams that previously lacked the resources or expertise to operate it reliably.

Scaling LLMs: How Bedrock Handles Load and Performance

Large language models are inherently **resource-intensive**. Their demand patterns are often unpredictable marked by high concurrency, sudden traffic bursts, and complex agentic pipelines that may invoke multiple model calls for a single user request. This makes traditional capacity planning difficult and, in many cases, impractical. Left unmanaged, LLM workloads can quickly become a source of performance instability and runaway costs.

Amazon Bedrock addresses these challenges through a combination of flexible scaling and workload-aware execution models.

a. On-Demand Auto-Scaling

For applications with highly variable or unpredictable usage patterns, Bedrock offers **on-demand auto-scaling**. As request volume increases,

Bedrock automatically provisions the required compute capacity without any manual intervention. Developers do not need to estimate peak load, pre-provision infrastructure, or manage scaling policies. This elasticity is backed by AWS's massive global infrastructure, allowing systems to absorb sudden traffic spikes while maintaining availability and performance.

This model is particularly well suited for experimental workloads, early-stage applications, and agentic systems where usage patterns are still evolving..

b. Provisioned Throughput

For production systems that require **consistent latency, high throughput, and predictable performance**, Bedrock supports **provisioned throughput**. Organizations can reserve dedicated inference capacity for periods ranging from one to six months, ensuring that model responses remain fast and reliable even under sustained load.

This capability is critical for:

- Field-force and frontline applications
- Consumer-facing GenAI chatbots
- RAG-powered enterprise search portals
- Agentic systems that invoke models multiple times per user query

By locking in capacity, provisioned throughput transforms LLM inference from a volatile, usage-driven expense into a **predictable and budgetable operational cost,** making large-scale deployment financially viable.

c. Multi-Model Workflows

A further advantage of Bedrock is its support for **multi-model workflows** through a unified API interface. Developers can route different tasks to the most appropriate model based on performance and cost considerations:

- Complex reasoning → Claude 3.5 Sonnet
- High-volume text generation → Llama 3.1

- Embeddings and semantic search → Amazon Titan
- Image generation and processing → Stability AI or Titan Image

This selective routing allows teams to optimize cost without compromising on quality or capability. This optimization is extremely difficult to achieve in custom, self-managed deployments. By abstracting infrastructure complexity and model diversity behind a single interface, Bedrock enables scalable, efficient, and economically sustainable LLM-driven systems.

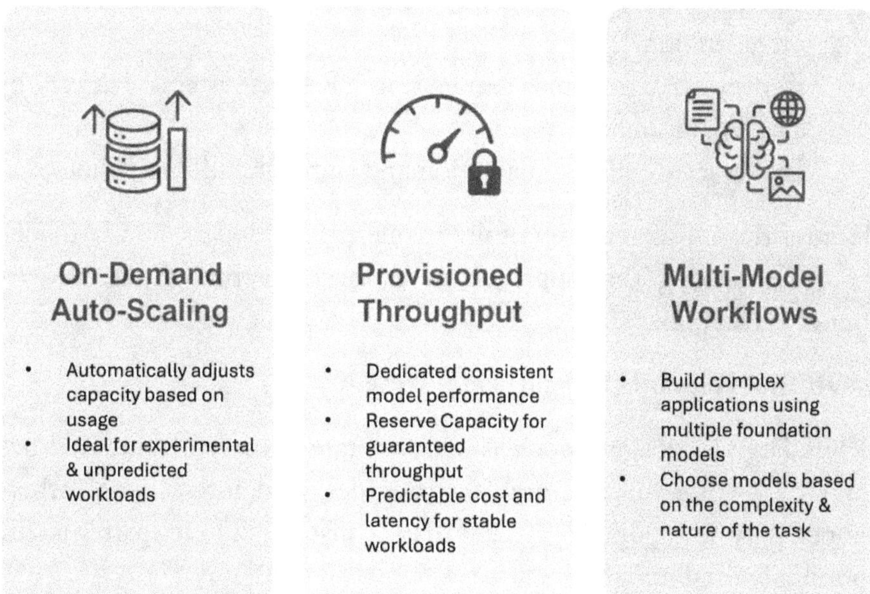

Deployment Environments: Online, Offline-tolerant (Hybrid) Architectures

A distinctive strength of Amazon Bedrock is its flexibility in supporting both **fully online cloud-native deployments** and **offline-tolerant (hybrid) architectures**—a critical capability for environments where network connectivity is unreliable or intermittent.

a. Online Cloud Deployment (Standard)

In the standard deployment model, applications interact with foundation models directly through the **Bedrock API**. AWS manages all underlying infrastructure, including scaling, availability, and model hosting, allowing developers to focus solely on application logic and integration.

This model is well suited for use cases such as:

- AI copilots embedded in enterprise applications
- Agentic workflows that require continuous reasoning and tool orchestration
- Retrieval-Augmented Generation (RAG) systems backed by cloud data sources
- Large-scale content generation and summarization pipelines

Because the infrastructure is fully managed, developers simply invoke the API, making this approach ideal for high-throughput, always-connected workloads.

b. Offline-Tolerant (Hybrid) Deployment

While large language models cannot operate entirely offline, Bedrock supports **offline-tolerant architectures** designed for scenarios where connectivity is sporadic rather than constant. These patterns are commonly used in:

- Remote sales and distribution operations
- Rural or low-bandwidth field-force applications
- Edge-style workflows where only selective reasoning requires cloud access

This approach relies on a combination of techniques, including:

- Local caching of invariant or frequently used data
- Pre-computation of prompts and embeddings
- Transmitting only minimal, high-value context snippets to the cloud

- Running lightweight predictive or rules-based models locally
- Invoking Bedrock selectively for complex reasoning or generative tasks

Such designs align naturally with **hybrid AI patterns**, where deterministic or predictive models operate at the edge, and generative models in the cloud add intelligence, reasoning, and synthesis when connectivity permits. This enables resilient, cost-efficient AI systems that remain functional even when always-on cloud access is not guaranteed.

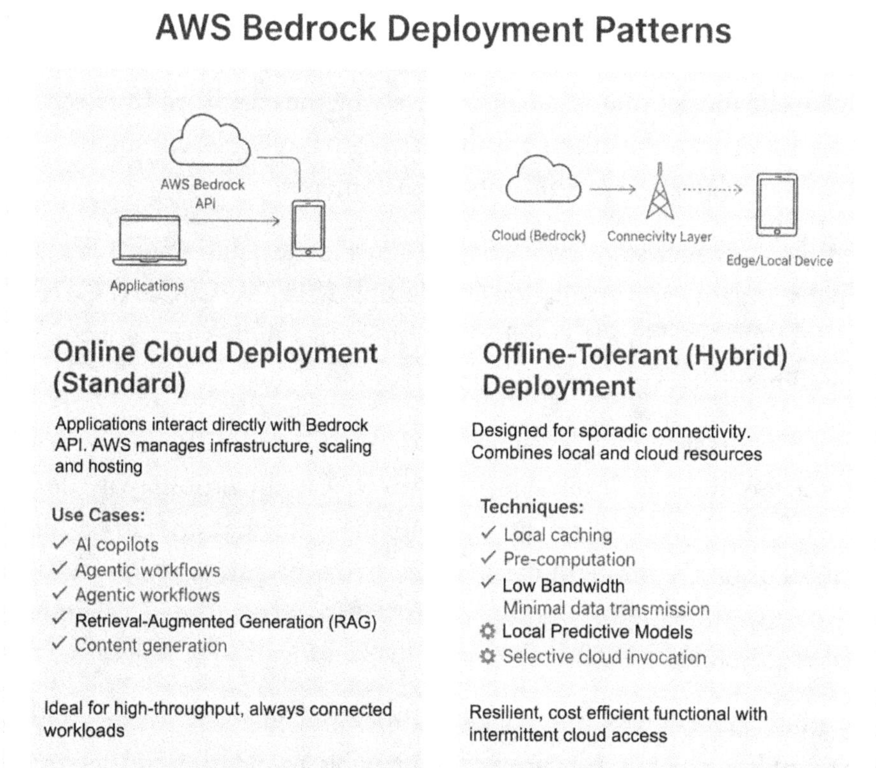

Security, Privacy, and Governance: Enterprise-Grade Guardrails

Amazon Bedrock adopts a clear and uncompromising stance on data privacy and security that is explicitly designed for enterprise and regulated environments. All customer data remains strictly within the customer's AWS boundary; inputs provided to models never leave the account and are not stored, logged, or reused for training any foundation model. This ensures that sensitive prompts, proprietary documents, and business logic remain fully under the customer's control.

Network isolation is enforced through support for **VPC endpoints (AWS PrivateLink)**, allowing all inference and retrieval traffic to flow entirely within a private network. Data is **encrypted both at rest and in transit**, aligning with industry best practices for secure data handling.

When fine-tuning is performed, Bedrock creates a **dedicated, private copy of the model** that is used exclusively by the customer. Importantly, proprietary data never alters the underlying base model, eliminating the risk of data leakage across tenants or customers.

From a compliance standpoint, Bedrock meets the requirements of major global standards and regulations, including **ISO, SOC, CSA, GDPR, and HIPAA**, making it suitable for industries with strict governance obligations.

Beyond infrastructure-level protections, **Guardrails for Bedrock** provide application-level safety controls. Organizations can define policies to redact personally identifiable information (PII), block harmful or non-compliant content, enforce tone and brand guidelines, and ensure that model outputs align with organizational values and legal requirements.

Together, these capabilities make Bedrock not just a powerful model-hosting platform, but a secure and governable foundation for deploying AI systems in production.

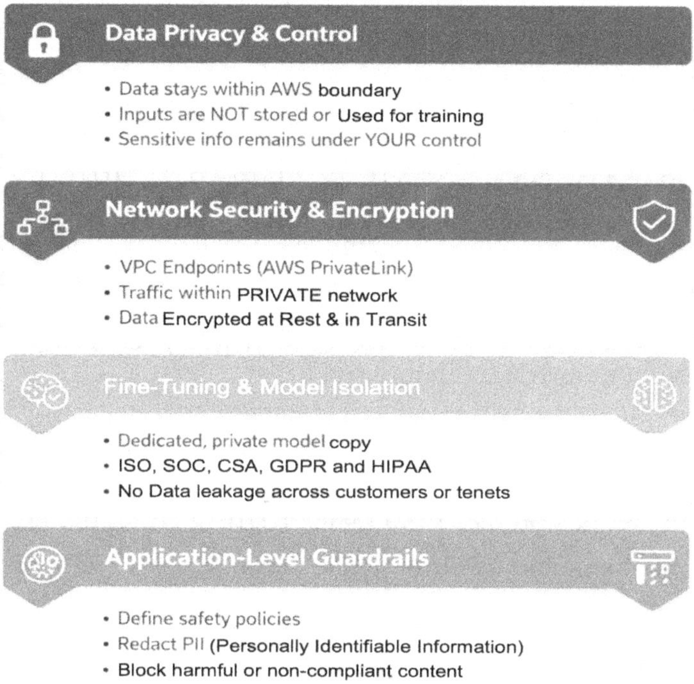

Customization: Fine-Tuning and Retrieval-Augmented Generation (RAG)

What makes Bedrock production-ready is the ease with which organizations can specialize models:

Fine-Tuning

Amazon Bedrock allows developers to adapt foundation models to their specific needs without undertaking the prohibitive effort of training large models from scratch. Instead of building a model end-to-end, teams can upload **proprietary datasets**, such as internal documents, transaction logs, or domain-specific records and use them to fine-tune existing foundation models.

Through fine-tuning, developers can **shape the model's behavior** to align with organizational terminology, business rules, and preferred response styles. This makes the model more accurate and consistent in specialized contexts, reducing hallucinations and improving relevance. Over time, this process enables the creation of **domain-specific expertise**, whether in retail (SKU hierarchies, promotions, supply chains), finance (risk metrics, compliance language), or healthcare (clinical terminology, workflows, and guidelines).

A key advantage is that fine-tuned models remain accessible through the **same Bedrock APIs** used for base models. This minimizes integration overhead and allows teams to switch between base and customized variants without rewriting application logic.

Most importantly, this approach avoids the massive computational and operational cost of training large language models from the ground up. By building on pre-trained foundations, organizations gain the benefits of customization and control while keeping costs, complexity, and infrastructure requirements manageable.

RAG (Retrieval-Augmented Generation)

Amazon Bedrock provides native support for **Retrieval-Augmented Generation (RAG)** by integrating seamlessly with widely used AWS data services such as **Amazon OpenSearch Serverless, Amazon Aurora, Amazon DynamoDB**, and **Amazon S3**. This native integration allows organizations to connect foundation models directly to their existing data stores without building complex retrieval pipelines from scratch.

By grounding generation in retrieved enterprise data, RAG enables **factual and up-to-date responses**, even when the underlying model's training data is static or outdated. Instead of relying solely on parametric memory, the model is augmented with real-time, contextually relevant information fetched from trusted sources at inference time. This significantly reduces hallucinations and improves accuracy.

Equally important, RAG improves **explainability**. Because responses are based on identifiable documents or records, outputs can be traced back to their sources, which is an essential requirement in regulated domains such as finance, healthcare, and enterprise analytics. Teams can audit which data influenced a response and apply governance policies consistently.

Finally, RAG delivers **domain-grounded results**. Whether the knowledge resides in relational databases, NoSQL stores, or object storage, the model's reasoning remains anchored in organizational context rather than generic training data.

Together, **RAG and Bedrock form a foundational building block for production-grade AI copilots and agentic systems** that are not only intelligent, but also accurate, transparent, and ready to operate at enterprise scale.

Agents in Bedrock: Automating Multi-Step Reasoning

Amazon Bedrock includes a managed **Agents** capability designed to simplify the construction of intelligent systems that require **multi-step reasoning and coordinated action**. Instead of treating every user request as a single prompt-response interaction, Bedrock Agents are built to handle tasks that unfold over multiple steps and require decision-making along the way.

At a high level, Bedrock Agents can:

- Break complex user requests into smaller, manageable subtasks
- Orchestrate sequences of actions in the correct order
- Invoke external APIs and internal services as needed
- Retrieve relevant documents or data sources to ground decisions
- Execute chains of tools where each step depends on the output of the previous one

Rather than hard-coding this logic, developers configure an agent declaratively by defining:

- The **overall goal** the agent is trying to achieve
- The **APIs and tools** it is permitted to call
- **Instructions and constraints** that guide its behavior

- **Memory sources** for retaining context or retrieving knowledge
- **Safety and policy boundaries** that limit what the agent can do

Once these elements are specified, Bedrock takes responsibility for the underlying **sequencing, reasoning, and execution flow**. The agent determines which actions to take, in what order, and when to stop without requiring developers to manually construct complex agentic pipelines or control loops.

This managed approach lowers the barrier to building agentic systems, allowing teams to focus on defining intent and governance rather than implementing orchestration logic. As a result, Bedrock Agents provide a practical path to deploying reliable, multi-step AI workflows in production environments.

Cost Models: Flexible Options for Every Workload

One of the most important considerations when moving generative AI from experimentation to production is **cost predictability**. Amazon Bedrock addresses this directly by offering a tiered pricing model that aligns with different stages of adoption and workload patterns, rather than forcing a one-size-fits-all approach.

Bedrock organizes its pricing into three primary categories:

1. On-Demand Inference

The on-demand model follows a **pay-as-you-go** approach, where costs are based on the number of input and output tokens processed by the model. This option is particularly well-suited for:

- Prototyping and proof-of-concept work
- Low- to moderate-volume applications
- Irregular or unpredictable usage patterns

Bedrock also supports **batch inference** under this model, allowing teams to process large datasets asynchronously at a lower effective cost. This makes it ideal for offline workloads such as document processing, data enrichment, or periodic analytics, without the need to reserve capacity in advance.

2. Provisioned Throughput

For production systems with **consistent, high-volume, or latency-sensitive workloads**, Bedrock offers provisioned throughput. In this model, organizations reserve a fixed amount of inference capacity for a defined period typically ranging from **one to six months**.

Provisioned throughput is critical for use cases such as:

- Consumer-facing generative AI applications
- Field-force or operational systems with steady traffic
- RAG-based search portals and copilots
- Agentic workflows that invoke models multiple times per request

By reserving capacity, teams gain predictable performance and pricing, transforming LLM inference from a volatile cost into a budgetable operational expense.

3. Model Customization and Fine-Tuning

When organizations choose to fine-tune models with proprietary data, additional costs apply. These include:

- Charges for training tokens used during customization
- Ongoing storage costs for the fine-tuned model artifacts

Inference on fine-tuned models requires provisioned throughput, ensuring stable performance and isolation. While this option introduces additional cost, it enables domain-specific behavior and higher accuracy often reducing downstream inference usage and improving overall system efficiency.

Taken together, this tiered pricing structure allows teams to **start small, scale deliberately, and optimize cost as workloads mature**. It supports a disciplined transition from experimentation to production, aligning technical ambition with financial control.

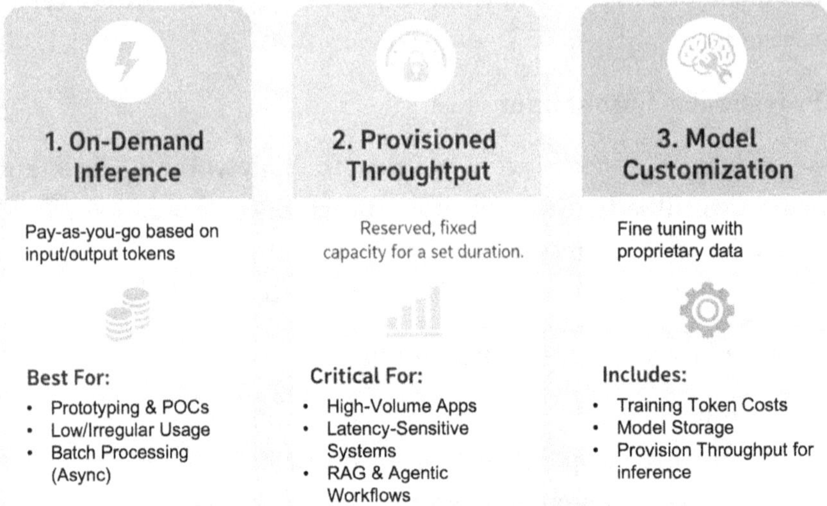

Bedrock in Hybrid-AI Architectures

One of the most practical strengths of Amazon Bedrock is how naturally it fits into **hybrid AI architectures** that deliberately combine different classes of models, each used where it performs best. Rather than forcing generative AI to solve every problem, hybrid designs assign roles based on cost, determinism, and operational constraints.

In such architectures:

- **Generative AI** is used to enrich data, interpret unstructured inputs, and reason across context
- **Predictive or classical ML models** handle structured, deterministic tasks such as scoring, classification, or forecasting
- **Edge or local models** support offline execution, low-latency inference, and cost-sensitive environments

Bedrock acts as the **reasoning and orchestration layer** in this setup. High-compute, context-heavy tasks, such as summarization, explanation, planning, or cross-source reasoning, are delegated to foundation models hosted in Bedrock. Meanwhile, lightweight models continue to run closer to the data, either on-device or in regional services, handling frequent or latency-critical operations.

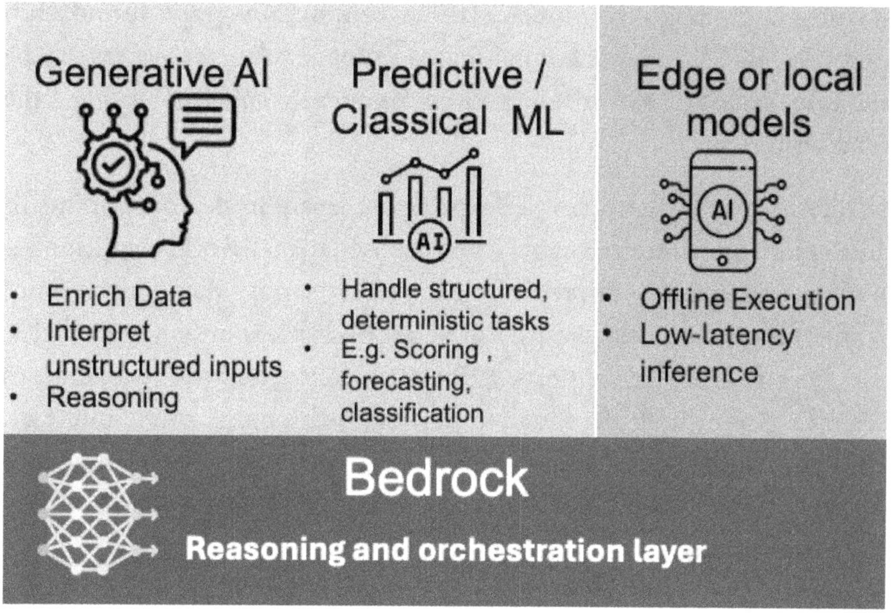

This pattern makes Bedrock valuable far beyond standalone GenAI applications. It enables intelligent pipelines such as:

- Outlet image verification workflows in FMCG, where edge models detect visual signals and Bedrock interprets anomalies
- Geospatial summarization systems that combine spatial analytics with narrative explanations
- Multi-step, agentic sales insights that blend transactional data with contextual reasoning
- Scalable quality checks and automated audits, where rules flag issues and Bedrock explains, prioritizes, and summarizes findings

By offloading reasoning-heavy workloads to Bedrock while keeping routine inference local, organizations achieve a powerful balance: **higher intelligence without runaway costs**, and **scalability without sacrificing control**. This hybrid approach represents one of the most sustainable ways to operationalize generative AI in real-world systems.

Conclusion

Amazon Bedrock should not be viewed as just another platform for hosting large language models. It is a **production-grade foundation** purpose-built for organizations that need generative AI systems to be **reliable, scalable, governed, and economically sustainable** over the long term.

While many AI platforms perform impressively in demonstrations or small pilots, they often struggle when exposed to real-world conditions—high concurrency, unpredictable traffic, strict data governance requirements, and cost pressure at scale. Bedrock is designed explicitly for these realities. It supports millions of concurrent requests, enables seamless use of multiple foundation models through a single interface, enforces strong privacy and compliance guarantees, and integrates naturally into hybrid AI architectures that blend generative reasoning with deterministic systems.

For enterprises operating with:

- Large and diverse user bases
- Distributed or field-force-driven operations
- Massive volumes of structured and unstructured data
- Stringent regulatory and compliance constraints
- Highly cost-sensitive deployment environments

Bedrock offers the architectural stability and scalability required to take generative AI **from POC to production at global scale**.

Appendix C
Cost Estimates for Amazon Bedrock in Production

A Sales Force Automation (SFA) Perspective

To properly understand generative AI costs in production, it is essential to anchor them in a **real operational workflow** rather than abstract token counts. The following estimates are based on a **Sales Force Automation (SFA)** use case—a domain where agentic workflows are invoked at massive scale, often multiple times per day.

Two Levels of Agentic Workflows

In a typical SFA system, agentic intelligence operates at **two distinct levels**:

1. User-Level Workflows (Salesperson-Centric)

These workflows are executed **per salesperson** and focus on insights such as:

- Target vs. achievement tracking
- Performance trends
- Route efficiency and task completion summaries
- Personalized recommendations
- End of Day Summary

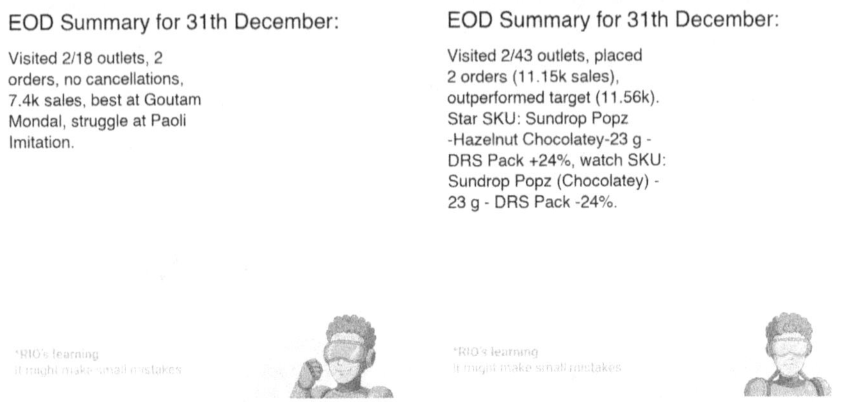

Figure: Sample End Of the Day Agent which is run for ~250K salesman

2. Outlet-Level Workflows (Outlet-Centric)

These workflows are executed **per outlet** and are significantly more expensive due to volume. Typical tasks include:

- Outlet performance summaries
- Sales and inventory insights
- Exception detection (low stock rotation, abnormal trends)
- Automated quality or compliance checks

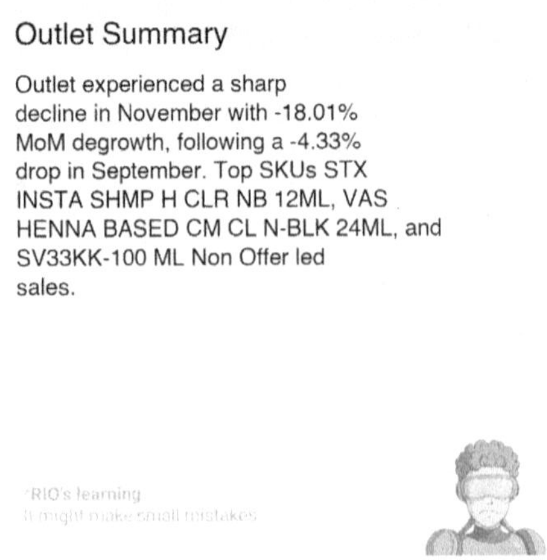

Figure: Sample output of Outlet Agent which is run daily for 5Mn Outlets

Cost Estimates Calculations

Lets work on the cost of calculating the user level agents.

Step 1: Define the Workload Assumptions

For this analysis, we assume:

- 250,000 sales users
- 10 user-level agents
- Each agent is run daily once per user

Total agent executions per day:

```
250,000 users × 10 agents = 2,500,000 runs/day =
2.5Mn runs/day
```

Step 2: Token Usage per Agent Execution

For each agent execution, we assume:

- **Input tokens per run:** 500
- **Output tokens per run:** 200

These are conservative, real-world numbers for:

- context injection (targets, history, KPIs),
- reasoning and planning,
- a summarized response

Step 3: Raw Token Volume per Day

Input Tokens

```
2,500,000 runs × 500 tokens = 1,250,000,000 input
tokens/day = 1.25Bn tokens/day
```

Output Tokens

```
2,500,000 runs × 200 tokens = 500,000,000 output
tokens/day = 500Mn tokens/day
```

Step 4: Effective Billable Tokens

In practice, batching, truncation, and internal Bedrock optimizations reduce billable tokens.

We assume a **1,000× reduction factor**:

Effective Input Tokens

```
1,250,000,000 input tokens/day ÷ 1,000 = 1,250,000
(1.25Mn) effective input tokens
```

Effective Output Tokens

```
500,000,000 output tokens/day ÷ 1,000 = 500,000
effective output tokens
```

Step 5: Apply Nova Lite Pricing

Using Nova Lite pricing (rounded for illustration):

- **Input tokens:** ~$0.00035 per 1K tokens
- **Output tokens:** ~$0.00295 per 1K tokens

Input Cost

```
1,250,000 tokens × $0.00035 ≈ $438
```

Output Cost

```
500,000 tokens × $0.00295 ≈ $1475
```

Step 6: Total Daily Cost (User-Level Agents)

```
Input cost ≈ $438

Output cost ≈ $1475

------------------

Total ≈ $1913 per day
```

At first glance:

- 500 input tokens
- 200 output tokens
- Low-cost Nova Lite model

all appear harmless. But when multiplied across:

- **250,000 users**
- **10 agents per user**
- **daily execution**

the system processes **billions of tokens per day**, turning micro-costs into **hundreds of dollars daily** *just for user-level workflows.*

Based on similar calculations, the cost for the outlet level agents comes to ~7650$ for a day.

User vs Outlet Cost Comparison

Dimension	User-Level Workflows	Outlet-Level Workflows
Entities	250,000 users	5,000,000 (5Mn) outlets
Agents per entity	10	4
Agent runs/day	2.5 million	20 million
Input tokens/run	500	250
Output tokens/run	200	100
Raw input tokens/day	1.25Bn	5Bn
Raw output tokens/day	500Mn	2Bn
Effective input tokens	1,250,000 or 1.25Mn	5Mn

Dimension	User-Level Workflows	Outlet-Level Workflows
Effective output tokens	500,000	2Mn
Input token cost (USD) @0.00035	**$438**	**$1750**
Output token cost (USD) @0.00295	**$1475**	**$5900**
Total cost	**~ $1900**	**~ $7650**

This effectively means ~200$ for a user level agent and ~1900$ for an outlet level agent. These estimates are based on the assumption that there are no failures where the agent is repeatedly making LLM calls. (The happiest flow!!!)

Conclusion

The calculations in this appendix reveal a pattern that is easy to miss during early experimentation but impossible to ignore in production: **Generative AI costs do not explode suddenly. They accumulate steadily and relentlessly with scale.**

At the level of a single agent execution, the numbers appear trivial. A few thousand tokens in, a few hundred tokens out, and fractions of a cent per call. But production systems are not built on single calls. They are built on **millions of entities, multiple agents per entity, and recurring daily execution**. When those dimensions multiply, even the most cost-efficient models begin to generate material operational spend.

In Sales Force Automation workflows, the effect is especially pronounced. User-level agents scale with hundreds of thousands of salespeople; outlet-level agents scale with millions of outlets. Each additional agent, each extra daily run, and each incremental reasoning step compounds token usage. The result is a cost curve driven not by model pricing, but by **architecture and workload design**.

This is the central takeaway: **cost in production GenAI systems is an emergent property of scale**. It is shaped by how often agents run, how broadly they are applied, and how much autonomy they are given not by per-token pricing alone.

Amazon Bedrock provides the infrastructure to support these workloads reliably, but controlling cost requires deliberate restraint: batching, selective execution, hybrid AI patterns, and disciplined agent design. Without these, even well-intentioned architectures can quietly become expensive at enterprise scale.

Appendix D
Parseboard Tool: Technical Guide

Introduction

DSL Parseboard (Domain-Specific Language Parseboard) is a **full-stack workflow visualization and analytics management platform** designed for data automation, orchestration, and analytical process governance.

Built using **Next.js**, **React**, and **TypeScript** on the frontend, with a **Python-based MCP (Model Context Protocol) backend**, Parseboard allows users to **visually design, execute, and monitor analytical workflows** without writing extensive scripts.

The platform bridges human reasoning with data-driven automation, providing a structured environment for designing **semantic graphs** that represent analytical logic, business flows, and decision pipelines.

Business Objectives and Value

- **Accelerate prototyping**: Build and test analytical workflows in minutes instead of hours of scripting.
- **Standardize tool usage**: Centralized management of approved "tools" or node actions ensures consistency and governance.
- **Enable repeatability**: Saved workflows can be re-executed, shared, and audited with version control.
- **Improve insight generation**: Rapidly surface operational and business metrics (e.g., SKU dips, outlet performance, demand fluctuations).

Core Features Overview

Visual Workflow Editor

A drag-and-drop interface for creating, connecting, and managing nodes that represent functions or data operations. Supports both analytical and operational pipelines.

Dynamic Node System

Nodes are dynamically populated and validated through backend MCP integration, ensuring that users only select valid operations for specific entities (e.g., SKU vs. Outlet).

DOT File Integration

Supports **import and export of Graphviz DOT files**, allowing seamless graph persistence, reconstruction, and interoperability with visualization tools such as Graphviz Online.

Real-Time Analytics Dashboard

Provides live tracking of workflow execution, including performance metrics, node success/failure status, and system health insights.

Natural Language Prompt Generation

Automatically generates workflow descriptions or execution prompts in natural language, helping users bridge analytical logic with explainable AI narratives.

Figure: Main editor interface overview

Core Components Details

This section describes the core components of the platform, providing guidance on how to use each module effectively.

Workbench Overview

The workbench overview allows users to interact with different aspects of the workflow. You can create, modify, or analyze workflows directly from this view.

The Workbench is the primary interaction surface for composing, editing, and running analytical workflows. It combines a large central canvas for graph editing with an easily accessible left node toolbar, a top control bar for global actions and environment toggles, and a right Results panel for inspection and iteration. The Workbench is optimized for quick composition: users add Action, Transform, and Result nodes from the left toolbar, connect them directly on the canvas, optionally import an existing Graphviz DOT file, and then execute the workflow to receive structured results in the Results panel.

UI callouts:

- **Top-center:** *Upload .dot File* button: prominent rounded button for import/export operations (useful when migrating from Graphviz assets).
- **Top-center (slightly right):** Database selector and *Data Mode* toggle (Actual / Dummy) used to change runtime context before running a flow. (in work)
- **Left panel:** Collapsible *Add Nodes* toolbar with searchable sections for Action, Transform, and Result nodes.
- **Center:** Graph canvas with user-made nodes and connecting edges.
- **Right panel:** *Results* pane containing Result/Saved Flows tabs, a summary card, and raw Final Answer text block.
- **Bottom-left:** Zoom controls and *Natural-Language Output* minimized card for free-text notes or generated prompts.
- **Top-right:** *Analytics* button to open the dashboard summary.

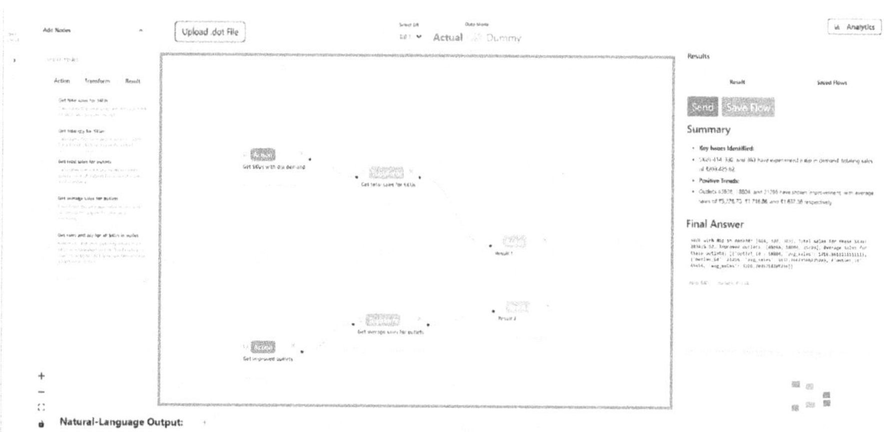

Figure: Workbench Area

Node Toolbar

The Node Toolbar organizes available building blocks (Action, Transform, Result) into a searchable list that supports both static definitions and dynamic tools fetched from the backend. Each entry includes a short description, icon, and a plus button to add it to the canvas. This design accelerates workflow assembly and reduces cognitive overhead.

UI callouts:

- Left panel (vertical): Search input at top of toolbar for quickly locating a node.
- Under search: tabs for Action, Transform, and Result.
- Node cards: concise title and explanatory two-line description (e.g., "Get total sales for SKUs: Calculates total sales amount for a list of SKUs at a specific outlet").

Node behavior & conventions:

Action nodes: source nodes that fetch raw entities (e.g., "Get SKUs with dip demand").

Transform nodes: operate on data (aggregations, filters, join operations).

Result nodes: terminal nodes that represent outputs or endpoints for display/save.

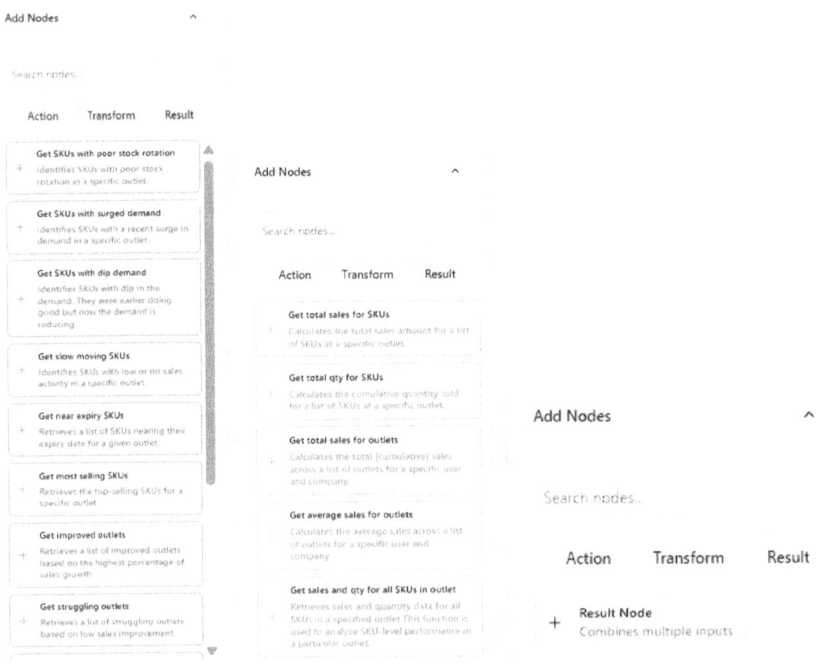

Figure: Different types of nodes – Action, Transform, Result

DOT File Import

The dot file import helps upload existing workflow graph (.dot) to pre-populate nodes/edges.

Graphviz DOT import is available via the *Upload .dot File* control (top-center). The import pipeline sanitizes DOT content, maps nodes to UI types (using color/label heuristics), and places nodes on the canvas with a readable layout. Exports serialize the current canvas back to DOT for round-trip compatibility.

UI callouts:

- **Top-center button:** clearly labeled "Upload .dot File" with rounded outline — primary entry for import.
- After import, nodes appear on the canvas and the left toolbar may highlight any unmapped or custom nodes.

User flow:

1. Click *Upload .dot File*.
2. Confirm or preview sanitized DOT; the app reports parsing warnings.
3. Import nodes are placed and the editor enters a temporary "import review" mode.
4. If heuristics fail to categorize a node, it is created as custom with the raw label preserved.

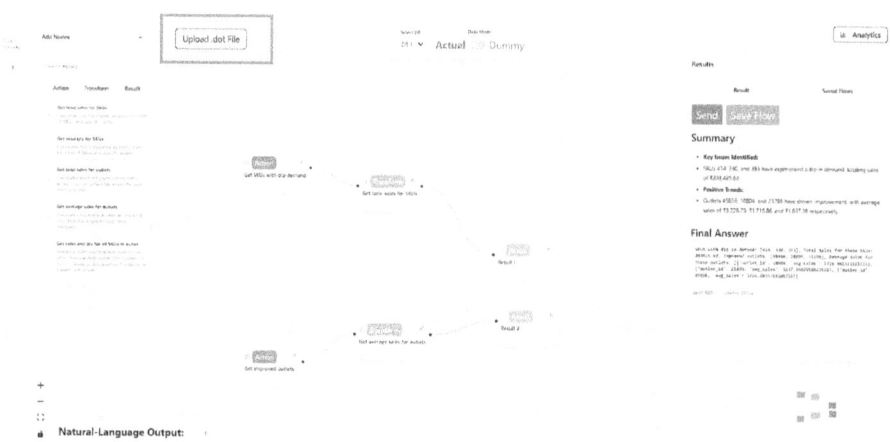

Figure: Button to import .dot format files

Results View

The Results panel (right side) is the single place to run flows and inspect outputs. It contains two tabs: ***Result*** and ***Saved Flows***.

The *Result* tab shows high-level summary cards (Key Issues, Positive Trends), a Final Answer raw JSON/text block, and action buttons (*Send*, *Save Flow*).

Execution is initiated from the Results pane to ensure context (DB, Data Mode) is captured.

The *Saved Flows tab is used to load workflows directly from the dynamic DB.*

UI callouts (from the image):

- **Right column:** panel with a white card showing *Send* (blue) and *Save Flow* (green) buttons near the top of the panel.
- **Summary block:** mid panel showing bullet lists — Key Issues Identified and Positive Trends.
- **Final Answer box:** scrollable area with raw output and small tags at the bottom indicating dbId and outletId.
- **Saved Flows tab:** accessible next to *Result* for loading & quick re-run of previously stored flows.

Figure: (A) Result

Figure: (B) Load Saved Flows

Sidebar

The left sidebar which is initially collapsed can be opened by clicking the button or using the shortcut key **Ctrl+B** or **Command+B** (on Mac).

It provides an extra glimpse mostly for developers or someone who wants to deeply understand the node structure. It includes the Action-Transform Pairs available, Final prompt that would potentially make sense and **Button to export as .dot file.**

There is a debugging section also present.

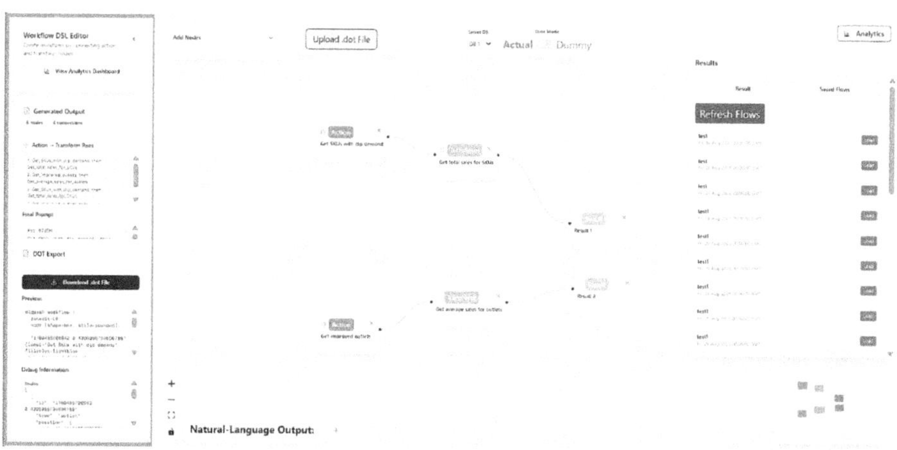

Figure: Left Sidebar

Analytics Dashboard Insights and Use Cases

The Analytics Dashboard offers detailed metrics that help users understand workflow performance, SKU analysis, and operational efficiency. It provides visual insights into key business processes. It lies in the path **"/dashboard"** relative to the current domain.

Workflows can be:

✓ Viewed

✓ Loaded into the workbench

✓ Directly be run for extreme simplicity

Switching between Dashboard and Workbench happens through a prominent button on top right of the website.

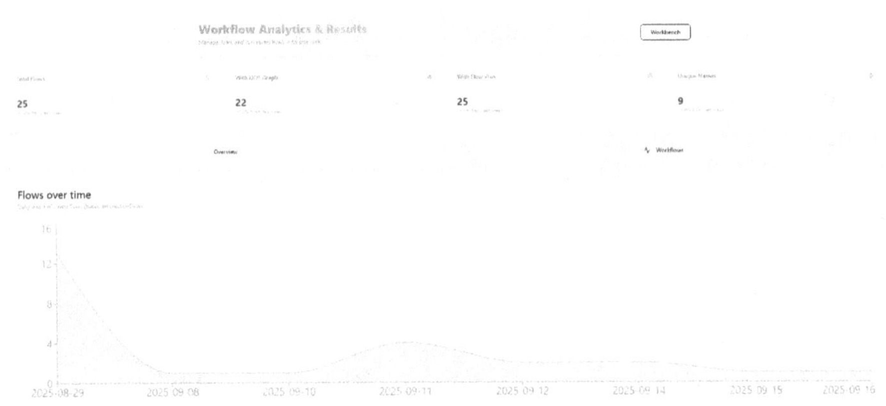

Figure: Graph Overview

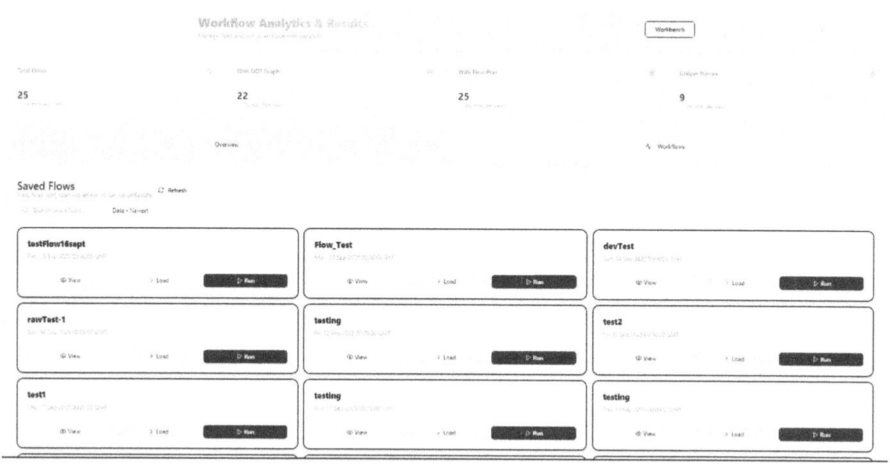

Figure: Saved Workflows

Some of the capabilities of the Dashboard include:

- SKU performance tracking
- Outlet revenue analysis
- Stock-level monitoring
- Workflow error rate tracking

API Capabilities

DSL Parseboard integrates with backend APIs that enable data exchange between the frontend and the MCP backend.

Endpoint	Purpose	Notes
/api/getTools	Fetch dynamic node (tool) catalog	Returned tools fill the Node toolbar
/api/getResults	Execute the current graph	Sends serialized structure (possibly DOT + JSON).
/api/saveFlow	Persist flow definition & metadata	Stores name, graph, timestamps.
/api/getAllFlows	Retrieve saved flow list	Powers Saved Flows tab & Dashboard.
/api/getFlow	Fetch single flow for load	Used when the user clicks Load/View.

Main Flow Tutorial

Step1: Open the application and navigate to the main workbench.

Step2: Use the Node Toolbar to add Action, Transform, and Result nodes.

Step3: Connect nodes using the drag connectors to define relationships.

Step4: Click 'Upload DOT File' to import an existing graph structure. (if required)

Step5: Click 'Run Workflow' to send the workflow for execution and view results in the Results Panel.

Step6: Save workflow if necessary, so it can be saved in the database.

Step7: Switch to the Dashboard tab to analyze results and performance metrics.

Technical Overview

The overall system architecture integrates multiple logical layers that work together to provide an interactive, data-driven workflow editor and dashboard experience. The architecture focuses on modularity, maintainability, and scalability across both frontend and backend integration points.

High-Level Components

- **Frontend Application:** Developed using Next.js 15 (App Router) with the main files located under src/app and src/components.
- **Workflow Editor:** Built using ReactFlow with custom node components in src/components/nodes. This component enables node-based flow creation and editing.
- **API Route Proxies:** Reside under src/app/api/* and forward requests to an external backend. The key routes include:
    - /api/getTools → retrieves a list of dynamic tool definitions.

- /api/getResults → executes a flow and returns structured results.
- /api/getAllFlows, /api/getFlow, /api/saveFlow, /api/runFlow → handle flow creation, retrieval, updates, and execution.

- **Utilities:**
  - src/utils/sanitizeDot.ts handles DOT file sanitization and formatting.
  - src/utils/parseMcpTools.ts parses backend tool text and descriptions into usable summaries.
  - src/utils/generatePrompts.ts manages prompt creation for various flows.
- **Visualization and Analytics:** Implemented with Recharts to visualize saved flows, results, and analytical metrics on the Dashboard.

Data Flow

1. Users create and manipulate nodes and edges on the canvas; these are stored locally in React state.
2. When importing a DOT file, the system sanitizes the file through sanitizeDotGraph, parses it via graphlib-dot, and constructs nodes and edges automatically.
3. Dynamic tools are fetched from the backend through /api/getTools, parsed with parseDynamicToolsResponse, and displayed in the toolbar for quick access.
4. On running a flow, the app constructs a payload and sends it to /api/getResults; results are displayed in the ResultsView panel.
5. The Dashboard retrieves saved flows through /api/getAllFlows and allows re-execution through /api/getResults.

Technology Stack

- **Framework:** Next.js 15 (App Router), React 19, TypeScript 5
- **UI Library:** Tailwind CSS 4, Radix UI primitives (Dropdown, Select, Tabs, Separator, Slot), and shadcn/ui components

- **Graph Engine:** ReactFlow 11 with graphlib-dot for DOT parsing and dagre-d3 reserved for future layout automation
- **Charts and Analytics:** Recharts 3 for dashboard visualization
- **Utility Libraries:** clsx, class-variance-authority, lucide-react, and framer-motion

Conclusion

DSL Parseboard successfully combines a user-friendly interface with backend intelligence to simplify workflow management. It bridges the gap between technical and non-technical users by enabling drag-and-drop analytics creation thus enabling non-technical people to create functions on the go. Future Changes may occur on the extensibility and scalability side of the architecture to support a large and real time audience with specific roles.

www.ingramcontent.com/pod-product-compliance
Lightning Source LLC
LaVergne TN
LVHW052031200926
848481LV00005B/1642